EUROPEAN UNION DISCOURSES
ON UN/EMPLOYMENT

Dialogues on Work and Innovation

The book series *Dialogues on Work and Innovation* presents empirically based studies as well as theoretical discussions on the practice of organizational renewal.
Its publications reflect the increasingly urgent need for the development of new forms of work organization. In today's interdependent world, workplace reform and organizational effectiveness are no longer solely the concern of individual organizations; the local and the global have become closely interconnected.
Dialogues on Work and Innovation mirrors the fact that enterprise development and societal development cannot be kept separate. Furthermore, the Series focuses on the dialogue between theory and practice, and thus on the mutuality of knowledge and action, of research and development. The *Dialogues* stress the critical significance of joint reflexivity in action-oriented research and the necessity for participatory processes in organizational change.

Editors

Hans van Beinum, *Halmstad University* (Editor-in-Chief)
Richard Ennals, *Kingston University*
Werner Fricke, *Friedrich Ebert Stiftung, Bonn*
Øyvind Pålshaugen, *Work Research Institute, Oslo*

Editorial Board

Volume 12

Peter Muntigl, Gilbert Weiss and Ruth Wodak

European Union Discourses on Un/employment
An interdisciplinary approach to
employment policy-making and organizational change

European Union Discourses on Un/employment

An interdisciplinary approach to employment policy-making and organizational change

PETER MUNTIGL

GILBERT WEISS

RUTH WODAK

JOHN BENJAMINS PUBLISHING COMPANY

AMSTERDAM/PHILADELPHIA

The paper used in this publication meets the minimum requirements of American National Standard for Information Sciences — Permanence of Paper for Printed Library Materials, ANSI Z39.48–1984.

Library of Congress Cataloging-in-Publication Data

Muntigl, Peter.
European Union discourses on un/employment : an interdisciplinary approach to employment policy-making and organizational change / Peter Muntigl, Gilbert Weiss, Ruth Wodak.
p.   cm. -- (Dialogues on work and innovation, ISSN 1384-6671 ; V.12)
Includes bibliographical references and index.
1. Manpower policy--European Union countries. 2. Unemployment--European Union countries.
I. Weiss, Gilbert. II. Wodak, Ruth, 1950- III. Title. IV. Series.
HD5764M86   2000
331.12'042'094--dc21   00-056432
ISBN 90 272 1782 3 (Eur.) / 1 55619 774 8 (US) (Pb.)

John Benjamins Publishing Co. · P.O.Box 75577 · 1070 AN Amsterdam · The Netherlands
John Benjamins North America · P.O.Box 27519 · Philadelphia PA 19118–0519 · USA

Contents

Acknowledgements

This book is part of a project on discursive processes and organizational change of European Union institutions (Peter Muntigl, Gilbert Weiss, Ruth Wodak) at the Research Centre: Discourse, Politics, Identity directed by Ruth Wodak and situated at the Austrian Academy of Sciences. Support from the Austrian Science Fund is gratefully acknowledged. Web-site: www.oeaw.ac.at/wittgenstein.

Our many thanks go to the following people and institutions that were of invaluable help to us in conducting our research. Without their help, this study would have been impossible. Our apologies in advance to anyone we have forgotten to mention.

Jan Andersson, Irene Bellier, Johanna Boogerd-Quaak, Joachim Born, Hans Borstlap, Hans Brunmayr, Pierluigi Castagnetti, Andrew Chapman, Aaron Cicourel, Peter Coldrick, Julie de Groote, Alfred Ebenbaucher, Konrad Ehlich, Jakob Engel-Wodak, Marianne Eriksson, Harald Ettl, Irene Etzersdorfer, Norman Fairclough, Georg Fischer, Pádraig Flynn, Herwig Friesinger, Karin Gayer, Judith Gebetsroithner, Anne-Karin Glase, Ilona Graenitz, Helmut Gruber, Marie-Thérèse Hermange, Patricia Herzberger, Reiner Hoffmann, Barbara Hufnagl, Stephen Hughes, Rick Iedema, Thomas Jansen, Marjorie Jouen, Werner Kallmeyer, Raoul Kneucker, Andras Kovacs, Verena Krausneker, Gunter Kress, Margit Kurka, Ferdinand Lacina, Allan Larsson, Jay Lemke, Karl Lönnroth, Christoph Ludwig, Betina Agathanos-Mähr, Bernie Malone, Thomas Mann, Jim Martin, Lieselotte Martin, Sabine Mayr, Winfried Menrad, Michael Meyer, Mieke Schuurmann, Richard Mitten, Karl-Heinz Nachtnebel, Ewald Nowotny, Helga Nowotny, Outi Ojala, David O'Sullivan, Jean-Claude Paye, Lucio Pench, Helwin Peter, Wolgang Petritsch, Karl Pichelmann, Franz Pichler, Hannes Porias, Bartho Pronk, Martin Reisigl, Peter Rosner, Dagmar Rothwandl, Edith Saurer, Edgar Josef Schiedermeier, Inger Schoerling, Rudolf Scholten, Arnold Schmidt, Bojan Schnabl, Antonia Schwaighofer, Johannes Schweighofer, Maria Sedlak, Peter Skinner, Günther Steinbach, Carolyn & Stephan Straehle, Johannes Swoboda, Georg Winckler, Alexander van der Bellen, Teun van Dijk, Anne van Lancker, Theo van Leeuwen, Wim van Velzen, Jerome Vignon, Susan Waddington, Werner Wanschura, Barbara Weiler, Friedrich Wolf, David Wright, Gustav Zöhrer, Heinz Zourek.

Austrian Academy of Sciences, Austrian Ministry of Science and Transport, Austrian Ministry of Social Affairs, Austrian Science Fund, Bank Austria, Department of Linguistics (University of Vienna), European Commission, European Parliament, Forward Studies Unit, University of Vienna, ZIIS.

Chapter 1

The European Union: Policy-making through organizational discursive practices

Peter Muntigl

1. Introduction

A central function of polities is making and implementing policies. Richardson (1996: 3) argues that the European Union (EU) has, since the Maastricht Treaty, increasingly concerned itself with policy-making. It has even been suggested that the EU, the European Commission in particular, because of its preoccupation with policy-making, has taken on the features of an over-regulating and over-controlling 'nanny' state. However, as pointed out by Richardson (1996), EU policy-making involves numerous groups and organizations (including the Member States, lobbyists and expert groups) and it is therefore difficult to pinpoint exactly which organization at any given time is exerting the most influence over EU policy. That is, influence over EU policy-making will depend upon the policy being negotiated and the organizations involved in shaping that policy. This emphasis on policy-*making* implies that in order to understand the workings of a polity, it is not sufficient merely to examine policy as an outcome. Of more importance is to examine the (organizational) *practices* involved in how polities come to produce policies. These organizational practices involve the use of discursive resources and technologies by organizational members to produce and reproduce the organization. Discursive resources such as talk and print provide the basic means with which policies are constructed, negotiated, and rendered into an enduring form.

Richardson (1996: 5) suggests that EU policy-making involves four general stages: agenda setting, policy formulation, policy decision and policy implementation. This book mainly focuses on the first three stages of this process since the last stage is, to a large extent, taken up by the Member States. The authors examine how specific EU members are invited into policy-making and how EU employment policy is then drawn up in some incipient, negotiable form and then transformed and recontextualized into a final form. The prime focus, therefore, is on how policy is discursively produced and transformed or recontextualized along the various stages of policy-making and what differences in the textual make-up of the policy we can detect along the way. Changes in the linguistic form of policy are also related to changes in its content. More specifically, our interest is in how ideologies are reflected and constructed through the stages of policy making and how certain ideological strands become highlighted while others become concealed. A final focus of our analyses is the command aspect of policies. Policies organize EU members (i.e., direct various sub-parts of the EU such as the Parliament and Commission), attempt to organize those whom their policies target, and, for this reason, may be seen as a form of social control. Since EU policies encode directives, linguistic abstractions and generalizations and are increasingly time-space distanciated from their original interactive forms of production, policies appear natural, universal, and acceptable; that is, persuasive. Policies are therefore rhetorical in that they, through their *naturalness* and *completeness*, achieve common ground with their addressees. Policies, however, do not solely perpetuate control over their subjects. Policies may also enable. They do not act deterministically, producing a single set of outcomes. Through EU policies for example, Member States (MS) may interpret the EU's guidelines in light of their own circumstances. This means that MSs have some flexibility in interpreting and responding to the EU's directives. Whether the targets of MS policies also have the same flexibility in interpreting the MSs' policies depends, ultimately, on how the MSs end up constructing their policies.

The area of policy-making under the scope of our analyses is unemployment and employment. It should be mentioned right at the outset that this is not a book about the unemployed or employed per se. Instead, it is about the discursive construction of employment policy measures that position organizations (i.e., EU, MSs, industry) and groups (i.e., employed, unemployed) as actors who do things or as the recipients of certain kinds of doings. For instance, on the recipient end of un/employment policy, critical issues for the unemployed such as who is (and who is not) to receive job retraining and who is to receive unemployment benefits and for how long may be decided. It should also be noted that the terms 'employment' and 'unemployment' are anything but straightforward. According to Grint (1991), characterizations of unemployment reinforce and reproduce typical 'Western' notions of what is and is not classified as work. Some of the consequences of the ways in which unemployment is typically characterized are nicely summed up by Grint (1991: 40):

> it marks out the conventional Western boundary between work and non-work; it poses questions about the centrality of paid labour in contemporary society; it often has catastrophic consequences for the individual and household concerned; and its definition — as those seeking work and signed on for unemployment benefit — mirrors the state-supported ideology of work as a full-time non-domestic, and hence masculine, phenomenon.

Employment policy-making is therefore not a neutral affair. Employment and unemployment are socially constructed and ideology-imbued terms and so the way in which these terms are used and what actions are to be performed based on these descriptions have real social consequences.

The general approach used in this book to studying the EU's organizational practices of policy-making draws largely from the discourse historical arm of critical discourse analysis (for other examples of studies that have used this approach see de Cilia, Reisigl, & Wodak 1999; Wodak, de Cillia, Reisigl, Liebhart, Hofstätter, & Kargl 1998; Wodak, Menz, Mitten, & Stern 1994; Wodak, Nowak, Pelikan, Gruber, de Cillia, & Mitten 1990; Wodak & Reisigl, 2000; Wodak, Titscher, Meyer, & Vetter 1997). Some of the distinguishing features of the discourse historical approach include: (1) ethnographic observation; (2) analyzing data corpora that extend over a period of time; (3) using a variety of research methods to examine an issue; (4) interdisciplinarity; and (5) critical and problem-oriented analyses. The first point, ethnographic observation, implies that discourse historical studies involve going *inside* of organizations. This entails that a general understanding of the workings of the organization and its practices is needed before focusing on any specific aspect of the organization. The second point insists on examining organizational practices that span across time. For instance, when studying policy-making, both the steps leading up to the policy (i.e., the process) and the policy itself (i.e., the outcome) are important. Texts, therefore, do not stand in isolation but instead are intertextually linked to prior and present texts. The third point argues for adopting a variety of methods in order to examine an issue from a variety of perspectives. This point mirrors Cicourel's (1964) principle of triangulation in which various interdisciplinary and methodological approaches are used to shed as much light as possible on discourse phenomena. The interdisciplinary approach of this book is also mirrored in the differing backgrounds of each of the authors in which a novel mixture of linguistic (e.g., functional systemic linguistic, critical discourse analysis), rhetorical (Burke) and social theory (e.g., Luhmann) has resulted. This interdisciplinarity, however, was not imposed on the research nor was it determined at the outset. When the project began in 1997,[1] the main focus was placed on ethnographic work on the various EU sub-organizations (e.g., Parliament, Commission, Council), data collection and the linguistic analysis of texts (published work on the earlier stages of the project include Muntigl 1999, forthcoming; Straehle, Weiss, Wodak, Muntigl, & Sedlak 1999; Weiss 1999; Wodak & Weiss, 2000). This prior work enabled the authors to combine their analyses of the different sub-organizations of the EU to offer a more comprehensive view of EU policy-making.

---

1. Researching the EU was made possible through the Ludwig Wittgenstein Prize awarded to Ruth Wodak in 1996. With this money, Ruth Wodak started up the research centre: discourse, politics, identity and hired on the research associates who make up the other 2 co-authors of the book.

Discourse historical approaches are also critical approaches — for a discussion see Wodak & Reisigl (2000). Critical implies a *problem*-oriented focus. Unemployment, as argued above, is not a neutral categorization but is socially constructed by EU organizational members. This socially constructed categorization, therefore, will have consequences for those individuals whom the categorization — and the policies resulting from this categorization — applies to. Put differently, treating the terms unemployment and employment as problematic translates into examining the social implications of categories and how they benefit some groups while negatively affecting others.

The remainder of this chapter sets out to situate the EU in terms of an organization. Policy-making is integrally tied up with organizing practices that direct people and their interests.

2.   Organizations and organizational practices

So far, the EU has been referred to as a polity and an organization. *Polity* tends to emphasize the policy aspect of the EU whereas *organization*, more generally, emphasizes the EU's role as organizing human conduct, experience, and relationships. Also, the term organization may be seen as reflecting a wider array of tasks that EU members engage in. That is, while policy-making is a central task of the EU, it is not their only task. EU members (especially Members of the European Parliament (MEPs)) also must meet, for example, with members of their constituency and special interest groups. Such interactions do not necessarily play a pivotal role in policy-making but rather may serve more general interpersonal requirements. In effect, since the functions of the EU are not solely restricted to policy-making, the EU should be referred to as an organization so that a range of other practices may also be subsumed under what EU members *do*.

We begin our discussion of organizations by drawing on some insights derived from studies in ethnomethodology (see also Iedema & Wodak 1999; Mumby & Clair 1997; Wodak 1987, 1996 for a more comprehensive review of organizational discourse). Boden (1994: 47), in her analysis of business meetings, draws principally from ethnomethodological and conversation analytic work by placing the focus of organizations "on the nature of organizing and on the temporal and sequential details of organizatio*n*." This ethnomethodological premise places people and their ethnomethods (i.e., their rational, practical, and accountable activities) at the center of what constitutes organizing. So, an organization is, for ethnomethodologists, not to be viewed as independent of individuals and their ethnomethods nor as having deterministic properties but as a contingent accomplishment in which people locally and accountably produce and reproduce settings for themselves and others. Garfinkel (1984: 33) emphasizes this point when he argues that:

> any social setting be viewed as self-organizing with respect to the intelligible character of its own appearances as either representations of or as evidences-of-a-social-order. Any setting organizes its activities to make its properties as an organized environment of practical activities detectable, countable, recordable, reportable, tell-a-story-aboutable, analyzable — in short, accountable.

Using the ethnomethodological notion of contingent accomplishment as a starting point for considering what organizations are means that our analyses should be grounded in actors' rational, practical and accountable activities in organizing their own settings. Placing the focus of organizations on the organization of social interaction requires an in-depth understanding of the kinds of practices that enable and constrain this day-to-day organizing process. These organizational (discursive) practices make use of numerous resources in producing and reproducing the organization. Some practices may appear informal (i.e., chatting with a colleague) or formal (i.e., chaired meetings, writing up reports, debates). That is, organizational practices tend to lie on a continuum of informal and everyday on the one side and formal, repetitive, and enduring on the other. The latter are often referred to as institutional practices. Giddens (1984: 17), for instance, refers to institutions as "those practices which have the greatest time-space extension." Similarly, Ehlich and Rehbein (1994) also speak of institution as combinations of complex interactive patterns, as stable and as goal-oriented. These views on institutions are discursively and interactively based. Institution is, therefore, not a complex of norms that regulate behavior in Parsons' sense, nor is it an organization in the sense just put forward. Institutions are instead the enduring, time-space distanciated practices used by people to organize their social world. But, in this book, rather than referring to institutions, we refer to institutionalized or institutional practices.

Much recent discourse-oriented work has displayed the numerous types of institutional practices that occur in various organizations and work environments (see for example, Drew & Heritage 1992; Drew & Sorjonen 1997; Firth 1995a; Wodak 1996 for talk in work settings; Gunnarsson, Linell, & Nordberg 1997 and Linell & Sarangi 1998 for talk in 'professional' settings; and Christie & Martin 1997 and Iedema 1995 for talk in school and workplace settings). Conversation analysts, basing their work on spoken face-to-face interaction, argue that to capture the institutional aspects of talk, one must compare conversational or everyday talk to its more formal and institutional occurrences. Institutional talk, as argued in Drew & Heritage (1992), may be identified along three general dimensions: participants' orientations to goals, constraints on contributions, and specific inferential frameworks. A few relationships can be drawn here with respect to the EU. If we consider Parliamentary debates, we can say that the participants in the debate broadly orient their talk to the organizational task of creating an EU employment policy. In addition, the participants' contributions are constrained temporally and sequentially since the order of the participants' contributions is determined in advance and the amount of time given to them to present their views may not be exceeded. Finally, conduct that deviates from the 'orderly' turn-taking of the debate — interrupting, taking too long a turn — is met with specific inferences that usually translate into sanctions from the presiding officer.

So far, this discussion of organizational practices has centered on talk. These practices, however, also involve the use of a number of other representation systems that make use of visual and material resources. Talk, therefore, is not the only medium in which information is negotiated. As Streeck (1996: 366) argues, "meaning and information are not only inherent in linguistic and embodied components of the communicative process — talk and gesture — but are *distributed* across a variety of "places" ... and representation systems." Put another way, information is distributed and stored across a variety of material and non-material resources such as language, print, objects, and constructed "material" spaces (c.f. Goodwin 1994; Kress & van Leeuwen 1996; Lebaron & Streeck 1997; Streeck 1996; Suchman & Trigg 1993). Analyses of organizational practices should, therefore, consider the range of interactional resources that organizational members make use of. Following Callon & Latour (1981) and Latour & Woolgar (1986), organizational members are seen as part of and constantly associating with an eco-social system. Social action is not seen merely as interactions between individuals but as interactions that are embedded within and associated with a multitude of ecological components.

The EU is a prime example of such an eco-social system. Here, EU members negotiate information in party and committee meetings and debates. This, in turn, is accomplished in and across a variety of geographic spaces (i.e., Brussels, Luxembourg, Strasbourg, MSs) using a host of interactional resources such as talk, written documents, and technologies (e.g., communication technology such as cell-phones and fax machines or 'writing' technologies such as computers and printers). Thus, in order to grasp the workings of the EU, an understanding of how EU members organize their discursive practices is of utmost importance.

3.   Some enduring features of organizational practices

Ethnographic studies of scientists' fact-making practices have shown how statements undergo transformations as they move from non-facts to facts (Latour & Woolgar 1986; Latour 1987). At the initial stages of fact production, statements are modally weak and appear in such forms as "I guess/think/believe that X." Through the later stages of fact production, statements increase in modal strength to the point that they become fact-like. At this stage, statements appear in such forms as "X is the case" or merely as "X." Later on in time, as the fact-like status of a statement has gained general acceptance, it need no longer be explicitly referred to and so becomes part of a community's tacit knowledge. There is no guarantee, however, that facts always remain facts. It is always possible to challenge a fact and by doing so reduce its status. Because of this, Latour (1987: 23) suggests that there always exists the potential to increase a statement's solidity by leading it away from its conditions of production (i.e., "X") or to weaken it by leading it towards its conditions of production ("I guess that X").

Another observation made by Latour & Woolgar (1986) is that pre-facts begin in an ephemeral state as people talking about what might be the case and end up, if they achieve fact-like status, embedded in more enduring media such as print — examples being journal articles or books. Latour (1987) discusses a number of discursive practices that work to maintain and build up the solidity of facts. One may, for instance, cite other authors to back up one's premises or strengthen a claim through visual representations such as figures. The idea is that as more referents (citations, articles, research laboratories) are brought in to 'surround' a claim, the harder it will be to attack the claim. This is so because in order to successfully undermine the claim, one now also has to undermine the citations, articles, and research laboratories that are associated with the claim. Latour metaphorically relates the practice of increasing the durability of statements to a black box. That is, by associating claims with a number of referents and by strengthening the modality of a claim, one black boxes its contents. In this way, the negotiability of the claim's contents is reduced.

The discursive construction of facts has also been taken up by more conversation-analytic orientations to fact making (Edwards & Potter 1992; Potter 1996). Drawing on the insights of Latour & Woolgar (1986), they suggest a number of discursive practices that bolster or undermine a description's factuality. This is referred to, respectively, as reifying or ironizing discourse (Potter 1996: 107). In order to examine fact making, Potter recommends that descriptions be analyzed along two levels. The first refers to the *action orientation* of descriptions. This means that descriptions should first be analyzed for the kind of discursive work that they are doing. For instance, a description may be making an argument or disagreeing with a claim, or accounting for a refusal to an invitation and so on. What is being recommended, therefore, is that descriptions be first examined in relation to their discursive context and for the number of discursive functions they may be performing. The second level refers to the *epistemological orientation* of descriptions. That is, descriptions may be made to appear more or less factual (i.e., reified or ironized) and these discursive practices are often bound up with stake and interest. The facticity of a description, for example, may be undermined by associating the producer of the description with certain interests. Edwards &

Potter (1992) refer to this as the *dilemma of stake*: Any description made by a speaker can appear dilemmatic since it may be refuted on the grounds that it is the product of the speaker's stake or interest. Speakers therefore, when doing descriptions, may engage in a lot of discursive work that either confesses stake in a matter or inoculates or distances them from being perceived as having stake.

One of the ways in which speakers/writers can guard against stake or interest is what Potter (1996: 150) describes as constructing *out-there-ness*. This would include all those discursive practices in which agency is transferred from the source of production — usually the one who produced the description — to another entity. Some ways in which this is done include distancing oneself from the source of one's description and constructing consensus and corroboration around one's claims. The former is often taken up under the rubric of *footing* (Goffman 1979). More specifically, speaker/writer roles may be negotiated along the lines of who has scripted the text (i.e., author) and whose point of view the text is meant to represent (i.e., principal). Impersonal forms such as "it is said that ..." or "the report urges that ..." may distance the speaker/writer from author and principal roles by aligning the scripting of the words onto an unknown collective or a report and by making them responsible for the words. The latter, constructing consensus and corroboration, occurs through discursive practices that position a number of individuals as having independently reached the same conclusion. In this way, one bolsters a description through the implication that some or many agree and that stake or interest cannot be involved since individuals, independent of one another, all claim the same thing.

Making descriptions more solid or more fact-like is also done within the clause. Latour & Woolgar (1986) alluded to this in their discussion of modality. A more extensive treatment of clause constructions is provided in an approach known as Functional Grammar (FG) (see Halliday 1994). We will, however, restrict ourselves to those discursive practices in FG that work to obscure agency and make descriptions more solid and durable. These practices include: abstraction, generalization, modalization/ modulation and technicality. A brief overview of each practice follows:

Abstraction

Abstraction is referred to by Martin (1991: 313–314) as buried reasoning, when "reasoning is realized inside rather than between clauses." Common linguistic manifestations of abstraction occur when processes are nominalized and embedded within a single clause. Consider the nominalized process *coordination* in the example "At the Amsterdam European Council, important instruments were adopted for the coordination of European employment policy." The prepositional phrase expressing the purpose of adopting important instruments can be unpacked to form a clause such as *so that European employment policy can be coordinated*:

Prepositional Phrase: for the coordination of European employment policy.
Separate Clause: so that European employment policy can be coordinated.

Martin refers to the first case as an instance of buried reasoning since information is being conveyed intraclausally that could have been expressed in a separate clause.

Generalization

Generalization refers to terms that 'collect' meaning. van Leeuwen (1995: 99) sees generalization as a form of abstraction since "they abstract away from the more specific 'micro-actions' that make up meaning." Those parts of the grammar where generalizations are often expressed are in nominalizations or in *processes*. Halliday (1994: 106) describes processes as representing the 'goings-on' of a clause. Such 'goings-on' include doing, happening, sensing, meaning, being, and becoming. Processes of doing, for example, refer to such verbs as run, give, and build whereas processes of sensing refer to think, believe, and know. Now, the idea behind generalization is that the generalized term implies a range of goings-on. An example can be found in this chapter when reference is made to *policy making*. Recall that policy making was divided up into four stages: setting an agenda, formulating a policy, deciding on a policy and implementing the policy. Using these terms, we can construct a taxonomy (Figure 1) in which policy making is the supraordinate term:

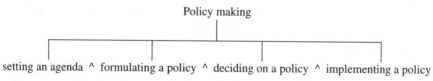

Policy making

setting an agenda ^ formulating a policy ^ deciding on a policy ^ implementing a policy

Figure 1: Taxonomy of policy making

So, policy making can be seen as a set of actions that, taken together, constitute what it means to make policy. In addition, van Leeuwen (1995) sees such a composition of actions as temporally organized. That is, the subordinate actions do not occur in a random order but must occur in the order depicted by the taxonomy for them to be recognizable as an instance of policy making. Generalization, however, does not stop there. What, for instance, is to be inferred from *setting, formulating, deciding*, or *implementing*? These processes are also generalized in that they cover a range of actions. Take *setting an agenda* as an example.

This would involve a number of actions such as choosing people for a meeting, briefing people on a topic to be discussed, bringing these people together, etc. As our work will show, generalizations often appear in policy reports.

Modality: Modalization and Modulation

Halliday (1994: 356) argues that clauses are of two types. They are either about exchanging information or goods-&-services. The modality of the former, information exchange, involves modalization. These clauses lie on a continuum between what is the case and what is not the case. Between these positive and negative poles lie weaker modal forms such as *may be*, *will be*, or *must be*. Modalization is expressed either through probability (i.e., possibly, probably, or certainly) or usuality (i.e., sometimes, usually, or always). Modulation, on the other hand, refers to the continuum between doing and not doing something. Weaker modal forms include *will do*, *may do*, and *must do*. Modulation is expressed through clauses that convey obligation (i.e., allowed to, supposed to, required to) or inclination (willing, keen, determined). Modality, according to Halliday, may also have an objective orientation in which the speaker or writer is disassociated from the modality expressed in the clause. For example, in a command such as *It is required for all Member States to reach agreements*, the commander is not specified. So, although it is clear that Member States are required to do something, what is not clear is who is doing the requiring.

Technicality

Important for understanding technicality is what Martin (1993b: 86) refers to as common and uncommon sense categories or taxonomies. Martin (1993b) suggests that people construct taxonomies in reference to their common sense knowledge which is, in turn, derived from their daily experiences. As an example, Martin claims that his common sense taxonomy of sea mammals would include whales, dolphins, and seals whereas a biologist's uncommon sense taxonomy would include categories such as placental, marsupial, and monotreme. The point here is that professional taxonomies arise out of the experiences and interactions with one's professional community and, because of this, bear little resemblance to more everyday notions of what people might have about, say, sea mammals.

The above discursive practices, by increasing the fact-like status of descriptions, can be seen to play a role in guarding against stake and making one less accountable for the claims being put forward. That is, through abstraction, generalization, modalization, technicality, distanced footing, and consensus, one can package a description so that issues of stake and the chances of being held accountable for a text are minimized. However, not all descriptions are about stake and accountability. It may well be the case that scientific texts such as journal articles make use of abstraction and modalization in order to guard against stake or, more generally, possible counter-claims from opponents. Other texts may be doing other things in addition to claim-making and, for this reason, it is necessary to examine the action orientation of descriptions as recommended by Potter (1996). For instance, policy is written up as a set of commands. So, in terms of its action orientation, policy is designed to get others to do things. In order to examine the above discursive practices in relation to a policy's action orientation, consider the following example from the EU parliamentary resolution (see Appendix 4(12)):

> The European Parliament, ... urges that decisions be taken without delay to reduce taxation of labour by means of European agreements on transferring taxation to the environment, natural resources, energy and capital-intensive production, as proposed in the White Paper on Growth, Competitiveness and Employment;

In this bit of text, the European Parliament (EP) proposed that instead of taxing labor, taxation should increasingly target other sources (i.e., the environment, natural resources, energy and capital-intensive production). What we propose doing in this example is to link up the above mentioned discursive practices with the action orientation of the policy. Let us first examine how generalization functions in this text. The EP proposes that *decisions be taken*. Taking decisions glosses over the number of implicit actions needed to take a decision, such as groups meeting to discuss, decide, and agree on whom is to be taxed. It should be pointed out that we are not suggesting that there exists a set of terms that are semantically complete. All terms, in Garfinkel's (1984) sense, are *indexical* and therefore only to be understood and appreciated for their relevance in their context of use. We *are* suggesting, however, that information that otherwise may be present can be backgrounded or buried within terms. The way in which *decisions be taken* obscures information may be better understood in conjunction with modulation. In this case, the EP issues a command with a relatively high positive modal value (i.e., urges). Note also that this process is passivized. Through passivization, the proposee can be (and in this case is) deleted. That is, those groups who are being directed to take decisions are not mentioned. In sum, unnamed groups are being directed to engage in a generalized activity (i.e., take decisions) in order to reduce the taxation of labor. If, however, we unpack this generalization and abstraction, we begin our search for the missing actors and the complex set of social activities that constitute *taking decisions*. It is also quite plausible to imagine that those whom this policy targets must go through this kind of unpacking process to find out what is to be done and, in this case since the propossees are not mentioned, if it applies to them. Further abstraction is achieved through the means by which these unnamed agents are to take decisions: *Euro-*

pean agreements. Agreements occurs in nominalized form which embeds the process of agreeing. In addition, the classifier *European* imbues agreements with a specific quality. The agreements are therefore European ones which implies that MSs are to be somehow involved. Perhaps in this way, the actors who are being targeted by the policy are able to sneak back into the clause. They do so, however, not as a participant of a process (i.e., as the one who is to negotiate agreements) but as a manner circumstance.

This brief examination of the practices of generalization, modulation, and abstraction has shown how the proposees of directives and what they are directed to do is backgrounded, obscured, and buried within linguistic forms. Although it could be argued that these practices relate to stake and accountability since reducing taxation of labor and shifting taxation to the environment and natural resources serves certain interests, there is another reading possible here. Not specifying who is to do something and not specifying how it is to be done may leave a certain amount of room open for those who will end up shifting taxation to these other areas. Nor are these formulations necessary a stalling tactic to shift the burden of responsibility on to others since the EU does not want to decide. Commanding others does not necessarily mean spelling out in great detail what needs to be done. There are advantages in leaving others a degree a room to perform their duties. Constraining others' actions may lead to dead ends since there is not enough flexibility to try another approach. So, it may be that this use of generalizations and abstractions in EU policy is to help enable the execution of policy rather than hindering its execution by narrowing the choices of those being commanded. These issues are taken up in more detail in Chapter 6.

Another possible reading to the frequent occurrences of generalizations and abstractions in policies are that these practices effect social control. Hodge & Kress (1993), for instance, suggest that abstractions such as nominalizations and passives tend to mystify meaning. This process of mystification tends to control people since they more readily accept the simplified information. As they put it:

> Reducing the complexity of an argument and limiting the terms which it can contain is a drastic intervention. Showing less means someone else sees less. And seeing less means thinking less. (Hodge & Kress 1993: 22)

Extending Hodge & Kress' line of argument to the above example, we could suggest that the policy attempts to control some unspecified others through abstraction and generalization since they are only vaguely told what to do. More specifically, as long as, say, MSs are not told precisely how to shift taxation to the environment, they may, through subtle discursive practices of control, be tricked into doing so. Now, one of the problems with this argument is that it assumes that those being commanded are not part of the professional community of policy makers. Hodge & Kress' claim may have plausibility in situations where an expert community is able to command others who do not have access to the same kind of (un)common sense knowledge. The situation, however, is very different for the EU and the Member States — or even for that matter the Social Partners, Enterprise, or Industry. The MSs also make use of abstractions and generalizations when drafting up policy and, therefore, *know* how to go about interpreting and executing EU policy. This does not mean that the language used in policy does not influence the way in which social reality may be perceived. Technicality or the use of uncommon sense categories, for instance, may influence the way in which terms such as employment are interpreted. Take another example from the EP resolution:

> The European Parliament, ... Calls on the Commission and the two sides of industry to make proposals concerning 'atypical' employment to ensure that the irregular work which is prevalent in it is accompanied by adequate social security and employees' rights which are equivalent to those for full working-time

In this example, attention is given to three sets of terms: atypical employment, irregular work, and full working-time. The EP uses a taxonomy that contrasts atypical employment and irregular work with full working-time. Notwithstanding the differences between employment and work (for a discussion see Grint (1991)), atypical and irregular is placed in opposition to full working-time. Working-time is classified as either full or atypical and irregular. The taxonomy is uncommensensical because the oppositions are not constructed as full-part, typical-atypical, or regular-irregular; that is words that share a common root or an opposition-pair are not contrasted. In other words, it is not necessarily part of our common sense to think of full as regular or typical, or *not* full as atypical or irregular. Rather, the juxtapositioning of atypical/irregular and full provides the implication that whatever form of work is not full time is atypical or irregular (further discussion of this example is provided in Chapter 6). This uncommon sense taxonomy allows for the interpretation that full-time work is regular, typical and, by implication, desirable, and non full-time work is atypical, irregular and therefore not desirable.

4.   Ideology

Abstraction is often taken as indexing ideological practices. Hodge & Kress (1993) suggest that ideology is related to discursive transformations such as passivization and nominalization. Surface forms of utterances that result from these transformations are therefore distortions of an underlying, semantically complete and undistorted, form. In addition, these transformations are not random but are linked to a systematically organized presentation of reality; a distorted reality in which information has been suppressed, reordered, or joined. Linguistic transformations of this kind, according to Hodge & Kress, also play a fundamental role in social control. Abstracted utterances that provide a systematically distorted view of reality get people to believe in the distortions. For this reason, ideology is closely connected to and inseparable from issues of domination or hegemony. The connection between ideology and hegemony is made explicit by Mumby who suggests that hegemonic relations are achieved through the active consent of all organizational members to certain sectional interests (i.e., the dominant ideology). In this view, a dominant ideology exercises control over others by perpetuating subtly persuasive — abstracted, mystifying — messages that get others to actively agree with them. How is it that ideology functions to reproduce hegemonic relations? Giddens (1979), also summarized in Mumby (1988: 86), proposes three functions of ideology that achieve this aim: (1) The representation of sectional interests as universal; (2) The denial or transmutations of contradictions; and (3) The naturalization of the present through reification. The first point suggests that certain interests are articulated as universally valid and applicable to all members. Members actively consent to these interests by accepting them as universal and therefore relevant to themselves. The second point implies that contradiction or opposing interests within an organization are reformulated as superficial or unimportant. Mumby (1988: 87) illustrates this tendency in regard to capitalism by claiming that a contradiction exists "between privatized appropriation (capital) and socialized production (labor)." Workers, for instance, tend to be kept at arms length from participating in organizational decision-making and therefore are not furnished with the same rights as management. Management can legitimate and obscure these inequities by arguing that workers are either unqualified or that their involvement will hamper production. The last point involves the reification, objectification, and time-space distanciation of social relationships. In this way, hegemonic relations, hierarchies, unequal participation in organizational activities are socially constructed as natural, ahistorical, and devoid of time and space. It is merely something, which has always existed and will continue to exist.

Based on the above work, two basic claims can be made about ideologies: One is that ideologies are packaged in an abstracted and mystified form and the other is that (dominant) ideologies systematically influence an actively consenting collective. The rest of this section will examine some of the problems with this conceptualization of ideology. We will first deal with the former point: *ideologies are packaged in an abstracted and mystified form.* In the previous section, reference was made to Potter's (1996) claim that descriptions be examined for their action orientation. There it was argued that abstracted, generalized, or modalized forms of descriptions may do a lot of discursive work related to stake, accountability and, in the case of EU policy, providing an increased and more flexible frame for interpreting the policy. That is, abstracted linguistic forms do not necessarily index social control. It is not the case that passive constructions or nominalizations are inherently mystifying and work merely to persuade individuals to see the world in a *distorted* fashion. Potter's point is that abstractions may do a range of discursive work and so it is important to first consider the range of discursive functions that abstractions are doing in the text before coming to the conclusion that there is a hidden motive behind the abstraction (see Potter 1996: 224–227 for an extensive critique of Hodge & Kress' claims).

The second point, *ideologies systematically influence an actively consenting collective*, is taken up by Billig et al. (1988) and Billig (1991). To begin, Billig views ideology as rooted in paradoxes or dilemmas and in the more general paradox found in language. In situations of language use, for instance, the individual is neither free to produce any utterance nor completely limited in making a choice. Or, to frame the issue somewhat differently, social action is not a purely cognitive phenomenon in which individuals make use of internalized scripts to interpret the world; But nor is it a purely 'socially constrained' phenomenon in which individuals are agentless, governed by forces internal or external to the actor. Billig sees this as a dilemma between individual versus social accounts of human action or thought. So, by focusing on one side of the issue, the individual, questions of how the individual relates to his/her environment will become salient. At the same time, focusing only on societal factors will generate queries about the role of human agency. For this reason, Billig suggests that one should not attempt to resolve or dissolve the paradox but to express or expose the paradox. So, at a general level, uncovering ideological uses in texts does not translate into the discovery of instances of universal, natural, or abstracted claims that are devoid of contradiction. As Billig et al. (1988: 2) argue:

> Ideology is not seen as a complete, unified system of beliefs which tells the individual how to react, feel and think. Instead ideology, and indeed common sense, are seen to comprise contrary themes. Without contrary themes, individuals could neither puzzle over their social worlds nor experience dilemmas. And without this, so much thought would be impossible.

By contrary themes, Billig et al. (1988) refer to contrary maxims or opposing pieces of folk wisdom that speakers make use of in their daily interactions. For instance, they argue that for every maxim there is an associated contrary maxim such as "nothing ventured nothing gained" versus "look before you leap" or "too many cooks spoil the broth" versus "many hands make light work." Their point is that in instances of common sense reasoning, speakers do not make use of *either* one or the other but of *both*. It is not that one excludes the other; rather, the use of one maxim will often implicate the relevance of the contrary maxim. Billig et al. (1988: 10) provide the example of a specialty cook who is faced with a sudden increase in requests for consommés. In order to meet the demands of the increased orders, the cook must recruit more help and, in order to ensure that the quality of the product is not jeopardized, hire on competent people. If the cook does not find the necessary experts, the quality of the consommés might decrease. However, if the cook decides to do the work alone, the orders might not be met and the customers will be disappointed. So, in this situation, the cook is forced to work within the commonsense dilemma of hiring on sub-standard help to complete the orders — making the maxim "many hands make light work" enter into force — or of going at it alone to ensure that the quality of the consommé is not compromised — "too many cooks spoil the broth."

Billig's interest in ideology is not only in speakers' uses of or orientations to commonsense maxims but of how speakers' practices also orient to what Billig et al. (1988: 27) refer to as *intellectual* ideologies. The intellectual ideology that they devoted the most attention to was liberalism. As with commonsense maxims, they see liberalism as rooted in dilemmas. That is, traditional equations of liberalism with individualism also contain contrary themes since questions of individual interests often raise the competing question of social interests. Edelman's (1977) study of poverty, for instance, shows how the poor are characterized in paradoxical ways. On the one hand they are characterized as individually responsible for their situation because they are lazy or weak. On the other hand, they are depicted as victims of an unjust society. In this case also, concentrating too much on the individual's responsibility for their situation will give rise to questions of how others or society might also have played a role. Or, turning the argument around, blaming society for an individual's ills will cause people to wonder about the individual's role in bringing about this state of affairs. By intellectual ideologies, Billig et al. (1988) do not mean to imply that these ideologies are passed on from philosophical or religious traditions to individuals in a uni-directional manner. Ideologies such as liberalism, used in everyday contexts, may also influence the theory makers. What is important to stress, however, is that ideologies are historical in that they may be passed along — as a form of commonsense thinking that is paradoxical in nature — from generation to generation. What *happens* to ideologies is not known in advance but is negotiated in the arenas of organizational and everyday activities.

Our interest in this book is on the intellectual ideology known as Neo-liberalism (discussed in more detail in Chapter 2). We argue that Neo-liberalism carries with it a number of contrary themes. One, as already mentioned above, involves the paradox between individual freedom and egalitarianism versus social necessity and authority. Other dimensions involve the Neo-liberal tenet of free markets against the Keynesian tenet of state intervention. Although the texts that we analyzed do reveal the paradoxical nature of Neo-liberal ideology, what we sometimes found is that one side of the paradox tends to be highlighted at the expense of the other. For example, claims of individualism may be constructed through abstractions and modalizations that make these claims seem fact-like or, in Giddens' terminology, natural and universally applicable. Often coupled with

Neo-liberalism, and therefore to free markets, is globalization. Neo-liberalism is linked to globalization through the argument that economic independence from the state, and therefore economic prosperity, can only occur in a global market. To provide a basic flavor of how globalization is used discursively, consider this extract from a topics' list on globalization written up by the Chair of the Competitiveness Advisory Group (CAG) — please refer to Chapter 4 for the history of the CAG and for a more detailed analysis of this topics' list:

> This globalisation process
> (a) is natural: it is the continuation and spread of the process of economic development and social progress on which the prosperity of our countries is based;
> (b) is a good thing since it
> – helps to satisfy consumer needs,
> – enables an increasing number of countries throughout the world to take part in the economic development process, thereby raising their living standards and thus giving us increasingly attractive trading partners;
> (c) is therefore inevitable and irreversible.

The CAG is an expert group that was requested by the European Commission in 1997 to send a policy paper to the 1997 Extraordinary Council summit on Employment. The purpose of this brief analysis is to tease out some of the ideological elements of this text. The text is thematically about globalization or the globalization process. It is also an argument *for* the globalization process and the argument is structured so as to provide reasons for the readers to accept its contents. One of the first things to consider in regard to globalization, then, is the possible dilemmas or paradoxes that talk about globalization might entail. If, for instance, there is such a thing as a globalization process, there might also exist a localizing or nationalizing process. So, the dilemma might be framed somewhat simplistically as follows: Globalizing an economy made up of national players might at some point produce situations in which it is in the nations' better interests — a contentious point but let us assume that a nation may have an interest and that this interest may be represented by some majority — to not act globally but instead act locally. Globalization, whether this refers to markets, enterprises, information, or some other phenomenon, can therefore be framed in the more general paradox of collective (in this case a federation of nations) versus individual (nations) interests. So, given that there exists this dilemma between global and local, one of the ways in which this dilemma can be effaced is to obscure the opposing tendency and present only one tendency as the possible one. Let us now turn to the discursive practices that make globalization appear as an unproblematic and non-paradoxical phenomenon. First, the term *globalization process* occurs in abstracted form. Since *process* suggests a number of *doings* that have beginnings, middle points and outcomes, we suggest that *process* is a generalized term. In turn, globalization may be seen as the nominalized form of *to globalize*.

Therefore, *globalization process* incorporates a number of meanings through abstraction and is, for this reason, fact-like. More discursive work is done in this text by relating the globalization process to a number of positive attributes, most of which are expressed through relational processes (i.e., the verb *is*). It is (a) natural; (b) the continuation and spread of the process of economic development ...; (c) a good thing; and (d) inevitable and irreversible. Note that expressing the relationship through *is* backgrounds the strength of the clauses' high-value positive modality. It is not that it might or must be the case, it merely *is* the case. Therefore, the clauses are made to appear as if the globalization process is simply being related to certain 'natural' characteristics. The positive aspects of the globalization process are also supported by a number of processes of *doing* in which globalization *helps* to satisfy customer needs, *enables* an increasing number of countries throughout the world to take part in the economic development process, and *gives* us increasingly attractive trading partners. Discursively packaging globalization in this way — as an abstracted and generalized term and by associating globalization with positive attributes — deflects from viewing economic relations in more local ways. However, even if other tendencies were considered, these tendencies would be, in contrast to globalization as natural, good and inevitable, seen as unnatural, bad and avoidable. How discourses on globalization work rhetorically is discussed in Chapters 2 and 4.

5. Recontextualizing

Much of the previous discussion on organizational practices has focused on transformative discursive practices. Latour's references to modalization, Potter's references to reifying or ironizing discourse and the number of discursive practices mentioned in Functional Grammar such as abstraction and generalization (see van Leeuwen 1995 for a more extensive list of these transformations) all imply movement towards a certain kind of linguistic form. What is assumed here is that discursive constructions *begin* in some form and get transformed into some other form and that there are sets of describable discursive practices that can be mobilized to bring about these transformations. The suggestion that discursive forms can be altered implies that discursive forms stand in relationships to other forms. The notion that texts may be discursively interrelated is often dubbed *intertextuality* (Bahktin 1981). Transformations of texts, however, more often fall under the rubric of *recontextualization*.

Recontextualization has become the focus of much discourse analytic research (for overviews see Iedema & Wodak 1999; Linell 1998; and Sarangi 1998). Much of this work focuses on recontextualizations at the *intra*textual (i.e., within texts) and *inter*textual levels. Recontextualization at the *intra*textual level has received much attention in Sack's (1992) lectures on conversation and also in

M. Goodwin's (1990) examination of children's arguing exchanges. These recontextualizations are referred to as *format tying* in which a speaker ties some semantic, syntactic, propositional or phonological aspect of a prior speaker's turn to his or her present turn. In this way, the present speaker modifies, through repetition, substitution, addition, or deletion, some part of the speaker's prior utterance. To briefly illustrate these processes, consider the following exchange — taken from Chapter 6 — between two speakers in a parliamentary debate:

> Hermange: …Moi j'ai vraiment peur qu'aujourd'hui, l'expression réduction du temps de travail ne soit à la mode dans certain pays européens et qu'elle se révèle quelque part à terme, peut-être pas a court terme, mais à terme antinomique et antisociale si elle est appliquée selon des modalités contraignants à toutes des entreprises …
> '…I really fear that today, the term working time reduction is only in fashion in certain European countries and that it will reveal in time, maybe not in the short term, but in time, to be antinomical and antisocial if its enforced, according to a restricting mode, onto all companies …'
>
> .
> .
> .
>
> Moreau: Ce n'est pas une mode, Madame Hermange, les 35 heures, c'est un grand objectif de civilisation pour vivre mieux et pour créer d'emploi. …
> '… This is not in fashion, Madame Hermange, these 35 hours, its a big objective of civilization for the better living and to create jobs. …'

In this exchange, two positions in regards to working time reduction are put forward: Hermange is against whereas Moreau is for working time reduction. Leaving aside important questions of ideology concerning working time (see Chapter 6) let us focus exclusively on how a fragment of Hermange's text is tied and recontextualized by Moreau. Hermange argues that working time reduction is in fashion (*l'expression réduction du temps de travail ne soit à la mode dans certain pays européens*) whereas Moreau argues that it is not in fashion (*Ce n'est pas une mode, Madame Hermange, les 35 heures*). Moreau does a lot of interesting linguistic work in the following turn by recontextualizing Moreau's statement through substitution or adding and deleting. First, *soit à la mode* becomes *Ce n'est pas une mode*. That is, Moreau negates Hermange's statement. In addition, Moreau substitutes Hermange's categorization of what is in fashion, *l'expression réduction du temps de travail*, to *les 35 heures*. The focus is no longer placed on the general term 'working time reduction' but instead on a concrete number, the 35 hours.

Our interest in recontextualization is also intertextual; that is, from print to print (e.g., one draft of a report to next) or from talk to print (e.g., negotiating in meetings to a written report). Processes of recontextualization at this level do not differ from intratextual ones. For instance, van Leeuwen & Wodak (1999), in analyses of written notices in which applications of family reunification of Austrian immigrants are rejected, suggest that recontextualizing transformations also occur through processes of deletion, rearrangement, substitution, and addition. So far our discussion social action and organizational practices has centered on transformational practices. Organizing may also be considered with respect to *activities* such as negotiating and decision-making. It is to these 'larger' processes of organizing that we now turn.

6.   Organizing as negotiating and decision-making

The '-*ing*' ending to the words negotiating, decision-making, and recontextualizing suggest an unfolding, dynamic, and interactive process. These connotations are, in our opinion, necessary for counteracting the tendency of viewing negotiation or decision-making as merely a static outcome of social action. Nonetheless, finding an adequate description of what these processes entail is no easy matter. The next few sections review some of the work that uses labels of negotiating and decision-making to describe organizational practices. We point to some inadequacies and inconsistencies in the way these terms are used and suggest some ways in which they may be used for studying the organizing practices within the EU.

6.1 *Negotiating*

An extensive overview of research on 'negotiation' is found in Firth (1995b). In this introductory chapter, Firth boldly sets out to provide a variety of working definitions on negotiation and a summary of a range of approaches (e.g., prescriptive, ethnographic, experimental, discourse) on negotiation research. Firth's chapter highlights the difficulties in supplying a single, comprehensive definition of negotiation. To illustrate this point, the first three pages of Firth's (1995b: 3–5) article provide no less than four definitions in which negotiation is viewed as a(n) "formal, problem-solving *event*," "*activity* of social decision-making on substantive matters," "discourse-based and situated *activity*, an *activity* that is interactionally constructed in concrete social settings," and "interplay of opposing and shared *interests* (the latter seemingly the more dominant) that compels the warring sides to engage in formal negotiations." A number of 'properties' may be teased out of Firth's definitions. First of all, he differentiates between negotiating as an *event* and negotiating as an *activity*. These two terms distinguish between highly formal and institutionalized practices of organizations such as peace negotiations between countries or ethnic groups and trade-union/management negotiations and the more informal, locally produced and sequentially accomplished negotiations that are constitutive of larger organizational (or everyday) practices. The former, negotiating as an event, generally takes place in the presence of a mediator, has a fixed time schedule and program, clearly articulated positions — usually conflicting — at the outset, pre-allocated turns, and is geared towards a specifiable outcome. In contrast, negotiating as an activity has little or no pre-agreed upon 'rules' of procedure and is locally, contingently, and accountably produced alongside other discursive practices.

So, on the one hand, we have negotiation as a highly structured and institutionalized event and, on the other hand, we have negotiation as a contingent and ephemeral activity that surfaces and disappears along with the moment-to-moment contingencies of talk. What binds the two together? Firth provides at least two substantive characteristics that can be applied to both: problem-solving/decision-making and outcome. Problem-solving implies that there exists opposing interests or views on an issue — or, at the very least, a not-yet-agreed-upon perspective on an issue. Problem-solving also implies an outcome. That is, parties will engage in problem-solving activities to reach a 'solution.' This could mean that one of the opposing interests will win out, or a new perspective will emerge, or that the parties agree not to agree (also a type of solution). Notice, however, that the focus is now not so much on negotiating but on problem-solving or decision-making. With this move, the burden of definition is removed from negotiation and placed on problem-solving. To make matters worse, negotiating, problem-solving, and decision-making may be used interchangeably to define each other. For instance, we could define problem solving and decision-making as "a formal, negotiable event" or as "an activity of social negotiating on substantive matters." Recognizing the inherent difficulties of applying general labels to social activities, ethnomethodologists tend to adopt a cautious stance, examining first whether a process such as negotiation is oriented to and made relevant to the participants (see especially Schegloff (1992, 1997) who argues that analysts should demonstrate how participants orient to and reflexively constitute the *procedural consequentiality* of social categories):

> Ethnomethodologists have long insisted on the 'accomplished' rather than 'negotiated' nature of social order. This emphasis is grounded in an ethnomethodological 'indifference' to labels, which is to say an avoidance of *a priori* assumptions about the specific nature of social organization. To propose that certain activities constitute 'negotiation', or 'bargaining', or 'conflict resolution' entails clear assumptions about the goals, intentions and even presuppositions of the social actors involved. (Boden 1995: 84)

Specifying what aspects of negotiation social actors are orienting to brings us right back to the problem of what negotiation *is*. However, rather than abandoning any attempt at incorporating the term negotiation into our analyses, we recommend retaining Firth's associations to problem-solving, decision-making, and outcomes without necessarily defining them in these exact terms. Organizational practices *do* involve differing interests and differing perspectives on issues (or, they simply need *a* perspective so that they can begin to frame the issue in some way) and these differences are often attended to and made interactionally relevant by participants. In examining negotiating, focus should be directed to social actions such as formulating, reformulating, and disagreeing with claims and how such claims orient to specifiable outcomes (see also Maynard's (1984) analysis of plea bargaining). Of interest is also which positions are intensively 'negotiated' and which are not. That is, do certain aspects of ideologies remain unchallenged or are they so formulated so as to gain active consent and is this suggestive of a hegemonic relationship?

The question as to which positions are less easily challengeable, problem-solvable, or decision-makeable (i.e., non-negotiable) is of central interest here. Recall our discussion of Callon & Latour's (1981) black-boxing in the previous section. One of the practices of the EU (and virtually any other organization for that matter) is to black box propositions and, once black-boxed, they become more difficult to re-negotiate. By negotiated we mean reformulated, disagreed with, and redirected in terms of its final outcome. Analyses of non-negotiability should therefore focus more on those practices that resist attempts by others to renegotiate an issue and those institutionalized practices mentioned in previous sections that reify — through abstraction, generalization, modalization — social processes.

6.2 *Decision-making*

Similar difficulties arise for decision-making as they did for negotiating. That is, decision-making may also be viewed in terms of negotiating, problem-solving, outcomes, etc. Moreover, the connection between the process in which decisions are made and its outcome is far from clear. Boden (1994: 21) points out that "ideas about "decisions" (as a set of outcomes) are confused with "decision-making" (as a process) by a semantic presumption that the latter is connected to the former in some nonproblematic manner." Garfinkel's (1984) examination on juror's decision-making practices highlights the disparity between jurors' discursive practices used in reaching a decision and their reconstruction of the decision-making process after the decision was made. In other words, the account for how and why the decision was made came after, not before, the decision.

> In place of the view that decisions are made as the occasions require, an alternative formulation needs to be entertained. It consists of the possibility that the person defines retrospectively the decisions that have been made. *The outcome comes before the decision.* In the material reported here, jurors did not actually have an understanding of the conditions that defined a correct decision until after the decision had been made. Only in retrospect did they decide what they did that made their decision the correct ones. When the outcome was in hand they went

> back to find the "why," the things that led up to the outcome, and then in order to
> give their decisions some order, which namely, is the "officialness" of the
> decision. (Garfinkel 1984: 113–114)

Garfinkel is not suggesting that the retrospective accounting for how decisions came to be has nothing to do with the decision-making process. Actors will surely draw on past discussions when formulating their decisions. It is just that the steps leading up to the decisions will not be reflected in their entirety (perhaps not even partly) in the final decision. Therefore, when examining EU reports (i.e., the outcome of some negotiating and decision-making process) little can be said about how information in the report was arrived at (through discursive practices) unless these practices are somehow made available; that is, if, for example, transcripts of the meetings in which decisions were made are made available (see Chapter 4 for the relationship between the verbally negotiated information in meetings and the outcomes of these negotiations as made manifest in a policy paper).

Although all the chapters in this book deal with decision-making and decisions (i.e., process and outcome) both are not given equal weight in their analyses. Chapters 4 & 6 examine both the process and the outcome of policy-making — Chapter 4 examines the negotiation of policy in meetings and Chapter 6 a debate on EP policy — whereas Chapter 5 focuses exclusively on the genesis of written drafts of EP policy. The latter uses Luhmann's systems theory (1997) to show how 'decisions' (i.e., policy) relate to, frame, and contextualize other decisions and construe decision premises within one organizational system.

7. Outline of the book

Two components of EU policy-making have been highlighted in this chapter: the institutional, discursive practices used in formulating policy and the outcome of these discursive practices (i.e., the policy). The intertextual link between policy process and outcome is mediated through recontextualizations of the former into the latter. Furthermore, recontextualizations are the sites in which ideological dilemmas can be made salient or non-dilemmatic. That is, recontextualizing practices may reinforce possible contrary themes or may, through abstraction or generalization, etc., package an ideology so as to obscure its contray themes. The chapters in this book show how the policy-making process of the EU can be viewed in terms of recontextualizations and how recontextualizations reveal ideological dilemmas concerning (EU defined) employment issues.

So, at a broad level, this book examines the organizational practices used in policy-making. Of special interest are those organizational practices that are institutional, ideological, and rhetorical. Some of the questions guiding the analyses are which organizational practices index ideological dilemmas, which work rhetorically to gain widespread assent or challenge specific sectional interests and which are institutionalized and therefore contribute to the organization's set of enduring organizational practices? Other questions involve which ideological themes — Neo-liberal and Keynesian, or other — are most closely linked with employment policy and how unemployment and employment is discursively constructed in written and spoken texts. A most central question, however, is how these organizational practices transform or recontextualize information within and across texts. The discourse-historical approach enables us to investigate these questions and provides an insight into the complexity and intransparency of organizations: how do networks function, what are the functions of the various committees, of an EU committee regime? What is the impact of the decisions, who is affected, etc.?

The remainder of this book is divided into four sections: economic issues, ethnography & data, analyses, and discussion. The following chapter, Chapter 2 by Gilbert Weiss, provides an in-depth examination of the economic issues that surround both employment and unemployment. These include issues of globalization, Keynesianism, and Neo-liberalism. One of the main arguments put forward is that there exist competing ideas, as manifested in EU employment policy, in terms of viewing the markets as the only relevant force behind job creation (Neo-liberalism) and the state as being able to significantly contribute to the creation of jobs (Keynesianism). In other words, these contrary views entail 'letting the markets create jobs' vs. 'state intervention in job creation.'

Chapter 3 by Gilbert Weiss gives an overview of the EU's history and EU employment policy, summarizes our case study approach to analyzing EU policy-making and gives a brief description of the fieldwork in Brussels and Strasbourg and how we obtained our data. From the numerous interviews, meetings, reports, and debates that were collected in Brussels, we chose to focus on a single policy and the steps that led up to its final production. Specifically, we examine the contributions by the EP and CAG to the 1997 Extraordinary European Council Meeting on Unemployment.

The next section contains three papers that analyze various stages in EU employment policy-making. The approaches used in each of these chapters is multi-disciplinary. Ruth Wodak, in Chapter 4, uses a discourse historical and critical discourse analytic approach (see Wodak et al. 1990; Wodak et al. 1994; Wodak et al. 1998 for other examples of the discourse historical approach) to examine the CAG's contribution to the 1997 employment summit. Here, Wodak examines the conflict between management and trade-unionist perspectives in the negotiation of a policy paper. She shows that the recontextualization of conflicts between these two groups and their perspectives can be traced from the interactions in meetings to the final draft of the policy report. Instead of indexing the merging of multiple voices into a single voice, Wodak argues that multiple voices are still retained within the final document.

The following chapter, Chapter 5, analyzes the final and pre-final draft of an EP resolution. Here, Gilbert Weiss combines a systemic functional linguistic (SFL) approach with Luhmann's systems theory. SFL is used to examine the theme-rheme structure of these documents and Luhmann's systems theory to reveal the 'decision premises' of EP policy and how these 'decisions' connect intertextually to prior 'decisions.' His analysis shows how Keynesian and Neo-liberal views are weaved into and recontextualized into the final version of EP policy. Ultimately, argues Weiss, EP policy plays an insignificant role in EU policy-making.

Chapter 6 by Peter Muntigl also examines the pre-final and final drafts of the EP resolution but also includes an analysis of an EP debate that intervened between these drafts. Muntigl uses a Burkean-rhetorical and SFL approach to examine discursive and rhetorical practices of the EP. Special focus is placed on the ideological dilemmas concerning the organization of working time. It is shown that despite the clear opposition of views expressed in the penultimate EP draft and in parliamentary debate, the final draft tends to efface this opposition by highlighting one side of the dilemma and backgrounding the other.

The discussion, Chapter 7 by Gilbert Weiss and Ruth Wodak, compares the EP resolution with the CAG policy paper and discusses the role of the various organizational sub-parts (i.e., CAG, EP, and Commission) in relation to Arendt's 'agonistic,' Rawls' 'legalistic,' and Habermas' 'discursive' models of public space.

Chapter 2

Labor Markets, Unemployment and the Rhetoric of Globalization

Sociological and Economic Background

Gilbert Weiss

1. Introduction

In 1998 no fewer than 18 million people were unemployed in the member states of the European Union (EU), a rate of 10.5 per cent according to the definition of the unemployment rate by the International Labor Office (ILO). This rate defines as unemployed all those aged 15 years and over who

> are without work
> are available to start work within the next two weeks
> and have actively sought employment at some time during the previous four weeks.
> (Joint Employment Report 1998)

In this chapter, I will look a little more closely at European and international labor markets, give some numbers and 'hard facts', describe sociological and economic approaches to employment and unemployment, and outline what will be called globalization rhetoric and competitiveness discourse. I will contextualize these issues in what is more and more often being called 'new' Capitalism, globalization, dominance of financial markets, changing role of the nation state, etc. In this way the chapter will set out the necessary background for understanding EU discourses and policy discourses on un/employment. It will, therefore, serve as an ongoing frame of reference for the linguistic-analytical chapters.

2. Labor markets

From the early 1970s on, unemployment has been continuously growing in Europe. At the beginning of the 1990s, in the face of a global recession, the continent witnessed a return to mass unemployment — a situation "comparable to the 1930s" (Michie and Wilkinson 1994: 11; also Thurow 1996: 189). The percentage numbers of unemployed in the EU, however, differ widely with regard to (a) individual member states, with, for instance, 20.8 per cent in Spain (highest rate) and 2.6 per cent in Luxembourg (lowest) in 1997, (b) individual regions (e.g., Bavaria and Rhône-Alpes showing the lowest rates of the Union versus Southern Italy, Southern France, South-East England showing the highest rates). In 1993 the ten worst regions showed an average unemployment rate of 25.3 per cent, and the ten best a rate of 3.6 per cent (on the statistical measure of regional disparity in unemployment rate, Townsend 1997: 62). (c) gender (9.3 per cent male unemployed vs. 12.4 per cent female in 1997), (d) age groups (young [15–24], prime age [25–54] and older [55–64] people), and (e) sectors of the labor market (e.g. manufacturing vs. services) (Townsend 1997; Addison and Siebert 1997; Collier 1994; Tomaney 1994)

Another statistical indicator of changes in labor markets is the employment rate, i.e. the number employed relative to working-age population. In recent years, this has been taken more and more as the most effective measure of the performance of an economy in providing jobs. Using this rate focuses attention on both employment and the employment potential of the non-employed, which includes both the "economically inactive" and the unemployed. Unsurprisingly, the employment rate in the EU has also declined in the last three decades, from 65.5 per cent in 1973 to 60.5 per cent in 1997. This situation is particularly alarming when compared with the US and Japan. In the mid-1970s the employment rate in the US (62 per cent) was lower than in the EU (64.5 per cent). By 1997 the situation had been dramatically reversed, 74 per cent in the US versus the EU's 60.5 per cent. Whereas in the US and Japan the employment rate has been continuously growing (with short breaks), it has been falling in the EU (Employment Rates Report 1998). The different development in these major trade blocks is not less evident when the unemployment rates are compared: 4 per cent in the EU and 8 per cent in the US (mid-1970s) vs. 11.2 per cent in the EU and 5.4 per cent in the US (1996). In this context, it is interesting — as A. Townsend points out — that in the US "the chances of becoming unemployed in any one year are several times higher than in the main EU countries, but the chances of finding a job are even higher [...]" (Townsend 1997: 34). For this reason, B. Anderton and K. Mayhew draw the following conclusion: "Higher unemployment in the EC countries is not so much the result of people frequently losing jobs, it is more to do with a lower probability of finding a job having once become unemployed" (quoted from Townsend 1997: 34). The US economist L. Thurow provides a similar diagnosis: "The European problem is not created by job losses. In the 1980s the US lost 2 per cent of its jobs every month while Europe was losing only 0.4. per cent of its jobs. The problem is created by a lack of job expansion. While Western Europe reported no net new jobs from 1973 to 1994, the US generated 38 million net new jobs" (Thurow 1996: 37).

These statements show how important it is always to consider rates of both employment and unemployment, and not to construe a simple relation between these two major statistical indicators for labor market development. For instance, high unemployment in the EU is not the only reason for the difference of employment rates between the EU and the US: "If half of the people currently unemployed were in employment (bringing the EU unemployment rate to the level of the US), the employment rate would be 64 per cent, still well below the levels of the US and Japan" (Employment Rates Report 1998: 4). Similarly to the unemployment rate, the employment rate also differs widely with regard to individual member states, regions, gender, age and economic sectors. With 48.6 per cent, Spain again brings up the rear, whereas Denmark, with 77.5 per cent, is the leader. In six member states (Netherlands, Ireland, Spain, Portugal, Belgium and UK) the employment rates increased more than the average over the period 1985–97; in Italy, Germany and France they fell slightly, in Finland and Sweden sharply. As a consequence, the overall EU employment rate remained virtually unchanged over this period. The increases were mainly in female employment, while male employment was stagnating or even falling. Nevertheless, in the prime age (25–54) and older people (55–64) groups standard employment rates for women are still around 22 percentage points lower than for men. In other words, there is still a significant employment potential for women in the EU. This also becomes evident when comparing the employment rates for women with those in the US:

	EU	US
prime age	61.9%	73.6%
older women	25.9%	49.5%

In general, employment rates for women, young people (15–24) and older people are much lower in the EU than in the US. Only the rate of prime age males (84 per cent) is slightly below the one of the respective group in the US (88 per cent). A particularly significant trend in the EU labor market is the decrease in employment rates for young people and the over-55s. In the period 1985–1997, the rate for the first group declined by nearly 2 per cent per year both for women and men — reaching a level as low as 36 per cent in 1997 (15 percentage points below that of the US). In this group the differences between the member states are also enormous, ranging from 24.4 per cent in France to 69.4 per cent in Denmark. With 46.5 per cent in 1997, the overall EU employment rate for older people is 8 percentage points below the year 1985. The decline in employment of the 55–64 age group, however, seems to be a trend common to all capitalist economies. In this group men are particularly hard hit: in the US the employment rate for male over-55s declined from almost 80 per cent in 1970 to 65 per cent in 1990. In the big member states of the EU it was still worse: e.g. in France from 75 per cent to around 40 per cent, in Germany from almost 80 per cent to 50 per cent (Sennett 1998: 123). This development is primarily due to a dramatic increase in early retirements because of disabilities and widespread 'downsizing' of companies. Finally, when we look at employment rates by sector (share of total employment) in the EU, we see that the services sector, with 65.6 per cent, is overwhelmingly predominant, compared to 5 per cent in agriculture and 29.5 per cent in industry. Needless to say, employment in services has substantially increased over the last 20 years, which does not mean that there is not still potential for further increase. For instance, the US rate in the services has increased to 73.3 per cent (Employment Rates Report 1998: 10).

The employment rate, however, does not only include full time but also part time work. If it were to include only full time jobs, it would be much lower. This counts particularly for women, young and older people (in the Netherlands, for instance, the difference in the group of prime age women is about 20 percentage points). In recent years, the increase of part time jobs has often been interpreted as a signal for growing "flexibility" in the labor markets, and therefore as a positive and necessary development. This might indeed be true from the point of view of the employers. It is much less true from the point of view of employees: "In the EU in 1997, 20 per cent of those working part time say they do so because they could not find a full time job [...]" (Employment Rates Report 1998: 13). This discontent is of course not so much due to working hours as to salary. I will consider the problem of flexibility more fully below. Let me now conclude the survey of numbers by stressing again the most crucial components of EU unemployment rates: namely "the persistence of long-term unemployment (some 50 per cent [of total unemployment]), the widening gender gap (unemployment is falling faster among males than among females for all age brackets), the high level of youth unemployment (twice the average: 19.8 per cent in May 1998), and the skills gap (some half of the stock of unemployed over 25, both males and females, had no educational qualifications beyond basic schooling)." (Joint Employment Report 1998: 9)

3. Unemployment, employment and society

The sociological implications of unemployment go far beyond what numbers and statistics of labor markets can say. What does unemployment mean for the individual as well as the society affected by it? To answer this question we first have to realize that — in a time of mass unemployment — unemployment is a "social condition as much as an individual problem" (Grint 1991: 42) — one that is accompanied by "psychological and material hardship" (Giddens 1989: 502) which can ultimately lead to a "tragedy of everyday-life" (Bourdieu 1997: 142).

3.1 The Marienthal study

With regard to the socio-psychological consequences of unemployment, the study of the "Arbeitslosen von Marienthal" by M. Jahoda, P. Lazarsfeld and H. Zeisel in 1933 was the first systematic sociological approach to the life-world — or rather: the changes in the life-world — of unemployed people. For the first time two genres were brought to a synthesis, namely the statistics of sociographic data on the one hand and the 'social report' on the other. In other words: the central aim of the project was (a) to understand how unemployed people *experi-ence* their state of being unemployed and (b) to relate this subjective perspective continuously to the objective sociographic frame (age, gender, marital status, social status, local circumstances, etc.).

At the beginning of this century, Marienthal, located in Lower Austria, was a small village completely dependent on a cotton-mill which had started there in the 1830s and had become bigger and bigger over the years. In 1926 the factory went through a serious crisis and half of the workers lost their jobs. In the following years it managed to keep the production running; but in 1930 it was finally closed. Marienthal became a community of unemployed. The public life of the community rapidly changed, it turned into a form of *agonia*. The authors described this state — which was a state of mind as much as a state of social life — as "the tired community" (*die müde Gemeinschaft*). Relations within the family (between husband and wife, father and child) deteriorated and were described by the interviewees with a sense of helplessness: e.g., they suffered greatly from the increasing conflicts and quarrels and nevertheless could not avoid them. Social activities and the engagement in the community were reduced to a minimum: the kindergarten was closed down, several cultural associations and clubs fell into decay, borrowings from the library decreased, the reading of newspapers equally, and the political parties complained about a loss of members, etc. (Jahoda, Lazarsfeld and Zeisel 1975: 55ff).

Without going into the many interesting details of the study, let us briefly point to the four types of 'attitudes' which the researchers discovered in the families/households affected by unemployment: (a) *unbroken* (maintenance of household and child-care, subjective feeling of well-being, activity, hopes and plans for the future, continuous attempts to find a new job); (b) *resignation* (also maintenance of house-hold and child-care, feeling of relative well-being, but: no plans and hopes, no relation to future, maximum reduction of all needs and wants which go beyond the pure maintenance of the household, only sporadic attempts at finding a new job); (c) *broken: despair* (household and child-care is still maintained but accompanied by the feeling of despair, depression, all efforts to overcome the status quo are regarded as hopeless, no more search for jobs, 'escape' into a better past); (d) *broken: apathy* (no more maintenance of ordered family life, lodgings and children are dirty and uncared-for, indolence, lacking energy for performing any activities, 'irrational' householding, men start to drink) (ibid: 70ff).

What turned out to be significant in all four categories was the experience of helplessness in dealing with the new *temporal* order of daily life. Men simply did not know how to spend the time, they were hanging around in the streets to avoid staying at home during 'working hours', mostly they could not handle the new 'slowness' of their life; idleness dominated daily life. Needless to say, the material situation was extremely difficult for all unemployed households.

3.2 *The flexibility of jobs*

Although times have changed since the early 1930s and, compared with today's urban unemployment, the situation in Marienthal was untypical insofar as it showed a whole community of unemployed and, therefore, did not show the difficulties of unemployed individuals living within a community where most people are still employed (the latter is the rule in the 1990s), in its socio-psychological implications the Marienthal-study is still very relevant today and has been largely affirmed by more recent studies (e.g., Bostyn and Wright 1987; Archer and Rhodes 1987; Clark 1987). At the end of the present century, the material and psychological consequences of being unemployed still depend to an important extent on the class position of the unemployed. While, for instance, middle class unemployed — from a psychological point of view — seem to suffer greater 'status collapse' than those from the working class, because the former are more personally engaged and involved in work careers, the latter, especially young working class unemployed, are more hit by the financial consequences (Warr 1983; Grint 1991). Talking about careers, today's labor markets generally have a great impact on the life-plan of individuals, on what sociologists like A. Giddens and Z. Bauman call "life politics" or "life strategies" in the age of "second modernity" (Giddens 1991; Bauman 1995). Only very few people are still able to give their professional life the shape of a homogeneous and continu-ous career. Most of them have to be "flexible"; they are forced into job rotation; throughout their lives they must change not only their jobs but also their areas of work several times. The periods of transition are very often periods of temporary unemployment: those who are lucky find a new job rather quickly, those who are not become long-term unemployed. This is precisely the point at which the political and economic flexibility-discourse intervenes: "life-long learning" (see below) is supposed to make people's skills into flexible skills, their minds should become flexible minds. What they did in the past is not relevant for the present; there is a new "market situation", new "challenges" which require new skills. Discontinuity replaces continuity. Against this background postmodernist ideas such as "life in fragments" (Bauman) and "the end of the *grands recits*" (J.-F. Lyotard) indeed gain undeniable plausibility — although not in the enthusiastic sense often accompanying them. R. Sennett (1998: 163) points out that building a career in former years meant modeling something like a life-long meta-narrative (i.e. a *grand recit* of the individual) which provided sense and orientation for the individual's "social personality". The career was the "scarlet thread" of the biography — one which offered a continuous point of orientation and reference even when other biographical threads (private relations, marriage) have been broken. Things have changed however. Flexible Capitalism and its labor markets seem to exclude homogeneous careers in the old sense of life-long meta-narratives (the *grands recits* of the working individual). The employers, furthermore, push ahead the image that employees staying too long with one job do not show enough flexibility and ambition. Stability is interpreted as immovability, or, as Sennett puts it: "Those who do not move are out" (Sennett 1998: 115).

The frequent changing of jobs also has financial consequences: in the US 34 per cent of people changing jobs lose a significant amount of income, while 28 per cent gain (Sennett 1998: 222; also Thurow 1996: 28). It is a paradox that right at the moment when for most people homogeneous careers are no longer available, the notion of "career" is more popular than ever before. Magazines and newspapers have set up career-pages (for example the German "Die Zeit" or the Austrian "Der Standard"), students contact "career-planning" services, and women who enter into job domains which were previously dominated by men are automatically called "career women". And indeed, the more the traditional form of meta-narratives framing the biographies of individuals is being deconstructed, the greater "fictive" meaning they gain. This counts for work as well as for private relations — e.g. people statistically change their partners every three to five years (German sociologists speak of *Lebensabschnittspartnerschaft* instead of *Lebenspartnerschaft*), and it is the same people that answer the question of what values are most important for them by referring to: fidelity, love, marriage, family. However, the break-down of traditional meta-narratives is not necessarily a bad thing just as flexibility is not, but the consequences might be different from what Postmodernists expect. Most of the sociological, psychological and medical data indicate that a "life in fragments" is not something that individuals in Western societies seem yet to be ready for. The idea of "life politics" becomes rather questionable when we look at the growing rates of mental and social diseases, drug deaths or suicides.

Although unemployment has clearly become a structural problem and a mass experience in our societies, those affected by unemployment still tend to interprete it not primarly as a social but as an individual problem. Such individualizing of a social situation naturally causes a feeling of personal "failings" in the individual (Grint 1991: 42). From a political point of view, this individualizing means depoliticizing the problem:

> For example, if unemployment was experienced as the direct result of an ineffi-
> cient or inhumane economic system then the unemployed and the employed
> might attempt to restructure the system. However, if unemployment is perceived
> as the fault of individuals (and there is considerable evidence to show that it
> usually is perceived in this way [...]), then little in the way of collective action
> against it is likely. (Grint 1991: 43)

On the other hand, in recent years there has also been evidence that the unemployed themselves start to repoliticize the problem. Probably the most significant phenomenon in this respect was the emergence of an unemployed movement in France in 1997. The unemployed, whose interests are traditionally poorly represented by the trade unions, started — independently of the latter — to organize demonstrations, set up an executive committee and initiated all kinds of "political actions" (such as occupying labor exchanges, universities and highly symbolic places of Capitalism, e.g. luxury restaurants, etc.). What has become political jargon, namely "fighting unemployment" (see Straehle et al. 1999), was now realized in a very concrete and physical form — one which politicians using this phrase surely did not envisage. The unemployed broke their passive isolation, entered the public space and became visible social and political actors. This articulation had basically two important aspects: (a) it made the general public realize the crucial material and life-worldly circumstances of unemployment, and (b) it helped the unemployed to (re)gain self-confidence and some form of pride (Bourdieu 1998: 104). For sociologists, the coming into existence of such a movement which emerged out of the institutional nothing, as it were, and has meanwhile spread to Germany and other EU member states, was indeed a surprise; P. Bourdieu even called it a "societal miracle" (1998: 103). Furthermore, what was surprising in these events was the widespread support for the concerns and aims of the movement among the general public, i.e. the employed part of the population. Why is this? The answer is quite easy to give: it is the fear of the employed themselves of losing their jobs and becoming unemployed. For the greater part of the working population, unemployment is not perceived as something that is 'far away' from their lives, but rather as something that might affect everybody at any time. A kind of fundamental insecurity and anxiety has befallen European societies. Unlike the situation in former times, this insecurity is no longer related to 'extraordinary' historical catastrophes (like wars). It is rather caused by the 'ordinary' everyday-practices and manoeuvres of a flexible Capitalism (Sennett 1998: 38). Instability, insecurity, anxiety have become the norm that people have to live with. In this context, Sennett quotes an author from the

New York Times: "[...] the care for job has entered everywhere, it dissolves the ego, wrecks families, undermines communities and changes the atmosphere at the place of work" (1998: 129).

This seems to be the price for the new flexibility of jobs. For Bourdieu, permanent job insecurity has further consequences: it helps employers increasingly to exploit employees through the threat of dismissal (Bourdieu 1998: 105). New/old strategies of domination and exploitation enter the scene. People's anxiety and insecurity are instrumentalized for the interests of employers. Workers are re-disciplinized by 'economic' arguments and their rights are surreptitiously cut. The result is the destruction of the European model of the welfare state.

Even if we do not accept Bourdieu's rather extreme position, the main point of his argument (as well as Sennett's) cannot be denied: what makes unemployment such a crucial societal and political problem is not only the 10 or 11 per cent unemployed (in the case of the EU) but, over and above this, the fundamental anxiety affecting the other 90 per cent. It is precisely this anxiety which gives new power to employers and global capitalists who do not want to be disturbed by self-confident workers. Consequently, when talking about unemployment and its socio-psychological as well as its political implications, we have at the same time to talk about the fear of the employed of becoming unemployed.

3.3 *Beyond the distinction of unemployed and employed*

The distinction between employed and unemployed, however, is not the Archimedian point for understanding the recent development of labor markets. At best, it is simplifying, and at worst, it is misleading. There is a wide gray zone between employment and unemployment. Consider, for instance, the part-timers who want but do not find full-time work, the employment contracts that are called "precarious" or "critical", not to forget all those receiving public assistance who have not "actively sought employment at some time during the previous four weeks" (for whatever reason, e.g. illness), and who are therefore not officially counted as unemployed, or those who have been forced to take early retirement, and so on. In all these cases the official distinction between employed and unemployed does not say much about the 'real' situation in the labor markets. As L. Thurow reports for the US, there is "an enormous contingent underemployed workforce":

> There are 8.1 million American workers in temporary jobs, 2 million who work 'on call' and 8.3 million self-employed 'independent contractors' (many of them are downsized professionals who call themselves consultants because they are too proud to admit that they are unemployed but have very few clients). Together they account for another 14 per cent of the workforce. (Thurow 1996: 165)

Such a huge unemployed or underemployed workforce, of course, puts pressure on the labor market and on the wage structure in particular. In terms of supply and demand, this means an enormous surplus of labor which necessarily leads to falling wages. This is exactly what happened in the US: From 1973 to 1992 "male real wages were falling for all ages, industries, occupations, and every educational group including those with post-graduate degrees" (Thurow 1996: 22). From 1973 to 1995, the lower 80 per cent of American employees experienced a decline of 18 per cent in average income per week (inflation adjusted), while the upper 20 per cent saw an increase of 19 per cent, which, after tax consultants had done their work, even proved to be a 66 per cent increase. Sharpening the contrast even more: the top 1 per cent of the American employed were able to double their real income from 1979 to 1989 (Sennett 1998: 68).

The dividing line runs not only between top employees and 'normal' employees, but also and predominantly between work and capital. U. Beck reports that in Germany from 1987 to 1997, the income from work showed practically no increase, whereas the income from capital grew 56 per cent (Beck 1998: 27). What these numbers indicate is evident, namely an ever-increasing inequality in the wage structure ending in a 'bipartite society' (R. Reich) confronting some winners with a huge number of losers. Unlike the situation in the past, the decrease in real income of the majority of employees is not related to growth and productivity 'problems'; on the contrary, in the US the 1980s and 1990s have seen a historically unique increase in productivity and GDP.

Is this inequality of wages and income a specific American problem that cannot be compared with European labor markets? Yes, on the one hand it is. Increasing inequality of income seems to be the price America had to pay for keeping employment rates low. The so-called US "job miracle" is primarily due to the creation of a high number of badly paid jobs in the services (Schubert 1998: 28). More than anything else, it shows the necessity of an ever increasing number of people — old as well as young — willing to accept any kind of job in order to make a living. It seems that the US no longer permits people the 'luxury' of surviving without gainful employment. In Europe, the *existential pressure* has not yet become so strong. Institutionalized systems of social insurance, training and educational systems — social legislation in general — have prevented such a situation — so far. The differences are indeed still enormous; for instance, "the lowest decile of the workforce [in the EU] earns 80 per cent more than the lowest decile of the workforce in the United States" (Thurow 1996: 37). For Thurow, the European status quo has further economic implications:

> With both average and minimum wages high, European firms invested in the capital equipment necessary to raise efficiency and survive paying the wages they have to pay, but they have no interest in expanding employment in Europe. Total costs are simply to high relative to those being paid in the rest of the world. If a business needs to expand, there are more profitable, lower-wage places to do so. [...] Continental Europe essentially managed to protect the wages of those who remained employed [...] but at an enormous cost in higher unemployment and lost jobs. (Thurow 1996: 38)

However, there are clear indicators signaling that Europe is moving towards the 'American direction' of reducing (or, more neutrally speaking, of 'changing') social welfare systems, minimum wages, unemployment assistance, labor market regulations, union powers, and so on. The politics of 'flexibility' is apparently also beginning to dominate the EU political arena. Consider once more Thurow's interpretation:

> While no official wants to say it loud, 'flexibility' is simply a code word for 'falling wages'. If 'flexibility' were to occur, there is every reason to believe that the European wage structure would move rather rapidly toward the American pattern. When the United Kingdom abolished its Wage Councils, 40 per cent of the work force ended up working below the old minimum wages. (Thurow 1996: 39)

According to Thurow, Europe seems to be caught in the dilemma of either keeping social standards high and at the same time accepting high unemployment, or Americanizing the labor markets, i.e. deregulating them in order to create 'flexible' jobs — with the consequence of falling wages and rising income inequality (see Chapter 4). Is this really the only choice we have? Is this all that economic logic can offer at the end of the 20th century? In the following we will specifically pursue this question and look further for the economic and political reasons of unemployment.

4. Economic explanations of unemployment

When explaining unemployment, economic theory usually refers to two statistical relationships, namely (a) between inflation and unemployment, and (b) between GDP growth and unemployment. To understand the implications of these relationships and the logic that frames them, it is necessary to present briefly some common concepts of modern economics.

4.1 *Keynesianism versus monetarism. About invisible and visible hands in economics*

At the core of modern economic thought is the so-called "business circle", that is the relationship between an economy's potential output/GDP and its actual output/GDP measured over a certain period of years. The potential GDP is an estimate of what the economy could have produced in each year if optimally running, i.e. if it had been at more or less full employment. Those periods when the actual output slumps below the potential are called recessions; those when it grows rapidly and closes the gap are called recoveries. Now, what happens in a recession and what has to be done in order to boost the economy again? These are the primary questions economists have been puzzling over for many years. It was, however, the British economist John Maynard Keynes who provided an explanation which became the most influential one in post-war economic theory as well as policy. For Keynes, the reason for recessions was basically monetary. As P. Krugman puts it, a "smoothly functioning 'real' economy" requires "a smooth financial flow, as firms earn money from their sales, pay out their earnings in wages and dividends, and households spend these receipts on new purchases from the firms" (Krugman 1994: 27). Now, this "smooth financial flow" is going to be disturbed when — for whatever reason — firms/investors/households retain more money than they spend. When households, for instance, buy fewer products, then firms produce less, pay less in wages, households buy still less, etc. In other words, income — of all participants in an economy — falls along with spending:

> I try to accumulate cash by reducing my purchases from you, and you try to accumulate cash by reducing your purchases from me; the result is that both of our incomes fall along with our spending, and neither of us succeeds in increasing our cash holdings. If we remain determined to hold more cash, we will react to this disappointment by cutting our spending still further, with the same disappointing result; and so on and so on. Looking at the economy as a whole, you will see factories closing, workers laid off, stores empty, as firms and households throughout the economy cut back on spending in a collectively vain effort to accumulate more cash. (Krugman 1994: 27)

What Krugman describes here in rather simple words, is basically Keynes' explanation of what happens in a recession. Therefore, according to Keynes, the first thing to do in order to overcome such an economic crisis is to "make it possible for people to satisfy their demand for more cash without cutting their spending, preventing the downward spiral of shrinking spending and shrinking income" (Krugman 1994: 31). And this simply means to print more money, and get it into circulation. In a free market system, the usual way to do this is through the central banks; in the case of the US, for instance, "the Federal Reserve buys US government debt, paying for it with newly created money, which is thereby injected into the economy and put into circulation" (Krugman 1994: 31). For Keynes, the first necessary measure for overcoming a recession is expansionary monetary policy. If the situation is so bad that this is not enough (e. g. in a true "depression"), the next step would be fiscal expansion focusing on public works programs. Such governmental programs, of course, have to be financed, and they are usually financed by borrowing.

Conservative economists have criticized the Keynesian approach primarily because of the active role of government that it implied. Since conservatives always believed in the 'self-healing' capacity of the free market, they could never accept the idea of the state intervening in the market via expansionary monetary and fiscal policy. With reference to a famous metaphor, for them, the 'invisible hand' of the market was enough, the 'visible hand' of the state could only be disturbing. However, the intellectually most demanding as well as politically most influential criticism of Keynesian ideas was expressed in the 1960s by the American economist Milton Friedman, a strong advocate of free-market policies. Friedman's criticism basically consisted of two arguments: (1) governmental actions in monetary policy are not reflected in the economy until quite some time after they occur; and the time they need to become effective is itself rather unpredictable. Interventions might take effect when the situation has already changed, and might therefore end up by making it worse. For Friedman, it was clear that active policy should be "replaced by simple, mechanical monetary rules. This is the doctrine that came to be known as 'monetarism'." (Krugman 1994: 35). It meant to keep the money supply steady, growing slowly at a rate consistent with stable prices and long-run economic growth. Friedman's second argument was even more effective: against the Keynesian idea of providing enough cash in order to be able to get the economy back to a high level of employment, Friedman asked what happens if the government continues to print money in large quantities even when the economy is at full employment. "The answer is obvious: once there are no longer idle factories and workers to draw into production, printing money will no longer raise production; it will simply raise prices" (Krugman 1994: 40). In other words, inflation will become a serious problem. But how is "full employment" to be defined? When is an economy at full employment? There is no economy in the world (and there never has been in modern times) without some percentage points of unemployment. The reason for this is quite clear: even when the labor market conditions are best, there are always workers who give up jobs and look for new ones. Furthermore, there are always new workers entering the labor market looking for their first job, and there are others returning after some time of absence (e. g. women who became pregnant). So, where is the red line? Is it at 5 per cent unemployment, or at 6 per cent, 7 per cent? On the other hand, there is also no sharp dividing line above which an expansion in the money supply stops an increase in output and starts an increase in prices. The British economist A. W. Philips, however, proposed the following relationship between the unemployment rate and the rate of changes in wages, i.e. inflation:

> In years in which the unemployment rate was very high, wages had fallen; in years in which it was low, wages had risen, and the lower the unemployment rate the higher the rate of wage increase. American economists quickly found a similar relationship in US data. This so-called Phillips curve seemed to quantify the tradeoff between unemployment and inflation. [...] The evidence seemed to suggest that price stability would require something like a 7 percent unemployment rate, but that if the country was willing to accept an inflation rate of 3 or 4 percent, it could achieve an unemployment rate of only 4 percent. [...] Since full employment was no longer precisely defined, a value judgment appeared to be involved instead: 'Expand the economy up to the point where you think that the cost of higher inflation outweighs the benefit of lower unemployment. (Krugman 1994: 42)

This sounds quite convincing. The only problem is that the reality of the 1970s did not fit into this scheme. Throughout the 1970s unemployment was growing just as inflation was increasing. It was again Friedman who offered a thorough as well as a simple explanation. For him, the tradeoff between unemployment and inflation did not work primarily because of one reason: firms and workers are being fooled. Workers set their wage demands too low because they underestimate the coming rate of inflation. Firms set their prices too low because they underestimate the coming rise in their wage and supplier costs:

> Perhaps no single worker or firm makes a very big mistake, but all the mistakes are in the same direction, and they cumulate because my price is part of your cost, and vice versa. [...] And now comes the moral of the story: You can fool all of the people some of the time, but you can't fool them all of the time. Suppose that the government of a country were to try to follow the advice of some 1960s economists and to trade off, say, 5 percent inflation for 3 percent unemployment. This might work for a little while; but according to Friedman, markets would soon catch on. Workers and firms would start to build that 5 percent inflation rate into their expectations, so that to surprise them you would have to have more than 5 percent inflation — and anything less would represent a surprise in the opposite direction, leading to a recession. After a while you would need to accept 5 percent inflation just to keep unemployment at a level that used to be associated with stable prices, and 10 percent to get what you used to be able to achieve with 5. (Krugman 1994: 45)

Friedman's argument had further implications which we cannot deal with here. In any case, he was definitely right in showing that there is no simple tradeoff between inflation rates and unemployment rates. But accepting this point does not mean that his strict refusal of any government intervention into the 'free market' must also be accepted. On the contrary, it merely means that economic policy requires more complex instruments and measures ("policy mix"). Overall, Friedman's idea of a free market basically regulating and healing itself is very questionable for one reason: it presupposes an ideal market (with ideal supply-demand relations, ideal competition, etc.) which does simply not exist in reality. When we look for the priorities of European and American economic policy over the last three decades, inflation has indeed played a crucial role. In the 1970s, with extremely high inflation rates all around the world (caused mainly by the first and the second OPEC oil shock and their consequences), it was considered the most critical macro-economic issue. The reduction of inflation became the prior task of all economic policy. The "war against inflation" (Thurow) was declared, and even at the end of the 1990s, when inflation has been under control in almost all western economies for the last 5 to 10 years, this war still seems to be going on. The present overall dominance of the goal of price stability in the monetary policies of the EU and the US, the extremely powerful positions of the European Central Bank (ECB) and the US Federal Reserve, leave no doubt that inflation is still perceived as the major enemy. And indeed, even if there is no simple tradeoff between inflation and unemployment, the general focus on inflation has definitely contributed to the emergence of mass unemployment in the 1980s and 1990s. Thurow goes so far as to say that the decision for price stability was at the same time a deliberate decision to accept unemployment: "[...] all of the world's industrial countries came to the conclusion that the only cure for inflation was to use higher interest rates and tighter fiscal policies (higher taxes or lower expenditures) to deliberately slow growth, to push unemployment up, to force wages down, to keep prices under control" (Thurow 1996: 164). Growth was *deliberately* slowed, and unemployment was *deliberately* pushed up. This is an important point: in this perspective, unemployment is not some kind of "supernatural" fate that has overcome Europe. Rather it is the result of political actions. Moreover, it is not an unintentional product of political actions but an intentional one.

Here, a few more words must be devoted to the relationship between growth and unemployment. If there is any law in employment theory and policy, then it is the following: without economic growth there is no growth in employment; or, in other words: the lower the growth in GDP, i.e. growth of an economy's productive capacity, the more unemployment there will be. From a statistical point of view, the relationship is "remarkably exact": "an extra percentage point of economic growth is associated with about a 0.5 percentage point fall in the unemployment rate; equivalently, a 1-point fall in unemployment is associated with about 2 percentage points of economic growth" (Krugman 1994: 114). To take an example, if the EU economy grows by 4 per cent in 1999, there should be a fall of 2 percentage points in unemployment in the same year. This tradeoff, however, is again not as simple as it seems to be. First, if the GDP is growing constantly by several percentage points over, say, 10 years, the unemployment rate would have to approach zero or become even negative. This, of course, never happens since, as was said above, an unemployment rate below 3 per cent is unthinkable: there are always new workers entering the labor market and looking for jobs, workers quitting old jobs and looking for new ones, and so on. Secondly, we have to face a new phenomenon which is commonly called "jobless growth". The productivity of some EU member states like, for instance, Spain or the United Kingdom has been growing rapidly but this has had very little impact on their unemployment rates. So, although there may be economic growth, jobs do not automatically follow. There are several reasons for this, the most important of which is to be found in the changing structure of Capitalism itself. On the one hand, those companies which make the best profits are usually those that are very much engaged in 'downsizing' measures, in 'rationalizing' their structures: that is, in firing large numbers of employees. In the 1990s the emphasis on "short term profitability" has become the core of marketing strategies. Managers are under intense pressure to focus on profitability without giving much attention to other considerations. The profits which are then realized by a company are not — as in the past — (re-)invested in production (by buying new machines, hiring new workers, etc.). Rather they enter the international financial markets. They become speculative capital — in the form of shares, loans, derivatives and the like. In this way, the chances to make quick and large profits are much better than in the "classical" economy. This leads to the second characteristic of the 'new' Capitalism: it is becoming more and more what is called a "Shareholder Capitalism", that is a Capitalism where capital is best increased when it becomes speculative capital moving back and forth in the international financial markets. Today, the daily returns on the world's stock exchanges have reached the astronomic size of a thousand billions US Dollars, which is 50 times the value of today's world exports (Perraton et al. 1998: 149).

5.   The rhetoric of globalization

In talking about new Capitalism, short-term profitability, financial markets, flexibility on labor markets, changing international ramifications and so on, one notion has been given a very prominent position in economic and political as well as scientific discourse: "globalization" (see Chapter 4). Globalization seems to be the new magic formula; politicians use it, *Zeitgeist* magazines proclaim it, advocates as well as critics of the new Capitalism seem to take it as a given. What is this formula all about? In whatever context it is used, globalization mostly refers to processes of economic, political and (electronic) media development. In the social sciences, there are all kinds of positions to be found with regard to globalization. Some think it is almost a "myth" that has no evidence in economic and political reality (e.g. Hirst and Thompson 1996). Some think it does exist and has to be strongly criticized since it ultimately leads to the domination of international capital, financial markets and global players (e.g. Bourdieu 1997; 1998) on the one hand, or to the domination of the "McWorld" of mass consumption and mass infotainment on the other (e.g. Barber 1995). Some are quite enthusiastic about it because they see the chance now of finally realizing the *Weltbürger* and a new/old form of "cosmopolitical democracy" (e.g. Beck 1998). Some take an ambivalent position, seeing the (political) chances as well as the (economic) risks (e.g. Habermas 1997; 1998a). And some just soberly describe the emerging tensions between globalization on the one hand and fragmentation/regionalization on the other (e.g. Clark 1997; Luhmann 1997). Here, we cannot of course cover all of these positions in detail. What we want to do instead, is to sketch briefly the field of tensions that lies behind the notion of globalization — particularly with reference to economic and employment policies.

5.1 *Economic evidence*

There can be no doubt that, from an economic point of view, the world is more and more growing together. But this is less due to the world's commerce (in the classical sense) than to the international financial markets involving a small number of very effective global players who themselves are divided — basically through joint ventures — into a large number of closely interrelated local or regional players. The crash on the stock exchanges in South East Asia, for instance, had enormous consequences from South America to Scandinavia. When Allan Greenspan, President of the US Federal Reserve, mentions in a talk that the Federal Reserve might raise interest rates, the stock exchanges from Frankfort to Tokyo immediately react (Koch 1997). So from the point of view of, say, a consequentialist ethics, globalization has become a reality insofar as certain actions somewhere in the world can have enormous consequences in all parts of this world. But let us look a little more closely at international relations in product as well as capital markets, investigate whether, from an economic perspective, we are really living in a "global village".

Processes of economic internationalization can be differentiated into *transfers*, *networks* and *arbitrage businesses* (Huffschmid 1997: 233). Transfers mean that goods and factors are transmitted from country A to country B where they go into consumption or production. They can be further subdivided into (a) foreign trade, (b) direct investments, and (c) migration. Ad (a): goods are produced in country A and are exported to country B, where they remain or enter into individual or societal consumption. Ad (b): capital is transferred from country A to country B where it is directly — or indirectly via capital markets — invested in the productive realm. Ad (c): people from country A go to country B where they now live and work.

In the case of international networks, a company's production process itself is divided between several countries where employees work on certain components of one and the same product. Economists speak of "integrated international production". The most usual forms of this are (a) the so-called global sourcing, for instance in the automotive industry: different parts of one car are produced in different parts of the world — depending on where the production of a certain car component is cheapest. The final assembly might than take place in only one country; and (b) the so-called strategic alliances for the development of new products, most common in the high-tech area (Siemens, IBM, Microsoft).

Finally, arbitrage business refers to the short-term speculative movement of monetary capital, i.e. capital which is not used for production purposes but only for creating yield benefits. It mostly takes the form of (a) short-term transactions of securities between different countries, aiming to benefit from interest rate differentials; and (b) currency speculation, aiming to profit from fluctuations in exchange rates.

International transfers of trade and direct investments have definitely increased in the 1980s and 90s. From 1986 to 1990, for instance, the world's average annual growth rates in the exports of goods and services ran to 13 per cent, those of foreign investments even to 24 per cent. On the other hand, these transfers remained and still remain largely within the major trading blocks. In 1997 round 70 per cent of the export of EU member states went to other EU member states (Bourdieu 1998: 45; Huffschmid 1997: 239). To take another example, in 1990 71 per cent of Canadian foreign direct investments went to the US and Latin America, 74 per cent of Italian foreign investments to EU member states. Accordingly, when we speak of the internationalization of economic transfers, it would be more accurate to call it "intraregional internationalization" (Huffschmid). Extraregional transfers are still rather low: in 1992 only 7 per cent of EU exports went to the US and Canada, and around 8 per cent of US and Canadian exports came to the EU. Similarly, the migration of employees — if it exists at all — is also still rather an intraregional phenomenon: people might move from Germany to France, from New England to California. Something like a global migration of employees, however, cannot be demonstrated.

Quantitative data for "integrated international production" are not yet really available. Although global sourcing is a popular topic of globalization critics (e.g. Martin and Schumann 1996), it seems that it does not play a significant role in the Western economies. It is only a few large companies that systematically perform global sourcing. For most companies, transport costs are still too high. Nevertheless, what plays an important role, is the so-called outsourcing, i.e. the transferring of entire manufacturing plants to countries and regions where conditions are better, which basically means lower taxes and cheaper workers. But this outsourcing is again much more a phenomenon of intraregional internationalization than of globalization. From the EU perspective, it mostly takes place within the EU member states or within the continent (Eastern Europe) (Huffschmid 1997: 241f).

The most crucial point is certainly the arbitrage business. For good reasons, the movement of immense capital flows in stock exchanges and financial markets has become the focus of critics of globalization. These capital flows seem almost to be decoupled from the product markets of the 'real' economy. They have their own 'life' — a life where enormous short-term profits can be made. From 1979 to 1994, the exchange profits increased from 30 billion to 250 billion US Dollars. The speed is indeed breathtaking: in 1994 1200 billion, in 1995 1300 billion, and in 1996 1400 billion US Dollar per day were traded on the world's stock exchanges (Müller 1997: 810). The immense growth of speculative capital flow is not some mysterious economic occurrence. It is rather the consequence of political decisions to deregulate the financial markets in the 1980s. The result today is that the financial markets can operate with almost no political control.

Politics seems not to act but only to react to what happens in these highly dynamic markets. Since financial markets have become a decisive factor, if not *the* decisive factor, in the capitalist system ("stockholder capitalism"), it seems that, with the decoupling of capital markets from politics, the system as a whole has decoupled itself from politics. If this is so, then the new Capitalism is increasingly working beyond democratic rules. This is the reason why critical theorists such as J. Habermas want to force politics to catch up with globalized markets again (Habermas 1998a: 82).

5.2 *The end of the nation state?*

This of course raises an obvious problem: which political entity is to do that? On the one hand, the nation state is significantly losing political power and influence in the face of transnational financial markets, and on the other hand, adequate supranational political entities are not yet established. It is precisely this vacuum that enables global financial players to play their game without being 'disturbed' by political regulations. But are the nation states really as weak as they are described by many globalization theorists (Martin and Schumann 1996)? Will the nation state disappear from the historical map as the empires of the Middle Ages once disappeared? It may very well be, but for the present it is definitely not happening. The nation states still play a very vital and critical role in what is going on in the world. National borders still exist and governments are still without doubt powerful authorities — not least with regard to economic questions. It is true that the strong relation between sovereignty and territory — the nation state as "the sole political authority with exclusive possession of a defined territory" (Hirst and Thompson 1996: 171) — is apparently being superseded by combined forms of territorial and deterritorialized authorities. Today, nation states are indeed less autonomous, they have less exclusive control over the economic, cultural and social processes within their territories. In many respects this political entity has lost power, but:

> [...] it remains a controller of its borders and the movement of people across them. As we have seen, apart from a 'club class' of internationally mobile, highly skilled professionals, and the desperate poor migrants and refugees who will suffer almost any hardship to leave intolerable conditions, the bulk of the world's populations now cannot easily move. [...] the bulk of the world's population live in closed worlds, trapped by the lottery of their birth. For the average worker or farmer with a family, one's nation state is a community of fate. Wealth and income are not global, but are nationally and regionally distributed between poorer and richer states and localities. (Hirst and Thompson 1996: 181f)

It is important not to forget "the bulk of the world's population" when talking about the dissolution of borders, global mobility, etc. What is highly mobile is speculative capital. It is not production and consumption in the 'real' economy,

and it is definitely not — apart from the "club class" and maybe some globalization theorists — the world population. But again, the uncontrolled global mobility
of capital is not some supernatural phenomenon. It was not God who deregulated
the financial markets and decoupled them from political institutions. It was state
governments who did that. It was again nation states and their governments that
declared price stability — clearly a necessary precondition for the "confidence of
financial markets" in a currency — as the prime task of all economic policy. It
was nation states that agreed on keeping interest rates high to combat inflation. It
was nation states that deliberately decided to accept or even promote unemployment as a necessary measure in the "war against inflation". And it was nation
states within the frame of the European Union that decided in favor of the
Maastricht Treaty, with the overall dominance of price and monetary criteria
("convergence criteria") and the extremely powerful status of the European
Central Bank as the politically completely uncontrolled protector of the financial
markets. Now politics has to face the music.

However, politics has not come to an end, and neither has the nation state as
some theorists suggest (e.g. J.-M. Guéheno in his book *The End of Democracy*,
Dittgen 1997: 943). It is globalization rhetoric (Hirst and Thompson 1996) that
wants to make us believe in this direction (see Chapter 4). It is a 'myth' which is
created (a) by those who have to legitimize their para-political manoeuvres, and
(b) by those who have made these manoeuvres possible through political decisions, i.e. politicians of state governments. It is a great paradox that politicians
themselves — with the rhetoric of global economic constraints, pressure of
international competitiveness, confidence of financial markets and so on — serve
an anti-political liberalism. As Bourdieu points out, this neo-liberal discourse is a
doxa that sells subjective interests as objective conditions (Bourdieu 1998: 41).
However, what we are facing today is not the end of governmental politics. It is
rather the retreat of the latter from crucial parts of the economic system.

6.   Summary

Let us summarize: if something like globalization exists, it is widely limited to one
part of the economic system, namely the financial and capital markets (although
even here, it is only a handful of economies [EU, US, Japan, G 7] — mainly those
economies whose currencies are used as international reserve currencies, and who
therefore have greater opportunities — that predominate). To be sure, this part of
the economic system has become the driving force of the system as a whole. In this
respect, those who criticize the domination of shareholder values over the 'real'
economy of production and labor markets are right. Capitalism indeed is turning
more and more into a "Shareholder Capitalism". Political decisions of deregulating

financial markets not only prepared the ground for this development, they have also been subordinating all economic tasks to the one goal of price and monetary stability — fulfilling the demands of the financial markets. The subordination of economic policy to price and monetary policies has consequences for labor markets, although economists have different opinions about the character of these consequences. Neo-liberal Friedman-disciples argue that all you can do to promote employment is to keep prices and wages at a level at which inflation is under control, and otherwise let the market forces do what they have to do. Since, for Neo-liberals, employment cannot be "created" by any outside intervention (i.e. from politics) such as monetary expansion, lowering of interest rates, increasing wages, pushing the demand-side, establishing employment programs and so on; in other words, since employment can only be 'created' by the market itself, an economic policy that limits itself to the guarantee of price stability can have only good effects on labor markets, simply because all other forms of (more interventionist) economic policies have *per se* bad effects. From this neo-liberal position the fall or rise of unemployment is something about which the market decides. In practice, this means accepting a "natural rate" of unemployment, as Friedman called it, or a "non-accelerating-inflation rate of unemployment" (NAIRU) as his disciples have more technically called it (Krugman 1994: 46).

For Keynesian economists, the situation naturally looks quite different. They basically argue that unemployment has to be fought through demand-oriented policies. For them the reason for unemployment lies mainly in the fact that participants in an economy hold more cash than they spend. Consumers buy fewer products, firms produce fewer products, entrepreneurs invest less money, jobs are lost. This vicious circle must be broken by political intervention, i.e. by giving the participants what they require, namely more cash. This means first of all an expansionist monetary policy (central banks print more money) but it also means the lowering of interest rates (so that firms and households can more easily 'buy' money) and the raising of wages (so that consumers have more money to buy products). With regard to the last point, however, Keynesian economists are not so united; some, who call themselves Postkeynesians think that the raising of wages does indeed create employment, others who call themselves Neokeynesians think that it is precisely the other way round. In any case, for all Keynesian economists an economic policy that exclusively follows the goal of price stability, neglecting all kinds of interventionist measures, will push unemployment ever higher. Such a policy serves only one group — the financial elite: capital owners, shareholders, speculators, banks, that is, all those operating with capital flows. This group is continuously growing, for the opportunities to make short-term profits in financial markets are much better than those in 'classical' product markets (one reason for this being the high labor costs in the EU). Furthermore, the overall orientation to price and currency stability — the pressure of "budgetary consolidation" —

prevents governments from making public expenditure, for example for employment programs. Governments seem to be paralyzed. But in the long run, global
capital movement cannot conceal local poverty and hardship.

The last point leads us again to the problem of "globalization rhetoric" in
political and economic discourses which make the "confidence" of financial
markets the ultimate yardstick for decisions. This rhetoric has clearly become an
argumentative vehicle for disciplining the aims of workers and trade unions.
Usually the argumentation goes as follows: there are international/global constraints, and because of these constraints we cannot pay higher wages, we have to
cut jobs, we have to reduce social benefits; the social partners have to be
'realistic' in the face of a 'changing world', they must be 'cooperative'; international competitiveness is the precondition for growing employment. And, in order
to become competitive we have to use all available means to keep our currency
strong, and — more than anything else — we/you have to be flexible. The magic
formula is: competitiveness and flexibility. We all "must swim in the same
Darwinian ocean" (Thurow 1996: 166). Welcome to the revival of survival-of-
the-fittest capitalism.

Globalization rhetoric, finally, is marked by two constitutive discourse figures: (1) the de-politicization of socio-economic fields of activity; and (2) the
passing of the nation-state, which is also a passing of the welfare-state ('impotence' of the nation-state in the face of 'new economic constraints'). With regard
to (1), the role of the financial markets is particularly important. They have the
essential function of supporting globalization rhetoric. The development of the
financial markets is presented as an immutable constraint, as an almost supernatural phenomenon, to which one must simply adjust. Usually, however, this reference is less direct. The financial markets remain concealed behind 'new
economic constraints' and behind 'criteria', in other words behind the criteria of
price and monetary stability as necessary preconditions for the so-called 'confidence of the financial markets' in politics.

What is happening here, in simple terms, is the following: a particular sector
of the economy, the financial market, is being made into a universal horizon for
the whole of the economy. Simultaneously it is being depoliticized, since it is
explained as an inevitable destiny. It is no longer an area of control in the field of
political activity, but rather the inalienable framework for this field of activity.
Political action then no longer questions this framework but is content to fulfil it
adequately, i.e. by guaranteeing competition and flexibility.

The construction of economic constraints by the 'global' financial markets
leads directly to the second discourse figure, namely to the deconstruction of the
nation-state as an effective and above all responsible political entity. It thereby
leads simultaneously to the invocation of new supranational units of action.
Confronted by these economic constraints, the nation state is said to be overbur-

dened, or powerless, and supranational entities such as the EU must take its place. Now even if the nation-state is by no means as powerless as it is said to be, this type of argument does have a degree of plausibility. The snag with this is that an effective and integrated supranational entity of this sort does not yet exist — particularly in the area of social policy and welfare (Höffe 1999). Precisely in this area the EU is still a "project in a state of uncertainty" (Müller 1997: 817), in the uncertainty between intergovernmental co-operation and supranational institutionalization. This uncertainty between the end of the old model (nation-state) and the development of a new model (supranational institutions) opens up a political vacuum that permits the financial players in particular to play their game without too much interference from political regulations. In particular they are liberated from the uncomfortable corset of the welfare principle. If one ignores the intentions hidden behind this, it is a great paradox that political discourse itself — through the rhetoric of global economic constraints, competitive pressure and impotence of the nation-state — promotes an anti- or at least apolitical liberalism.

The core of globalization rhetoric can be summarized as follows: proceeding from a particular sector of the economy (the financial markets) a total economic development is established. If one overlooks the fact that the true state of affairs is already somewhat distorted by this manoeuvre, the next two steps in the argument are decisive: this contingent development is declared to be a necessity determined by destiny, and in a further step this necessity becomes a virtue. We are dealing, therefore, with a two-step argumentative transformation: contingency is transformed into necessity, and necessity into virtue (see Chapter 4).

It is this economic/political rhetoric of globalization that dominates today's political arena (Todd 1999). To put it even more provocatively: we are not so much living in a globalized economic and political world as in an economic and political world of globalization rhetoric. By this, I do not mean that there are not enormous processes of internationalization going on in many areas of social life. Nor do I want to deny the threatening emergence of a transpolitical and transnational space where "global players" of various kinds are becoming increasingly powerful. But, and this is the decisive point, state governments have not vanished into thin air, they still play important roles in the 'game' — maybe not as "imaginative communities" (B. Anderson) but definitely as 'real' communities with real power over real people. The unemployed, for instance, know quite well what this real power means when their benefits are cut. It might be that the nation state has stopped being the *grand-recit* of political modernity (Albrow 1998), but it has not stopped being a political entity making decisions that very much affect "the bulk of the world's population". Those who declare the end of the nation state and promote a "cosmopolitan model of democracy" (Held 1998) should be aware that it is precisely the political vacuum between the end of the 'old' model and the beginning of a 'new' model that gives international capitalists every opportunity to do what they aim to do without political control. Talking about the nation state means at the same time talking about the welfare state. In today's world, the end of the nation state would also mean the end of the distribution of welfare from rich to poor — another reason why capitalist elites promote 'global thinking'.

On the other hand, the world is indeed changing. New problems and risks — economic as well as social and environmental — have arisen which can clearly no longer be solved at the level of nation states. The "risk society" (U. Beck) transcends nation states and their territories; it requires international cooperation and multinational decision-making. This point is not questioned by anybody. Politics has to become more polycentric, it has to change from *unilateral government* to *multilateral governance* (Müller 1997; Hirst and Thompson 1996). The question which is primarily discussed is how this multilateral governance should be institutionalized, and how far it should go. Intergovernmentalists argue for institutionalized decision-making procedures *between* nation state governments — but with the latter remaining the final authorities. Supranationalists argue for decision-making institutions *above* the level of nation state governments — with the latter losing significant power and authority (Pedler and Schaefer 1996; O'Neill 1996). The European Union as it exists today seems to be a compromise between these two positions — a compromise, however, that is unique in its character:

> The Union is not and will not become a nation state writ large. Its development cannot be modeled on a continental-sized centralized federal state like the USA. Rather the Union is a new kind of political entity to which the conventional constitutional categories do not readily apply. Such categories have been derived from the institutions of the nation state: at the most basic level, the sovereignty of the principal legislature and the accountability of the central executive to that legislature. In contrast to this, the Union has no single and sovereign source of law nor does it possess a central multi-functional executive that is democratically accountable through a single channel to representatives of the people. (Hirst and Thompson 1996: 153)

But how does this "new kind of political entity" then look like? On the basis of what "categories" does it function? Is it an efficient political entity in the face of mass unemployment as the continent's number one problem? What are the goals and instruments of EU employment policies? Does the EU show a "visible hand" in dealing with unemployment, or does it limit itself to the guarantee of price stability and the flexibility of labor markets? We will try to answer at least parts of these questions in the following chapters.

Chapter 3

Researching the European Union

Data and Ethnography

Gilbert Weiss

The aim of this chapter is to provide background information on the structure of the EU organizational system, its employment policy-making in recent years as well as the ethnographic basis of the studies undertaken in the following chapters.

1. History of the European Union

The origin of today's EU goes back to the European Coal and Steel Community (ECSC) based on the plan of the French Foreign Minister Robert Schuman and established in 1951. Schuman's idea was to bind France and Germany together in crucial industries and thereby make a war between the two countries more unlikely. The ECSC was also joined by Italy, the Netherlands, Belgium and Luxembourg. This first community did not involve close political cooperation. In the mid-1950s, however, talks about the foundation of a European Economic Community (EEC) and a European Atomic Energy Community (EAEC) were initiated. Then, in March 1957, the heads of government of the six ECSC member states came together in Rome and signed the so-called Treaty of Rome establishing these two further Communities. As the principal aim of the EEC the treaty named the creation of a customs union and a common market based on the four freedoms of movement — persons, goods, services and capital.

In the early years, the three Communities had separate organs; in 1962, the Common Assembly of the ECSC turned into the European Parliament (EP). The Merger Treaty of 1967 changed the former EEC Commission into the European Commission (EC). At the same time, the Council of Ministers (CM) of the European Communities was established. With the development of these three common organs political cooperation became closer. In 1973, Denmark, Ireland

and the UK became members; Greece (1981), Spain and Portugal (1986) and finally Austria, Finland and Sweden (1995) followed. In the course of the years, the early idea of intergovernmental cooperation of sovereign nation states — based on agreements under international law — was widened to the project of European political integration which meant handing over sovereign rights to the suprana- tional European organs. The project of *political* integration via economic integra- tion became particularly visible in the 1980s when Greece, Spain and Portugal were allowed to become members although these three economically rather poor countries clearly put an economic burden on the other member states. The decision for accession was made in order to strengthen democracy in these three countries which had been suppressed by dictatorships up to the 1970s. Nevertheless, at that time a conflict over the aims of integration became virulent: should the integration primarily focus on enlarging or deepening the Community ("wider versus deeper")? Like many other conflicts, this question has not really been solved up to the present. However, the Single European Act (SEA) in 1986 was an important step — maybe *the* most important step — in deepening supranational integration. It included not only a commitment to establish the single market by the beginning of 1993, but also laid the foundation stone of the Economic and Monetary Union (EMU) and projected the transformation of the three Communities into one "European Union"; it simplified and quickened decision-making (majority deci- sion rather than unanimity); and, even more important from our point of view: the SEA developed the idea of Social Europe, with the explicit goal of reducing social disparities within the Community. Then, in 1993 the European Union came into existence through the ratification of the so-called Maastricht Treaty on European Union. Article A of this treaty says that the parties to the treaty are founding the European Union making the citizens of member states into Union citizens. The treaty is furthermore built on three "pillars": pillar one representing the area of the three European Communities (ECSC, EEC, EAEC) which continue to exist; here, EU competence is extended to subjects such as health, education, industrial policy and consumer protection; pillar two covering common foreign and defense poli- cies; and pillar three settling rules for cooperation in the area of justice and domestic policies. Only pillar one is guided by the idea of 'real' supranational decision- making, whereas pillars two and three remain largely limited to intergovernmental cooperation (Field 1995). With the Maastricht Treaty, the democratic legitimacy of EU decision-making was also further strengthened by giving the EP additional legislative powers. At the core of the Maastricht Treaty is, however, the EMU, or rather the aim for a high degree of convergence of the member states' economic performance as the basis for the "third stage" of EMU, namely the installation of a common currency — the Euro — in 1999. The formula that came to dominate economic policies of the member states after the treaty was "convergence criteria". The first of these four criteria refers to "a high degree of price stability [...] apparent from a rate of inflation which is close to that of the three best performing Member

States" (Article 109j). The second is the elimination of public sector deficits defined as "excessive". The third is observance of the "normal fluctuation margins" provided for in the Exchange-Rate Mechanism for at least two years, with no devaluation against the currency of any other member state. The fourth criterion, which relates to the sustainability of the convergence, is the level of long-term interest rates, which must not exceed by more than 2 per cent the average of interest rates in the three best-performing member states, assessed in terms of price stability. These criteria were to be fulfilled by those member states aiming to join the common currency. As the long-term guardian of the convergence the treaty established a politically independent European Central Bank (ECB). The ECB's "primary objective [is] to maintain price stability and its basic tasks are to 'define and implement' monetary policy, to conduct foreign exchange operations, [...], and 'to promote the smooth operation of payment systems'" (Bainbridge and Teasdale 1996: 155). Equipped with these tasks, the ECB has become the most powerful organ of EU economic policy. Apart from the implementation of EMU, the Maastricht Treaty also emphasized the need for "promoting social progress" and "easing the inequalities between people and regions" (Field 1995: 5). On January 1 1999, the "last stage" of EMU — the currency union — began with eleven member states (non-participants: UK, Sweden, Denmark, Greece).

A further step in EU integration, particularly with regard to employment policy, was the Amsterdam Treaty signed on October 2, 1997. For the first time, employment was included as a separate title into a Community/Union treaty. With the adoption of the employment title, the member states "agreed that employment should be considered as a matter of common concern". The treaty "reinforces the coordination of national employment policies and foresees the establishment of common guidelines which can in due course lead to recommendations to Member States" (European Commission 1997: 1–1). With respect to general decision-making procedures, the treaty extended the co-decision competences of the EP — concerning mainly policy areas such as employment, equal opportunities, public health, transparency and data protection. A new chapter on the free movement of persons, asylum and immigration was also included in the new treaty, although the UK, Ireland and Denmark have opted-out from these provisions. However, following the decision of the UK to opt-in to the social protocol agreed at Maastricht, this chapter was now included in the main body of the treaty.

2.   The EU decision-making dialogue

Here we cannot go into detail about the structures and functions of the various EU organs. What we want to do, however, is to describe briefly what can be called the "decision-making trialogue" of the EU, that is the decision-making interactions between Commission (EC), Parliament (EP) and Council (CM). To put it rather simply: the EC acts as the executive and administrative branch "supervising the daily running of the Union" (Goodman 1996: 9). Among the general public, its twenty members are seen as a kind of EU government. The EC has the image of the most supranational EU body, whose members do not represent member states' interests but only European ones. This perception is misleading, however, since the separation of powers typical of western nation states does not immediately fit the EU (see Chapter 7). Our investigations will furthermore show that the EC not only *administers* Europe, so to speak, and acts as "guardian of the treaties", it actually *makes policy*. The purely idealistic image of the EC as neutrally serving the "European idea" will have to be corrected. The EC's policy-making involves different political and ideological positions in the same way as any policy-making. With regard to the decision-making trialogue, EC's major function is to draft *Proposals* to the CM and the EP, where these Proposals are discussed and adopted or rejected. Or to put it differently, any legal acts produced by the EU are based on proposals of the EC — this is one of the reasons why the EC has such a big influence on what *political* direction the Union takes (see Chapter 7).

The CM, representing the member states, plays the principal legislative role in EU decision-making (although the EP has almost caught up with the CM). It consists, on the one hand, of the ministers and officials of the member state governments who, at different levels, regularly meet in Brussels or Luxembourg, and, on the other, of the *Permanent Representatives* who live and work in Brussels. The CM negotiates on the basis of the EC Proposals, with the aim of reaching an agreed position. Accordingly, the documents produced by the CM are called *Common Positions* (of the member states). In the Committee of Permanent Representatives (COREPER) most of the decisions formally taken by the ministers are pre-negotiated (see Weiss 1999). Some decisions can be made by a simple majority of eight of the 15 members, but some are made under a so-called qualified majority vote of the Council (Haynes-Renshaw and Wallace 1997). In recent years, the CM has often been accused of blocking European integration and of "putting narrow and parochial national interests ahead of collective European interests" (Hayes-Renshaw and Wallace 1997: 2).

The EP, composed of 626 members directly elected every five years by the population of member states, is the second legislative body of the EU. The Single European Act and particularly the Maastricht Treaty have significantly increased the powers of the EP. It has now joint decision-making procedures with the CM in many areas; it may propose amendments to legislation, draft opinions on EC and CM documents; it can insist on changes in the EU budget or even reject it, and has the power to dismiss the Commission through a censure vote. Finally, the EP can also adopt resolutions on recommendations for *Extraordinary European Council Summits* such as the Luxembourg employment summit in 1997.

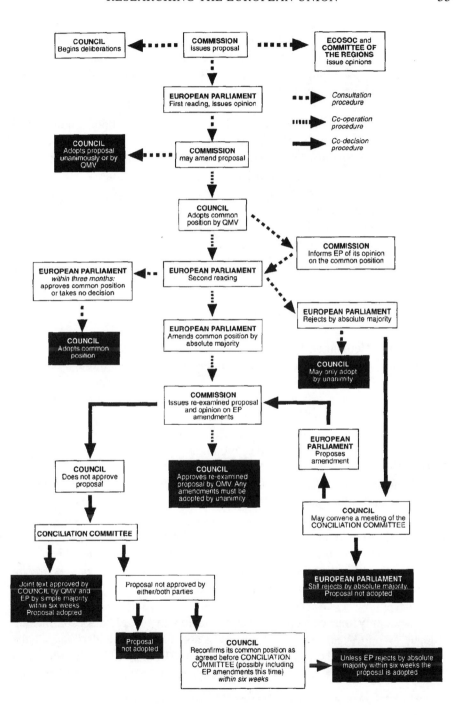

Figure 1. EU decision-making trialogue (Source: Field 1995: 11)

Above these three EU decision-making bodies there is the European Council as the overall guiding force of EU politics. Not formally a part of the EU decision-making trialogue, the European Council consists of the heads of state or government of the member states, and usually meets twice a year to set up the general political guidelines for the Union. It can also come together, however, for so-called Extraordinary Summits — as in the case of the Luxembourg summit. The foreign ministers and the president of the EC also participate in these meetings. From a procedural point of view, the European Council interacts with the other EU organs through recommendations, requests and instructions. After its meetings the results are issued by the respective Presidency of the Council and designated as *Presidency Conclusions*.[1]

An overview of the EU decision-making trialogue — which also involves so-called auxiliary organs like the Economic and Social Committee and the Committee of the Regions — is given in Figure 1.

3.   The EU as organizational system

Following the German sociologist N. Luhmann (1984, 1996, 1997), we understand organizations as social systems reproducing themselves through the communication of decisions. For Luhmann, communication consists of three components: *information, utterance* and *understanding* (Luhmann 1997: 190f). Each of these components represents a selection from a range of possibilities. Information is a selection from a repertoire of possible references, i.e. it selects the *what* of communication. In order to communicate information, a variety of possible "utterances" can be used; these include, for instance, oral language, written language, non-verbal behaviour; furthermore, oral, written and non-verbal communication can be further differentiated: e.g. oral communication can assume the form of command, demand, request, etc., each of them having its own grammatical structure and intonation; written communication can be a letter, a report, a directive, and so on. In other words, *utterance* designates the *how* of communication. Finally, the information being uttered can be *understood* in different ways. Without understanding, communication does not take place. Communication is a hermeneutic event, not a mechanical procedure.

If we apply this concept of communication to the EU decision-making trialogue as portrayed in the diagram given above, we can understand all the arrows between the EU organizational part systems (EC, EP, CM) as communicative acts which can be further analyzed with regard to the what (content/informa-

---

1. The Presidency rotates — in the same way as the Presidency of the CEU — every six months between the member states.

tion), the how (form/utterance) and the consequences of communication (under-standing). These communicative acts, however, must not be limited to the purely legal acts described in the diagram. The utterance aspect is so important precisely because there are so many different ways — formal and informal — in which the part systems communicate with each other. These include formal proposals, amendments and common positions as well as reports, requests of all kinds, letters, etc. Because of this variety of different possibilities of communicating with each other, it is interesting to see what forms of communication have what consequences in which policy fields. And it is particularly interesting in policy fields where the EU — because of the subsidiarity principle[2] — has little legal competence, for example, in employment policy. What forms of formal and informal communication are predominant in such a policy field and what organi-zational, legal, political consequences do they have? Is a report issued by the EC and transmitted to the EP taken into consideration in a resolution of the latter? How does the EC react to an EP request? Which role do rather informal "utter-ances" like letters play? And so forth. If adequately analyzed, there is a complex multitude of arrows occurring between the various part systems. A similar com-plexity of communicative relations is to be found within one part system. Imag-ine, for instance, the variety of communications between the various committees, parties and MEPs within the EP. Finally, the decision-making trialogue between EC, EP and CM must of course not be misunderstood as consisting primarily of written documents. Rather it represents a continuous process of discussing, negotiating, drafting and redrafting texts. For instance, the EC does not produce a proposal without being in permanent exchange with the CM and the EP, other-wise it would not be able to produce a "realistic" proposal, i.e. a proposal that has a good chance of being adopted. EU text production continuously has to inform itself about the difference between the possible and the impossible. Therefore, EC officials regularly participate at various levels of the negotiation process in the EP and the CM, and continuously redraft the proposals according to what turn out to be more realistic positions.

Although from an outside perspective, EU decision-making manifests itself primarily in written documents, the principal form of communication in complex organizations like the EU is oral interaction. As Luhmann says — in opposition to Max Weber's model of bureaucracy which determines written language as the predominating form of communication: "more than one commonly thinks, the culture of organizations is an oral culture" (Luhmann 1996: 159). In other words,

---

2. "Subsidiarity is the principle that decisions should be taken at the lowest level consistent with effective action within a political system" (Bainbridge and Teasdale 1995: 430). For the EU, this means that many policy fields (e.g. employment policy) remain subject to the "lower" decision-making level of the member states; in other words, the EU decision-making competences are rather limited in these fields; for the particular case of employment policy, see further below.

organizational decision-making is primarily "realized" by what Luhmann calls "interaction systems", i.e. communications under the condition of the spatial and temporal presence of participants. D. Mumby (1988) comes to a similar conclusion when emphasizing the importance of meetings in organizational life, particularly with regard to the reproduction of organizational power and hierarchy:

> [...] meetings are perceived as necessary and pervasive characteristics of organizational life — they are events that people are required to engage in if decisions are to be made and goals to be accomplished. While this is the ostensible rationale of meetings, they also function as one of the most important and visible sites of organizational power, and of the reification of organizational hierarchy (Mumby 1988: 68).

All the written documents with which we are confronted when dealing with EU decision-making have first been orally negotiated in committees and groups of various kinds.[3] Naturally, the chances of, but also constraints on immediate reaction of participants provided by meetings are important to figure out how a certain piece of information is "understood" by other participants. In this way, orientation is made easier and communication is accelerated. Of course, the aspect of utterance in meetings is particularly important in multilingual organizations like the EU. Which languages can be used in a meeting? Are all official languages translated or only French, English, German as *linguae francae*? Can the participant speak in his/her native language (as in parliamentary committees) or must s/he use a foreign language (like, for instance, a Greek delegate in COREPER)? Which language is used in informal talks in the Cafeteria or in the corridors? Consider, for example, a French and a German EC official — both knowing the language of the other — having a business lunch: when they speak French, then the French person clearly has an advantage in expressing his/her position; when they speak German, it is the other way round. So it might happen that both decide to speak a "third" language such as English (see Abélès, Bellier and McDonald 1993). These points are important with regard to how effectively information can be uttered, and, of course, how it is understood. Furthermore, we should not forget the different cultural backgrounds that come together in the EU organizational system; different cultures have different ways of expressing different things; this can involve intonation, non-verbal behavior, directness/indirectness, different forms of addressing things and persons, etc. This again plays an important role in how communication proceeds, i.e. how information is understood.

---

3. With regard to the importance of committee interaction for EU decision-making, Pedler and Schaefer speak of "government by committee" (1996: ix); for the role of committees in the EU, see also Weiss (1999).

4.   EU Decision-making and employment policy

Let us now turn from the formal perspective on EU decision-making procedures and communications to the *content* of the latter being relevant in this book, namely employment policies. The history of EU decision-making on employment is a rather short history — at least with regard to developing specific instruments for "creating" employment and "fighting" unemployment. For many years, purely economic goals had guided EU politics. This became even more evident since the mid-1980s when the preparation of the Economic and Monetary Union (EMU) reduced all other policy goals to secondary goals. The Maastricht treaty — dealing predominantly with economic "convergence criteria" — definitely represents the high point of this growing *Primat der Ökonomie* (see Schubert 1998; Koch 1997; Henningsen 1998). Employment policy was widely considered to be labor market policy only, and labor market policy, on the other hand, remained almost exclusively in the competence of the individual member states.

In 1993, the year of the ratification of the Maastricht treaty, the situation changed. Being under pressure by an ever increasing unemployment rate, the EU organs realized that they could not any more ignore the problem of unemployment. Accordingly, in December 1993, Jacques Delors, at that time President of the EC, presented a White Paper on *Growth, Competitiveness, Employment* to the heads of member state governments at the European Council summit in Brussels (European Commission 1994). As the title suggests, this paper focused on economic growth and competitiveness as necessary preconditions for higher employment-rates. The central idea can be summed up as follows: higher competitiveness leads to more growth and more growth on the other hand to more employment. The magic formula was "employment-intensive growth" (European Commission 1994: 139f). The latter was to be reached (1) by developing macro-economic conditions which would stimulate the "market forces"; (2) by establishing structural measures which help to increase the competitiveness of the EU-economy and (3) by pushing forward an "active" labor market policy and by making the labor market in general "more efficient".

Unsurprisingly, the White Paper frames the "necessity" of competitiveness by globalization rhetoric: "firms must achieve global competitiveness on open and competitive markets, both inside and outside Europe"; "the globalization of economies and markets, which involves the intensification of international competition through the emergence of a potentially unique worldwide market for an expanding range of goods, services and factors, brings out the full responsibility on the part of national and Community authorities as regards competitiveness" (European Commission 1994: 71).

Concerning so-called "active" labor market policy, the White Paper puts emphasis on "adaptation of education and vocational training" — "life-long learning", "training policies" — and on the "flexibility of work" (European Commission 1994: 133f). Consequently, "structural" measures for increasing competitiveness primarily refer to structural changes of labor markets; employment policy, to a large extent, is seen as labor market policy. As a whole, the White Paper represents a mixture of globalization, competitiveness and flexibility discourse being typical for the Neo-liberal common-sense in economic theory of the early 1990s. Nevertheless, the Delors-Paper can be regarded as a turning point in EU employment policy or rather non-policy: it is the first time that unemployment is considered as a problem that has to be solved at the political level and that can be solved politically *only*. It develops the idea that employment policy has to be an "integral part of the guidelines of economic policy", and, therefore, must not be limited to pure labor market policy only. Furthermore, it does not just list various reasons in the past for the present unemployment situation, it also offers clearly defined objectives for the future such as the halving of EU unemployment until the year 2000. From an economic theoretical perspective the White Paper tries to elaborate a synthesis of macro-economic and structural views on the problem of unemployment although, in the end, the "flexibility" of labor markets is predominating. In any case, the White paper became to be known as a political document that signals a change from almost exclusive orientation on financial and monetary matters to the economic "real facts" of growth and employment/ unemployment; and it made clear that failure on the unemployment front would create substantial threat to further European integration. It is however important to state that, in contrast to the Maastricht treaty, the White Paper was just a policy paper without any legal obligingness.

The next step in the development of a coordinated EU policy on employment was the European Council meeting in Essen 1994. In order to continue and strengthen the strategies of the White Paper, the Presidency Conclusions of the Essen summit mentioned five "key areas" for increasing employment:

1. Promoting investment in vocational training.
2. Increasing the employment-intensiveness of growth
3. Reducing non-wage labor costs
4. Improving the effectiveness of labor-market policy
5. Improving measures to help groups which are particularly hard hit by unemployment

The Essen catalogue indeed continued the "program" of the White Paper. The "employment-intensiveness of growth" remained the main focus; and the flexibility discourse remained the argumentative frame. The last point becomes evident when we look at the proposed measures for increasing the employment-intensiveness of growth: "[...] more flexible organization of work in a way which fulfils both the wishes of employees and the requirements of competition; — a wage policy which encourages job-creating investments and in the present situation requires moderate wage agreements below increases in productivity". Beside flexibility in the organization of work, it is flexibility of wage demands that is expected from workers. In practice, the rather neutral formula of "moderate wage agreements below increases in productivity" of course means that workers have to accept a fall in real income.

The Essen summit also agreed on multi-annual programs for employment and on a supranational monitoring system ("employment surveillance") obliging member states to annually report on the process of implementing the 5 key areas in national employment policies. The following years then were characterized by further elaborating and concretisizing this monitoring system. A system of country-comparable statistics and indicators was developed in order to identify "benchmarks" for comparison. The European Council summits in Madrid (December 1995), Florence (June 1996), and Dublin (December 1996) followed the idea of the *Essen Process* — each time on the basis of a Joint Report prepared by the EC and CM (ECOFIN and Social Affairs). Additionaly, in 1996, Jacques Santer, successor of Jacques Delors as President of the EC, presented a *Confidence pact* for further promoting an EU-wide "fight" against unemployment. The document brought nothing really new, it rather psychologized the problem, so to speak. Santer suggested that the labor market situation could only be improved when a "climate of confidence" was established between all economic and political participants at supranational, national and local levels so that investment and demand get going again. In the face of missing legal obligingness, psychological issues like confidence, trust, belief were emphasized.[4] In 1997, however, the Amsterdam treaty finally institutionalized the *Essen process* in a new title on employment. According to the EC which clearly served as the driving force in this development, the treaty introduced two "major innovations":

> Acting by a qualified majority on a proposal from the Commission, and after consulting the European Parliament, the Economic and Social Committee, the Committee of the Regions and the Employment Committee, the Council shall each year draw up guidelines on employment which shall be consistent with the broad economic policy guidelines. Acting by a qualified majority on a recommendation from the Commission, it may also make recommendations to Member States in the light of its yearly examination of their employment policies. In Amsterdam, the European Council decided to make the relevant provisions of the employment title immediately effective (European Commission 1997: 2–1)

In order to put the Amsterdam treaty "immediately" into effect, the heads of government decided at the Amsterdam Summit in June 1997 to have an "extraordinary" European Council meeting exclusively devoted to employment in Lux-

---

4. P. Muntigl has analyzed the specific form of the construction of "confidence" in speeches by EU Commissioners; see Muntigl (1999).

embourg in November 1997. With this Luxembourg Summit, the EU focus on employment as important part of the Union's political agenda definitely reached a highpoint. The member states agreed not only on establishing Union-wide employment guidelines but also on incorporating these guidelines into "national employment action plans". On 15 December 1997, the CM adopted the first guidelines for 1998. At the end of January 1998, the member states agreed on a common structure for the national action plans, and committed themselves to submit their plans by April 1998.

Now, how do the employment policy guidelines agreed on at the Luxembourg summit look like? They are based on "four pillars"

1. Improving employability
2. Developing entrepreneurship
3. Encouraging adaptability in businesses and their employees
4. Strengthening the policies for equal opportunities

The first pillar primarily refers to modernizing education and improving training systems ("lifelong learning"); main target groups are young and long-term unemployed. The idea is to develop preventive instruments "so as to reduce significantly the inflow of young and adult unemployed persons into long-term unemployment" (European Commission 1998: 7). Through a more active labor market policy people shall be "shifted" from "welfare dependency to work and training". Special emphasis is given to "facilitating the transition from school to work".

The second pillar covers a variety of measures in order to make it easier to start-up and run businesses. These include, for instance, reducing administrative burdens for business, reducing tax burdens on labor as well as VAT. Furthermore, the "development of self-employment" is emphasized.

The third pillar aims at modernizing the organization of work (working time, forms of work). Increasingly "diverse forms of employment" shall be taken into account through "more adaptable types" of labor contracts. Thereby, "flexibility" and "security" (for employees) should be balanced.

The fourth pillar gives priority to "tackling gender gaps in employment and unemployment". It mentions the reconciling of work and family, the facilitating of reintegration into the labor market and the promoting of the integration of people with disabilities into working life.

Each of these four pillars definitely represents plausible ideas and important measures to be taken in order to improve the employment situation in the EU. These ideas and measures, however, refer mainly to structural labor market policies in a more narrow sense. Their focus still is the "flexibility" of labor markets. They do not really mention macro-economic aspects such as inflation/deflation, price stability, interest rates, consumption/consumer demand, fiscal policies (public expenditures), wage distribution, etc. On the one hand, this is surprising when considering the EU common sense that employment policy has to be an "integral part of economic policy". On the other hand, it is not surprising because — as EU officials usually argue — the employment guidelines are naturally linked to the "economic guidelines" presented in various other documents such as the *European Council Resolution on Growth and Employment* in Amsterdam. This point is right but, nevertheless, what the Luxembourg Summit established were employment guidelines being separated from economic guidelines; and the national action plans of the member states are documents devoted to labor market questions only. As a consequence, we face a variety of documents and guidelines but no integrated economic *and* employment program. This has strongly to do with the tensions between national and supranational competences in the field of employment policy. According to the principle of subsidiarity, labor market policy is primarily a task of the member states and not of the Union. This indeed makes sense because labor market policies depend to a large degree on local and regional particularities. The problem is however the following: labor markets are a national concern, but unemployment is not. The latter is a macroeconomic issue as well as a structural (BEIGEWUM 1998: 17). Only if unemployment is limited to structural problems of labor markets, the idea of national action plans solving unemployment can be accepted. As Delors' White Paper put it, what is crucial for overcoming unemployment is "employment-intensive growth". And the question of how growth can be made "employment-intensive" is widely a macro-economic one. In an integrated economy like the EU's this question can only be considered at the supranational level. In other words, as long as the Union's economic policy — guided by the ECB and the demands of financial markets — remains primarily oriented to capital growth instead of employment growth, the proclamation of employment-intensive growth is just a proclamation, nothing else. Shareholder-Capitalism and "Employment-Capitalism" do not fit together very well, they rather contradict each other (BEIGEWUM 1997, 1998; Thurow 1996; Schubert 1998). Some of these contradictions will be presented in the following chapters.

All these questions lead us back to how unemployment is economically explained. Today, basically three forms of theories can be distinguished: (1) theories of friction which see the reasons of unemployment in insufficient adaptations at labor markets (to the 'new' economic circumstances); (2) theories of distribution and allocation fights which understand unemployment as a result of conflicts of distribution between capital and work; (3) Keynesian theories which derive unemployment from the lack of political coordination of decentralized economies (BEIGEWUM 1998: 55; Chapter 3). There is no doubt that, up to today, EU employment policy is primarily based on the first theory. That is why overall emphasis is given to the structural problems at labor markets. Naturally, an employment policy which is based on theories of friction is one that gives most freedom to financial markets' operations. From what was said in the preceding chapter, it is evident that the author of these lines favors a position which combines all three theories — putting however special emphasis to the approaches 2 and 3 (see Chapter 5).

5.   The case study approach

As researchers in this project we were immediately confronted with the dilemma of how to begin our studies in a realm as vast and an organizational system as complex as the European Union. Regardless what theoretical and methodological position one takes, most would probably agree that the investigation of the EU involves attempting to understand "complex social phenomena" tied to "contemporary events" (Yin 1989: 14). The case study method ends itself particularly well to examining just such types of issues. Specifically, it

> is preferred in examining contemporary events, but when the relevant behaviors cannot be manipulated. Thus, the case study relies on many of the same techniques as a history, but it adds two sources of evidence not usually included in the historian's repertoire: direct observation and systematic interviewing…the case study's unique strength is its ability to deal with a full variety of evidence — documents, artifacts, interviews, and observations (Yin 1989: 19–20).

To summarize,

> A case study is an empirical inquiry that: investigates a contemporary phenomenon within its real life context; when the boundaries between phenomenon and context are not clearly evident; and in which multiple sources of evidence are used (Yin 1989: 23).

In our project, we focus on one "critical event", namely the European Council Summit on employment in Luxembourg — as a point of culmination of several years of development in EU employment policy making — and use direct observation of European Union bodies, interviews with individuals working in them, and various documents produced in the EU organizational system as data to help us draw a holistic understanding of what we are studying. Another way of expressing this multi-dimensionality in the gathering and analysis of data is the principle of triangulation (Cicourel 1992 as cited in Wodak et al. 1998; Hammersly and Atkinson 1983.)

Building on this view that research on complex, contemporary events can be strengthened by analyzing a variety of evidence, textual and otherwise, is the idea that robustness can be built into a study by using multiple approaches to analysis. This is not to pave the way for a postmodern eclecticism, but to express a belief in the value of methodological flexibility in light of the multi-dimensionality of socio-discursive phenomena. In our project, such flexibility implies the weaving together of theoretical perspectives from linguistics and sociology (e.g., organization theory) and the implementation of a variety of analytical tools (i.e., rather than dogmatically using only one type of analysis) to examine various discourse genres (written texts, speeches, debates, interviews, etc.).

This study distinguishes itself from many others on the EU precisely because of its socio-linguistic and discourse-analytic orientation. While much literature has been produced on the EU from political, economic, and historical perspectives, our focus is on the centrality of language in constructing the EU as an organization and as an ever-evolving site for myriad competing political, national and organizational identities. In other words, we espouse the point of view that the EU is ultimately constructed (and constructs itself) through individuals interacting discursively, whether in the form of meetings, debates, speeches, reports, policies, or treaties. While a discourse socio-linguistic perspective is the main orientation of our research, each of the analyses are bound by their examination of different language genres generated around the much-debated topic of unemployment in Europe and a pivotal event in supranational EU policy-making: the 1997 Employment Summit.

6. Data collection

6.1 Preparation of field work

The investigations in the following chapters are ethnographic investigations, that is they are based on extensive fieldwork in the respective EU bodies in Brussels and Strasbourg. This fieldwork, of course, required a long phase of preparation. According to Fetterman, "An introduction by a member [of a given community] is the ethnographer's best ticket into the community" (1989: 43). Getting 'in' to the EU was clearly a problem we faced early on in our research endeavors, since much of our data-collection depended on the tools employed in ethnographic fieldwork, participant-observation and research interviewing (see Fetterman 1989: 45ff for description). Thus, even long before the 'official' launching of the project in March 1997, several members of the research team were engaged in extensive networking with people connected — either directly or indirectly — to the main decision-making bodies of the European Union (EC, CM, EP). In this preparatory period, contact was initiated with EC officials, among them the head of Forward Studies Unit (FSU), the EC's research branch; Members of the EP (MEPs) and their assistants, especially Austrian MEPs; delegates to the Austrian Permanent Representation in Brussels; representatives of the Economic and Social Affairs Committee in Brussels; the Austrian Ministry for Employment and

Social Affairs; and the Austrian Ministry for Science and Transport. Ultimately, these initial contacts and meetings led to our gaining access "into" the organizational bodies we wished to study. Needless to say, this networking was a very time-consuming enterprise which meant more than one year doing practically nothing else but initiating and maintaining contacts.

In addition to establishing contact with individuals and groups somehow affiliated with major EU sites, in the early stages of the project we also established relationships with (1) experts involved in EU labor issues (e.g., economists, political scientists, members of the European Federation of Trade Unions, etc.) and (2) international centers conducting research relevant to our own. While members of the first group have proved invaluable with regard to their insight into economic and labor market issues (e.g., indispensible for assisting us in understanding the economic topoi in certain texts), the latter group — comprising the Institut für Deutsche Sprache (IDS) in Mannheim, Germany, the Laboratoire d'anthropologique des institutions sociales (LAIOS) in Paris, France, and the University of Sydney in Sydney, Australia — are particularly important with regard to experience both in the EU and in understanding large bureaucratic systems.

Born & Schütte (1995) represents a major linguistic study conducted by the Mannheim group resulting from over a year spent as participant-observers at the Economic & Social Committee, one of the EU's advisory organs. This research ultimately focuses on "Eurotexts" — the documents generated in the EU's multicultural, multilingual environment — both on the special context in which these documents evolve and the qualities that mark them as such. The LAIOS group is represented by a team of anthropologists who spent over a year as participant-observers in the EC (e.g., Abélès, Bellier, MacDonald 1994; Abélès and Bellier 1996), following several years of similar work in the EP (e.g., Abélès 1994, 1996). The insights of these groups into the cultures of the respective EU organizations studied lay critical groundwork for our own investigations. Finally, the connection with the University of Sydney, especially the work of R. Iedema (e.g. 1995) is important for its insights into the nature of language in bureaucracies, in particular with regard to recontextualization and Systemic-Functional Linguistics (SFL; e.g., Halliday 1994) in general.

Once provided with an 'in' to the EU organizational system, our plan for conducting fieldwork on-site in Brussels emphasized breadth and variety: our aim was to collect as much data related to unemployment as possible in the three main organizations of the EU. The fieldwork itself would consist largely of participant-observation of meetings and debates (including the 'shadowing' of one MEP over a period of time) as well as interviews with MEPs, Commission officials (especially from Directorate General V, the DG handling employment issues) and representatives from COREPER, the secretariat for the Council of Ministers. As observed by Fettermann (1989: 45), participant-observation is a technique combining "participation in the lives of the people under study with the maintenance of a professional distance that allows adequate observation and recording of data". This combined with interviewing — a conversation-like genre that can help uncover a person's perception — can be a powerful resource for identifying those values shared by a particular community.

6.2 In the field

As a result of early contact with individuals in the Commission, we were given office space and access to basic infrastructure (telephone, fax, photocopiers, post) in the building that houses the Commission's FSU. As temporary affiliates of the FSU, we also received Commission IDs, which gave us access to Commission buildings, including the library, but not other organizations (e.g., Parliament), where we had to get day or week passes (depending on the "gatekeeper" on duty). The office gave us a much needed, centrally located, home base inside the EU, enabling us to pose as EU 'insiders' — e.g. being able to give an EU telephone number for call back purposes. Most of our appointments and meetings (e.g., at the Parliament, DGV, Council Building, etc.) were within 15 minutes' walking distance, but because appointments often had to be scheduled quite closely together — and because we generally carried a fairly heavy load with us, including a tape recorder, extra supply of tapes and cassettes, and various documents collected throughout the day — our days were frequently physically exhausting.

Once in Brussels we continued to attempt to contact/set up appointments with everyone we had written to prior to our arrival and to "cold call" others, especially members of the Austrian Permanent Representation or those who had been referred to us by people we had previously contacted. This turned out to be a rather time-consuming and frustrating endeavor, as it often seemed impossible to reach certain individuals; with others, appointments would be set up and then end up being postponed or cancelled, often on very short notice.

Because of the number of interviews, meetings, and diverse other tasks we arranged to undertake, it quickly became necessary for each of the two researchers located in Brussels to assume primary responsibility for gathering certain types of data and performing certain types of tasks. At the same time, we remained flexible enough so that one of us could take over for the other (e.g., an interview or the observation of a scheduled meeting) in the event that something unexpected arose. The general division of labor looked like this: one researcher focused on making/confirming contacts for interviews; collecting recorded and printed materials; making arrangements for and going to Strasbourg for two days (with a third colleague from Vienna) to observe EP plenary sessions; doing

Commission library work; and developing/maintaining ties with the FSU. The second researcher in Brussels focused more on attending and observing meetings in various EU committees; conducting interviews with members of the Austrian Delegation and "higher" level Commission officials; "shadowing" an MEP over a period of time, and gathering information connected to very specific topics in employment policies. Both fieldworkers took care of general administrative matters as needed and conferred regularly throughout the day.

6.2.1 Interviews

While in Brussels, we conducted a total of 40 interviews with MEPs, Assistants to MEPs, Commission officials (primarily from DGV, some members of President Santer's cabinet and 1 commissioner), officials working for the Council and translators/interpreters. Many of the others we had contacted by letter/phone expressed interest in being interviewed for our project, but ultimately there was insufficient time. In fact, several appointments had already been scheduled with several of 16 additional MEPs expressing interest in our project, but these had to be cancelled at the last minute because of unexpected changes in their schedules.

As in any fieldwork situation, interviews were often conducted under "less than ideal" circumstances. For example, it was not unusual for interviews to be delayed by ten or more minutes or interrupted repeatedly by telephone calls, questions from an assistant, or other factors. This inevitably cut into interview time (e.g., appointments scheduled for 45 minutes were often reduced to 20 or 30 minutes) and put additional pressure on the interviewer to cover ground as quickly and well as possible, yet without rendering the interview overly structured. This also meant that certain interesting points raised by an interviewee could only be probed more deeply at the expense of other topic areas. Moreover, many interviews took place in noisy, smoky areas such as cafes outside of formal meeting rooms, simply because they were most convenient for our interviewees. In the case of the MEPs, we also had to deal with the fact that their offices were being moved into a new — but not quite finished — building, which resulted in time lost in looking for poorly marked wings and offices, or for interviews held in spaces stripped of all contents except for a desk and a few chairs. Nevertheless, these "less than perfect" interview conditions accurately reflect the pace of daily life in many EU organizations, especially the European Parliament.

6.2.2 Participant-observation of meetings

Another major group of data was collected through participant-observation, specifically through the attendance of numerous meetings and debates. Here again, access to such meetings was gained primarily through the contacts we had made early in the pre-fieldwork stage. For instance, we observed meetings of COREPER I by accompanying one of the Austrian delegates, essentially incognito as part of the Austrian "team". Similarly, in the European Parliament it was possible to accompany one of the MEPs to a wide variety of meetings — committee, political group and plenary — quasi as an "assistant". Furthermore, one of our researchers spent two days accompanying ("shadowing") an MEP and observing committee meetings, lunchs, hosting visitors, informal conversations, phone calls, cocktail party, speech to non EP public, etc. — in the daily life of an MEP. In one case, however — and this was very early in our field-related endeavors, that is, before the extended period in Brussels — our real identities were discovered, resulting in our being asked not to return to the group. This major faux pas aside, our participant-observation was conducted without problem.

The meetings and debates that we observed — whether in the Parliament, Council, or elsewhere — most frequently took place in large, formal conference rooms or debating chambers where the seating arrangements for primary participants are more or less fixed. So, for example, in the conference room of the Justus Lipsius Building where COREPER meetings take place, delegates from the member state currently holding the Presidency sit on one side of the rectangular arrangement of tables, directly across from representatives from the Commission. Arranged along the other two sides are places for delegations from each of the member states. Just as seating arrangements are largely formal in these sessions, so, too, are their speaking protocols. In COREPER I meetings, sessions are presided over by a representative of the Member State currently holding the EU Presidency, and, among other things, this individual oversees the agenda and allocation of turns at the floor (see also Weiss 1999). In parliamentary debates — where sessions are chaired by the president of parliament or one of the vice-presidents — agendas are devised and speaking time is allocated according to strict Rules of Procedure. In advising committees of the Commission, such as the Competitiveness Advisory Group, the structure is more flexible, though also there the chairperson has a very powerful position.

Data collection during these meetings consisted of note-taking, tape-recording, and close observation, e.g., from the visitor's deck in the hemicycle of the Council of Europe where the Strasbourg plenary meetings of Parliament are held; seated behind the Austrian representatives at COREPER sessions (at tables reserved for individuals not directly involved in the discussion of a particular agenda point). In our notes we attempted to record the seating arrangement, flow of turns, the country represented by a speaker, gender of a speaker, the general content of the talk, background activity or other details concerning the context. However, because these meetings were fast-paced, involved constant changes in participants (i.e. beyond changes in turns at talk, movement of individuals in and out of the room) and generally ran for several hours without interruption, note-taking became increasingly strenuous over time. Moreover, from our own, stationary observers' positions, it was not always possible to see/identify who was currently speaking. Nevertheless, our notes do provide a sketch of the meetings we observed, and in some cases, we were able to tape-record sessions as well. In addition to notes and audio-recordings, we also collected — to the extent possible — the written materials that were distributed in or otherwise relevant for these debate sessions.

6.2.3 *Collection of written texts*

In addition to conducting interviews and acting as participant-observer to gain insight into the way in which the discourse of unemployment is constructed by individuals working in the three major organizational part systems of the EU, it was of interest to us to understand how EU texts on the subject come into being, what changes (drafts) texts go through, how arguments are recontextualized, what discussions/debates/decisions these changes are based on, which individuals/ organizations work on these texts and what is the nature of their interaction, what kinds of world views/identities are presented in these texts, etc. With these interests in mind, we gathered several "dossiers" of material. Gathering such documents was facilitated again by our "insider" status that gave us unlimited access to the Commission Library, for instance. In other cases, we were aided by our various contacts, such as interviewees who provided us with various drafts to a particular document.

6.2.4. *Primary focus*

To be sure, not all the data collected during our stays in Brussels entered into the present book. Some of them had been used for pilot studies, others had been analyzed and published elsewhere (see Chapter 1). On the other hand, even those ethnographic experiences — of interviewing people, observing committee work and collecting written materials — which are not directly followed up here, are *indirectly* very relevant for the case study presented in this book because — as said above — they helped us to draw a closer and better understanding of a subject as complex as EU decision-making and organizational discourse. In this sense, we will most likely use, for instance, the interview data to complement textual and other data types as part of a case study rather than a primary focus.

Ultimately, having decided to focus on the Luxembourg summit, its preparation and decision premises, we have restricted our analyses to the genesis and recontextualization from print to talk to print of two documents produced in the months before the summit and intended to be considered by the heads of state: (1) a policy-paper of the Competitiveness Advisory Group, a group of so-called experts who convened at the request of Commission President Jacques Santer (see Chapter 4); and (2) the European Parliament's so-called Van Velzen report and the subsequent resolution (see Chapters 5 and 6). These two documents were selected as primary foci because they represent two dimensions of EU policy-making: on the one hand, the "committee regime" (Pedler and Schaefer 1996)

consisting of a multitude of standing and ad hoc committees and groups producing policy-papers, making recommendations, giving advises behind closed doors,
so to speak; and on the other, the parliamentary-public space legitimated through
democratic vote. At the end of this book, in the final chapter, we will come back
to this basic distinction and summarize the differences and tensions between these
two different forms of political spaces. Let us now go into *medias res* and start
with the linguistic-analytical part.

Chapter 4

From conflict to consensus?

The co-construction of a policy paper

Ruth Wodak

1. Introduction: Theoretical assumptions, guiding questions and the importance of recontextualization

1.1 *A new "European economy"*

This paper analyzes the drafting process of a policy paper and the debates in an expert committee where the drafts were discussed, on new European employment policies. The policy paper was prepared for the European Council in Luxembourg, in November 1997. The committee, the Competitiveness Advisory Group, consists of delegates from the employer side, from the trade unions and some politicians and bureaucrats. However, as van Schendelen (1996) suggests, the borderlines between these professions become blurred more and more, and even the experts do not stay "objective and neutral", but convey ideologies, beliefs, political opinions and positions. The committee forms a very specific network which cuts across nations, interest groups and professions (Burt 1995). In our study, it forms a micro-cosmos which illustrates ongoing debates about unemployment and employment policies. This transnational expert group (Beck 1998), moreover, makes it possible to distinguish between two main economical positions, put forward by the employers and politicians, on the one hand, by the trade unions, on the other hand. The aim of the debates and the drafting process is to achieve and negotiate a consensus, a new concept to fight unemployment which should differ — as explicitly stated numerous times — from policies in the USA and Japan. The whole drafting process and the impact of the debates are studied elsewhere (Wodak and Weiss, in preparation); due to space restrictions, I will focus only on three dimensions which are interconnected with each other and will have to neglect other very interesting and important aspects:

1. The role of globalization rhetoric in the argumentation for new employment policies (see also Chapter 2, Chapter 7), in combination with "rhetoric of competitiveness" (Krugman 1997);
2. The achievement of consensus between conflicting positions in the committee;
3. The role of recontextualization in decision making and negotiation.

What do we mean by "globalization rhetoric"? We use this term to refer to the discursive construction of a state of affairs known as "globalization" that exists in a very close argument-relationship with other constitutive elements of EU employment discourse: e.g. competitiveness, location and flexibility. The "need" for competitiveness and liberalization, as a precondition for employment growth, is substantiated by globalization rhetoric — and this is true for both macro-economic and structural measures. Moreover such rhetoric is invoked to proclaim a European identity distinct from other "global players", particularly the USA and Japan.

Trade Unions and employers view globalization and the impact of globalization on unemployment very differently: the employer side is persuaded of the inevitability of globalization processes in economy and proposes to adapt the European nation states to new demands of the market. They emphasize competitiveness. Thus, flexibility, new labor laws and less intervention of the state (among other things) are proposed. Globalization is not questioned, it appears as presupposition to all economic concepts and ideas. It is used as legitimation device for severe changes of European economics.

The trade unions view globalization as a threat to the important achievements of the European Welfare States, of justice and democracy. They also are in favor of changes but prefer investment in "human capital" to facilitate flexibility and competitiveness. "Social cohesion" is the most important concept in their argumentation.

These two views form the basis of a very serious conflict throughout the whole drafting process and the debates in the committee. The analysis will make the negotiation process explicit and investigate which side wins in the conflict and which view lastly marks the policy paper in its final version.[1]

The main claim in this chapter is to view recontextualization as part of decision-making processes. Decisions always mark a choice between different opinions and meanings, decisions transform one argument to another through specific operations, they decontextualize and recontextualize items (see Chapter 1). Exactly this process can be viewed as recontextualization (see below), as transfer of meaning from one context to another context. Decisions mark the negotiation process and the solution of conflicts. The final draft is the outcome of

---

1. See Gruber (1996) and Antaki (1994) for overviews on the linguistic analysis of conflicts in face to face interaction and on conflict theories in neighbouring disciplines. I will not repeat this overview here. I restrict myself to those concepts (see below) which are adequate for analyzing conflicts in organizations.

decision processes, the final draft also recontextualises the voices (in the Bakhtinian sense) of the trade unions and the employers in unique ways which illustrate the power of certain arguments, speakers and positions.

Before presenting the ethnographic background of the data and the analysis of the drafts and meetings, it is important to elaborate and summarize some of the theoretical concepts employed in this study, mainly on decision making and on recontextualization. Other theoretical assumptions in relationship to the debate on economic concepts in the European Union and on the impact of globalization and competitiveness rhetorics are explained in detail elsewhere and will not be repeated here (Chapter 2).

1.2 *Decision-making in organizations*

The sociologist Niklas Luhmann characterizes organizations primarily in terms of their decisions and the processes of decision making. He claims that these decision processes determine the everyday life in organizations. Organizations, he says, are constantly reproduced through decisions: "Organizations produce decision options which otherwise would not exist. Decisions serve as contexts for decisions" (Luhmann 1997, 830). The EU is a very differentiated system with an extremely complex structure. "With increasing complexity of decision-making on decisions on decisions", Luhmann says about such organizations, "the autopoesis creates conforming structures and develops a growing tendency towards a decision not to decide" (ibid. 839). This may sound confusing at first, but what it means is that decisions are postponed, delegated, or shifted to other bodies by an organization. Organizations may even choose not to take any decision at all, and this also is a decision. Such processes happen at numerous meetings, as all of us know only too well. The feeling that yet again 'nothing has been achieved' simply means that there has been a decision not to decide anything definite and to postpone the decision.

Decisions are taken at many points in an organization, at meetings, in the corridors, during telephone conversations or on social and informal occasions. It is very difficult to reconstruct individual incidents. However, organizations tend to stage their decision processes, much like a drama, orally at meetings as well as through their protocols, directives and other written bureaucratic genres. At least for an insider these scenes are comprehensible; they are hierarchically structured as not everyone has unlimited access to everything, status and power are thus produced and reproduced. The linguist Denis Mumby characterizes the significance of meetings in organizations as follows:

> Meetings are perceived as a necessary and pervasive characteristic of organizational life — they are events that people are required to engage in if decisions are to be made and goals to be accomplished. While this is the ostensible rationale for meetings, they also function as the most important and visible sites of organizational power, and of the reification of organizational hierarchy. (Mumby 1988: 68)

1.3 Decisions, conflicts and consensus

Meetings are the sites where decisions are taken and where conflicts evolve and are resolved through decisions in more or less democratic ways (through debates, through voting procedures, through majorities or through the decisions of the powerful). These conflicts can be of different kinds. Balla (1989) distinguishes between two major types of conflicts, conflicts of interests and conflicts of values. The conflicts of interests, according to Balla (1989), are fights about resources, power and status, the conflict of values refers to priorities in different ideologies and connected value systems (see also Dahrendorf 1994). Referring to Seymour Lipset (1959), Dahrendorf concludes that not all conflicts in modern societies can be viewed in the traditional theory of Karl Marx, as *"Klassenkampf"* (Dahrendorf 1994: 162). Moreover, these conflicts do not have to erupt and explode or lead lastly to revolutions (summarized in a very brief and simplistic way):

> Der Gedanke ist einfach und schlagend. Es gibt soziale Gegensätze, die zu politischen Konflikten führen. Doch statt zunehmend gewaltsam und zerstörerisch zu werden, sind diese Konflikte von Organizationen und Institutionen gebändigt worden, durch die sie innerhalb der verfassungsmäßigen Ordnung Ausdruck finden können. Politische Parteien, Wahlen und Parlamente machen Konflikte ohne Revolutionen möglich (Dahrendorf 1994: 162).

This implies that organizations play a major role in the resolution of social and political conflicts. In this chapter, I will try to illustrate how the Competitiveness Advisory Group (the CAG) which was investigated in a course of 6 months arrives at certain compromises and resolves major value conflicts (in Balla's sense), conflicts between different interests and lobbies, conflicts between employers and representatives of the employees, members of the trade unions. A consensus is lastly achieved, in the form of the finalized document, then presented to the European Council, November 1997, but the conflict stays visible in the document, it is materialized in writing which will be analyzed in detail in the following sections. Decision-making and conflict resolutions are thus interwoven in a complex, but also systematic way. One could even argue, metaphorically, that in this particular case, the debate between employers and trade unions takes the form of a traditional *Klassenkampf.* The debate and the positions are not new! The major aim in this chapter is to show how this happens linguistically, how recontextualization as a central process of meaning and decision making is used to achieve consensus (see below).

Luhmann (1997: 467ff) discusses conflicts in terms of his theory of communication (see Chapter 2). He refers to three ways of coping with conflicts in complex systems and to three possibilities of conflict resolutions: First, the avoidance of conflicts through legitimate power. The powerful have the right, to say "no" without having to fight for their opinion. Secondly, Luhmann continues, conflicts are allowed to evolve, third persons are included to solve such conflicts (mediators for example, or judges). Thirdly, there is a different kind of mechanism in modern complex societies: the sources of conflicts are differentiated and new topics of conflicts are created. This means, that conflicts get delegated into other domains or into other levels of abstraction. In our case, there are at least two dimensions which interact: the chairperson acts as mediator, and the topics are also removed into other domains, as will become visible in the interview with the chairperson of the committee below. The first aspect which Luhmann mentions is also important: the chairperson is the most powerful member of the group and thus combines the first two of the above mentioned functions.

1.4 Recontextualization

The reconstruction of the genesis of the policy paper can make decision-making and conflict resolution on a very high level of bureaucracy and politics transparent (Figure 2). We can trace the negotiations on the exact formulations in the policy paper due to a complete set of drafts, the complete correspondence concerning the drafts, the recordings of two meetings, where drafts were discussed, and the minutes of the meetings which summarize the discussion and were used for redrafting. The analysis of such a large data set would naturally require much more space then available. Thus, I have decided to focus on several central research questions in this chapter (see above) and leave other possible studies of this material to future work. One interview with the chairperson of the meetings and at the same time the responsible author of the drafts will allow insight into the self-assessment of the CAG (Competitiveness Advisory Group) members.

- Contextualization - to provide a context to some discursive element
- Decontextualization - to take an element out of its context
- Recontextualization - to put an element in a new context
  ◆ Transfer and transformation of information

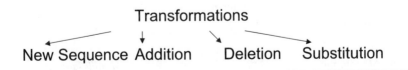

Figure 2. Definition of recontextualization

Basically, what we are dealing with here in these data sets are *recontextualizations* from one genre to another, synchronically and diachronically. The first draft, *"Outline"*, which already is based on the *"Topics List"*, puts forward a number of argumentative chains which should explain the present economic situation and should make recommendations possible. The topic of globalization and its consequences for European economic policies and for unemployment is central to the discussion and to the paper (see Beck 1998; Habermas 1998b; Waters 1995; also Chapter 2). The next two drafts reformulate these arguments, taking the discussions in the meeting into consideration and many expert opinions put forward by the committee members. It also relies on the employment guidelines of the Commission and on other important studies done by the commission or elsewhere. The final version can be regarded as a condensing of all these written and oral interventions, reformulating, adding, rearranging, deleting and substituting contents and formulations (see van Leeuwen and Wodak 1999; Iedema 1997, 1999; Linell and Sarangi 1999). The recontextualization passes from one semiotic genre to another, from written to verbal, to written in several recursive steps (Figure 3). Lastly, we will investigate if and how this document and its recommendations found its way into the Presidency Conclusions of the November Summit (Chapter 6).

The recontextualization takes place from the dialogic to the monologic, from verbal interaction to written, from concrete to abstract, from vertical to horizontal (Bernstein forthcoming), many voices in the Bakhtinian sense get condenced to a single voice or to distinguishable two voices in our case, the voice of the employers and the voice of the trade unions. Thus, the text does not get strictly monologic in this sense, but a monologizing process is at work (as every text

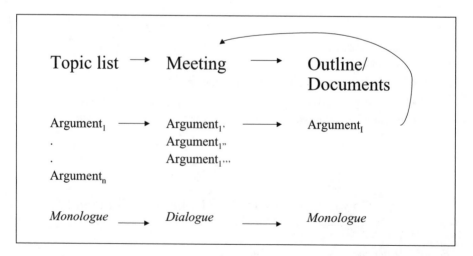

Figure 3. The recursive process of recontextualization

addresses an audience, it would be difficult to talk about a monologic text in the first place anyway). Another possible study could, moreover, investigate the transition into another semiotic genre, into concrete actions of the European Union and the member states which implement the recommendations of the policy paper. Thus, this unique data set allows the study of recontextualization in the complex organization of the EU and makes some aspects of decision- making and the achievement of consensus transparent.

Organizations imply power and hierarchy (Wodak 1996, 1997; Tannen 1998).[2] Moreover, the specific structure of the EU organizations is characterized by multiculturalism, multilingualism and by opposing political and ideological opinions coming together. Meetings manifest all these aspects of organizations in a particularly distinctive way (Mumby 1988; Mumby and Clair 1997; Iedema and Wodak 1999; van Schendelen 1996; Born and Schütte 1995; Born 1999), they are a quasi microcosm, where the interplay of organizational mechanisms becomes apparent. In studying the meetings of the CAG, I am most interested in the function of such meetings in the construction of a policy paper. The specific research questions are the following which elaborate the general aims and claims formulated at the outset of this chapter: Which issues are discussed? Which issues become "sensitive" issues, issues where conflicts occur? How does the CAG handle conflictual situations, how are they solved, how is consensus achieved, if at all? Is the redrafting process influenced by the meetings at all? Are the different ideological and political stances recontextualized into the draft? Does the final version of the policy paper manifest a consensus or only the opinion which was "strongest" in the debate?

These questions guided the analysis of the data set. On a meta-level, the central question of our whole book is always present: how does the shift from a traditional European economy or economies to an adaptation to globalization present itself? And how does the shift from a form of "Keynesianism" and a more state-oriented economy to neo-liberalism and competition manifest itself in this discursive construction of an important expertise on economic policy? (see Chapter 2)

The first section of this paper describes the CAG, its history, its functions, its members and its influence as viewed also by the chairperson of the CAG. This sets the scene for introducing the data set in its complexity, in a second section. Then, the "Topics List" and the "Outline" will be analyzed first, primarily using

---

2. Tannen (1998) has a very pessimistic view of modern societies. She argues that an "argument culture" has taken over, that metaphors of war and conflict are visible everywhere and that dialogues do not occur anymore. In my view, such generalizations are too simplistic. There are necessary sites of struggle (see Straehle et al. 1999) and the following sections. Politics do not only stage discussions, arguments and debates, politics are concerned with the confrontation of values and interests. Tannen proposes actually a model of the "ideal speech situation" (see Habermas 1981; Wodak 1986, 1996) which is only thinkable in interactions where no power relations exist. We do not have the space here to argue our point of view in detail, we would just like to mention that societies without contradictions and struggles are not possible and never were possible.

Functional Systemic Linguistics (Halliday 1994; Thompson 1996) and argumentation theory (van Leeuwen and Wodak 1999; Wodak and Reisigl, 2000; Wodak et al. 1998, 1999), and certain specific issues out of the drafts taken up in their recontextualization and reformulation process. These sequences from the four drafts and the final version will be complemented by extracts from the meetings which discuss issues of the drafts, and the influence of the meetings on the drafting process will be analyzed. Finally, the interpretative conclusions will analyze the possible implications of such a policy paper on the summit in November 1997. Chapter 7 of this book will compare the two policy papers presented in this section of the book in respect to their genre, their setting in public and private spaces, some of the recommendations and trace the recontextualization into the Presidency Conclusions and into other EU-documents.

2.   The CAG

Jean-Claude Paye, former president of the OECD and former member of the European commission as well as career diplomat characterized the beginning of the CAG as follows:

> I: when did you: get to be chairperson?
>
> P: äh: I was ASKed by président Santer, öh at the beginning of ninety SEVen,
>
> I: mhm,
>
> P: öh whether I would be prepared to chair a group of that KIND.... I said that I was interested, öh but äh: Santer TOLD me, it was probably in January or äh or February last year, I still HAVE to find the other MEMbers
>
> P: of the of the group, and ah — he said that he would get in
>
> I: yeah.
>
> P: touch with a number of people, — and I heard nothing about öh about the group for äh — let's say three to four MONTHS, so thought the idea had been DROPPed, and 'öh öh some time in May, or June, I got a phone call from äh (xxx) to to — to Santer, who told me, WELL the group is constituted, so
>
> P: [both laugh] are you prepared to to hold a session in in
>
> I: ja
>
> P: JuLY, I said all RIGHT, — so we MET for the first time in äh
>
> I: yeah.
>
> P: at the beginning of JuLY
>
> I: yeah.

The members of the group were recruited by President Santer himself. Also Paye was asked by Santer. As Paye recounts, the beginning was slow, and then became very fast and sudden. Including Paye, 13 members are assembled in this group. Three represent the trade unions, six the employers side (COs), two are university professors and former politicians, and one is a member of the commission.

I interviewed Paye in Paris, in his splendid apartment where we spent over two hours, drinking coffee and discussing the CAG, unemployment, the European Union and his own opinions and hopes, specifically his motivation to take up the very extensive work of a chairperson. The interview was held in English although Paye is native French speaker and also fluent in German. He himself chose the topic for the first policy paper and authored it himself, in English.

In the following, I would like to present some of Paye's opinions; first, the members of the CAG need to be introduced shortly, while protecting their anonymity:

MEMBERS OF THE COMPETITIVENESS ADVISORY GROUP 1997

Mr. Jean-Claude Paye, Chairman, Conseiller d'État,
  former General Secretary of the OECD.

M1 Member of the Conseil de la Politique Monétaire, Banque de France
  former Président Honoraire des Assurances Générales de France.

M2 General Secretary of Confederazione Italiana Sindacati Lavoratori (CISL),
  Vice-President of the International Confederation of Free Trade Unions.

M3 Deputy, former Prime Minister, Belgium.

M4 Honorary Chairman Repsol, SA. former Chairman Instituto Nacional de Hidrocarburos, SA. and Repsol, SA.

M5 President of the Federation of German Industries (BDI), former President of IBM Europe.

F1 President Nijenrode University, former Secretary of State for Transport and Public Works.

F2 First Vice President of the Swedish Trade Union Confederation.
  Member of the Executive Committee of the Council of Nordic Trade Unions.

M6 CEO BFE-Investimentos, former Portuguese Minister for Industry and Energy.

M7 General Secretary Trade Union Congress (TUC), Great Britain.

M8 Chairman and CE0 Pirelli S.p.A., Member of the Executive Council of Confindustria.

M9 Chairman British Telecom, Vice-Chairman of the Royal Bank of Scotland.

M 10 Commission Permanent Representative, Principal Adviser, European Commission.

Jean-Claude Paye comments the members in the following way:

> I: and do you have the impression that from a point-
>
> I: of view of the social partnership that (xxx xxx) BALanced the group?
>
> P: yes I think the group öh I find the group very well
>
> I: ja.
>
> P: BALanced. of COURSE öH in so small a group, öh the personalities and I öh do THINK this is äh of

Paye then hints at the conflicts between "strong personalities", specifically between the representatives of the trade unions and employers. We will illustrate these conflicts in the meetings below. It is naturally also difficult to get such busy people together who all have heavy schedules; this is why a lot of written correspondence is circulated and many statements are sent in, because the members sometimes can not attend the meetings. The chairperson emphasizes that he always took account of the written statements as well during the drafting process:

> P: are not (implied) öh: either they ha/ well often the have
>
> I: no TIME ja.
>
> P: no TIME but but more frequently they say that they will COME but they have an: urgent matter to deal with, äh and äh they drop out öh just öh öh the day beFORE,
>
> I: Yeah.
>
> P: so we have to to make recourse to: [*laughs*] written proCEDURE as äh as I said,

Another characteristic of the CAG and similar committees is the fact that only two or three working languages exist, and that most of the delegates have to speak in a language which is not their native mother tongue. This by itself is a manifestation of power, privileges some over others and implies that misunderstandings are bound to happen. In the case of the CAG, the languages were English and French, and — interestingly — Italian, because one delegate could speak no other language. The implications of language policies have to be neglected here and is left for further investigations (Born 1999).

Paye proceeds to describe the drafting process; particularly, he emphasizes that the problem of unemployment and the changes of societies due to globalization processes were developments with which he himself was concerned a lot. He had already worked and thought about this topic during his time in the OECD. And he had the impression that Europe should move fast now, that the discussion of strategies was very important.

Finally (after my question about the major conflict in the group) Paye talks about the debate between trade-unions and employers: one paragraph stayed conflictual, the trade-union members did not agree with the formulation of one aspect (see below) and insisted on the inclusion of a footnote to express their disagreement after having given in to many other formulations and proposals which certainly do not manifest the ideologies of the trade unions:

> P: if you have äh: objections, let me: — know by — such a DAte, — and we had PROBlems with the the three — ähm trade unionists. öh on only ONE–point, öh öhm which öh which was öh — [*signs*] I don't remember preCISEly — what it was, it ha/ it had to do with öh öh the connection between — ähm
>
> P: the — reduction of working TIME AND consequences on -
>
> I: yeah.
>
> P: employment if I remember — correctly.
>
> I: and and the labour laws. I think

P: probably so. probably so. öh there was only ONE

I: ja.

P: — point ah ah, and öh öh I made made a change öh öh (so I changed) but on the other HAND I had to take äh care of the %REST of the [laughing]% of the GROUP, a/ and find a a middle — middle way, — so, äh this was agreed with just öh

P: one öh reservation, which is in a foot note öh

I: yes

P: — in in the report, — and I must say I was — glad to SEE that it it proved possible to reach an aGREEment on äh on this.

The whole description of the procedures of the CAG fits well with the observations of van Schendelen (1996). The committees are costly, non transparent and the main function consists of networking. We will come back to the interview with the chairperson in the conclusions when we try to interpret the political impact of such a policy paper and the actual decision-making process which took place. The power of the chairperson and his role in the drafting process become very clear in these statements, as mentioned above, Paye himself chose the topic and wrote the topics list and all the drafts. He decided basically what to include and what to exclude or neglect. It was also Paye who finally achieved the version to which all members of the CAG agreed. Below, we will analyze some sequences of the meetings in detail to illustrate the decision-making and recontextualization with authentic data from the meeting and from the drafts and thus link the data sets with each other.

3. The data set

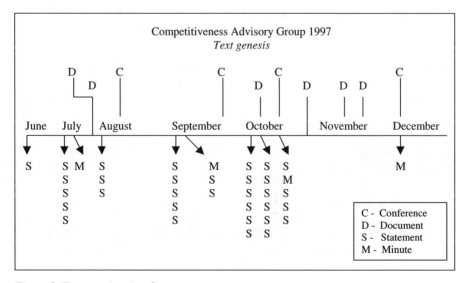

Figure 3. Textgenesis – time line

4.   The roots for the drafting process: The "list of topics" for the meeting on July 25th 1997, and the Outline for the meeting on September 19th, 1997

4.1 *Chronology*

On the 15th of July, the chairperson Jean-Claude Paye (P1) distributed the list of topics "Some possible topics for a report to the November 1997 European Council" and asked for comments by the other members of the CAG. After the first meeting, on July 25th 1997, a second discussion paper was sent out, "Outline" (D1) as basis for the second meeting in September. As to be seen in the timeline above, several members of the CAG sent in discussion papers (statements [S]), and finally the outline (D1) was debated in the second meeting of the CAG, on 19th September 1997. On the basis of this meeting, the minutes and the discussion papers, Paye drafted the first document (D2), dated 14th October, which reformulates the chain of arguments which was elaborated in the Outline and recontextualizes the Outline into a policy paper.

The topics list and the Outline (D1) are very important for our reconstruction task because they both condense the opinion of the most powerful person in the CAG, of the chairperson, and also allow insight into the concept and opinions on globalization, competitiveness, economy and unemployment which the politicians and experts endorse. The outline already refers to the meeting in July and to suggestions made there. It was heavily debated in the meeting in September 1997 where the trade union members were not present. D1 led to D2, the first reformulated draft as policy paper that was then discussed in the second meeting on October 17, 1997. At this meeting, the members of the trade unions were present, and thus the biggest changes in the drafting process occur from D2 to D3 (see below). This is also the meeting where most value conflicts between the groups of the employers and politicians, and the trade union members occur explicitly and where the recontextualization actually manifests these conflicting voices.

In a first step, we would like to present the topics list and the argumentation chain in the Outline (D1) focusing on the impact of globalization which allow us to detect which arguments are deleted later on, substituted or rearranged, and which arguments are added which were not present in D1. As we were not able to get hold of the tape recordings of the first meeting, we have to rely on the minutes, distributed on July 28th, 1997.

4.2 *The list of topics*

On the 20th of July, Paye sent the list of topics with an accompanying letter to all the members of the CAG. The letter explains the aims of the group and describes their workload.

PAYE 970720

TO ALL THE MEMBERS OF THE COMPETITIVENESS
ADVISORY GROUP

At its Amsterdam meeting, the European Council decided to
devote a special session to the problem of employment. This
session is to be held around 20 November. I feel — and this is
also the opinion of President Santer — that our group should
provide a contribution to the proceedings of this special session
rather than to those of the ordinary session in December.

I would like to discuss this idea at our meeting on Friday 25 July
and enclose a note setting out some possible topics for a short
report focusing on employment. The suggested approach is
deliberately simple and educational. The aim is to offer the
European Council a form of words it can use for a public that
has lost its bearings and has become highly critical. This is no
more than the bare bones and will have to be fleshed out
subsequently.

I look forward to our forthcoming meeting,

Jean-Claude Paye

This list of topics sets the tone for the first meeting and the resulting documents.
Already in this accompanying letter, Paye describes the function of the CAG and
the functions of the "contribution" by the CAG. By referring to the President of
the Commission, Santer, a topos of authority is initiated. Paye thus presents
himself as supported by the most powerful person in this setting and also as a
delegate of this person. Secondly, the main characteristics of the enclosed list are
formulated: "deliberately simple and educational". This means, that the paper
should be understood by the public (which remains anonymous, we do not know
who is meant and how widely this paper would be distributed) and it should also
contain arguments and "educate" the public which has become "critical" and has
also "lost its bearings", is thus afraid. The public needs to be convinced, which
makes it clear that a persuasive, argumentative mode will be selected for the
paper. Already at this point, a big distinction is constructed between the "public"
and the "experts"; the latter are seen as irrational and uneducated, the experts as
knowledgeable. The objectives of the CAG are not to be discussed as such, they

are set out from the beginning, the work of the CAG is defined: "our group should provide". Hierarchy is visible from the outset.

As it is not possible to analyze the whole documents in this chapter, I would like specifically to trace two main issues which are linked with each other throughout all the drafts, starting with the list of topics:

– globalization (and competitiveness) and related evaluations and definitions
– the proposed changes in economy and the resulting tensions between welfare states and a
– liberalized economy (see Chapter 7)

4.2.1 *Globalization*

Topic list
People have lost their bearings.
  a. They are under the impression:
      – that our countries have forgotten the recipe for satisfactory economic growth;
      – that we are subject to ever keener competition caused by trade liberalisation and technological progress;
      – that this competition imposes on us ever faster structural changes which result in:
      – massive job losses,
      – serious occupational instability,
      – growing inequality in wages and salaries,
      – more generally, increasing injustice in society;
      – that social welfare systems are increasingly unsuitable, to the point of being a handicap rather than an aid;
      – that no model for economy and society is entirely satisfactory;
      – that politicians have no effective and convincing answer.
  b. They tend to blame globalization for these difficulties.
This globalization process
  a. is natural: it is the continuation and spread of the process of economic development and social progress on which the prosperity of our countries is based;
  b. is a good thing since it
      – helps to satisfy consumer needs,
      – enables an increasing number of countries throughout the world to take part in the economic development process, thereby raising their living standards and thus giving us increasingly attractive trading partners;
  c. is therefore inevitable and irreversible.

The beginning of the topic list sets out the common sense beliefs of "people". Obviously, these "people" are not the experts, they are consumers, workers, retired, old and young, men and women in all the member states of the EU. Although the restriction to the EU is not made explicit, this can be inferred by the whole document because it relates to the situation in Western Europe and to resulting changes and possible recommendations. Thus, we find an argumentative structure from the start: the enumeration of a number of beliefs and fears which are related to globalization in the minds of "people". The second step is the expert characterization of globalization which should counteract these fears. And the third step are then the consequences which have to be faced realistically if globalization becomes an accepted fact of life and how to make the best of it. The beliefs which are enumerated at the beginning are not backed up by evidence, they are taken as facts which are built up as to be able to argue against them which is a known and old rhetorical device.

A number of impressions are listed under (a) (see above): Summarizing these "false" beliefs, the rhetorical argument goes as follows: Countries (as *pars pro toto*) have "forgotten" how to fight unemployment. Politicians have no answers. New developments cause unemployment and injustice; and finally it is argued that the European model is unsuitable (the social welfare systems). No where is it stated where these beliefs come from, how the people came to such opinions and why these opinions follow from each other. The enumeration as a list suggests that there is some kind of argumentational or causal link between these separate issues, the sequence is important. Thus, people believe that globalization is the cause for unemployment ("they tend to blame globalization for these difficulties"); and secondly, they believe that the politicians are useless. It follows clearly, that as a next step, the "topics list" will provide counter-arguments from experts and prove that globalization is used as a scapegoat, that the people do not understand the social and political changes correctly.

Thus, let us have a look at the next issue in the "topics list". Looking at the textual function, the theme of the whole next paragraph is "globalization process".[3] This is taken as a given and stays unexamined. Ideationally, it is an attributive process, an evaluative description which stays as presupposition in all the argumentation further on. This paragraph is a key point in the whole drafting process: it succeeds in marking "globalization" as a "good" thing which stays as a given in the whole debate and position put forward by the employer side and serves rhetorically as counterarguments to the listed "impressions" above:

The first attribution of globalization states that globalization is "natural". This implies that no other development is possible, this is unevitable and the flow of nature. Secondly, the positive sides of globalization are enumerated: it is good for the consumer, and it is good for the economic standard of countries. The third proposition states that globalization is irreversible and inevitable, again coming back to the claim that globalization is natural. From this statement follows that Europe has to accept this development and that the maximum benefits have to be

---

3. Halliday, by the way, took the distinction between theme and rheme from the Prague School. Theme and rheme organize a text according to the given, the assumed knowledge and the new information (see Thompson 1996). Thus the theme-rheme pattern in a sentence is of profound importance. Whatever is perceived as theme is taken for granted (also Chapter 5).

derived from this process and development. The proposal for the future is explicitly written as a sequence of these arguments: "We must be competitive and create jobs. Job creation is vital for social cohesion and political stability, but these jobs must not be artificial and must not be a liability for our economy". Thus, globalization is linked with competitiveness very closely. These clauses are characterized by explicit, unmitigated "mustness" (Iedema 1995). Job creation is perceived as the main tool against unemployment. Job creation is seen as vital, but only a certain type of jobs. The mentioning of artificial jobs and jobs which are liable for the economy stays vague, because we do not know which jobs are meant. Implied is thus, that job creation has not been successful upto now and that there are contradictions; contradictions between job creation and stability and social cohesion.

The following "comments" on these issues make the implications clearer and point to the most conflictual issue which will be taken up in the meetings as will be shown below: the tension between social cohesion and social institutions, on the one hand, and competitiveness, globalization and job creation, on the other.

In the minutes of the meeting from July 25th 1997, we can conclude that the topics list was accepted in a favorable manner: "the preliminary note from the Chairman was generally endorsed, both in its background analysis ('people have lost their bearings' faced with small growth, high unemployment and deep structural change; there is no turning back from globalization, but economic performance cannot be built on social fragmentation) and its broad objectives (improve individual life chances through strengthening of education and training systems......)". But on the other hand, already in these very formal minutes which summarize the discussion and do not relate opinions to certain individual speakers, it becomes evident that there were debates and conflicts about some issues: "the importance of the welfare state (pension, health and education systems, unemployment benefits, labor market regulations and policies) and its reform, particularly to make it more employment-friendly, was recognized by most members. There was not a consensus, however, on the message the report should give. Some members stressed the function of 'social infrastructure' in making people more willing to accept change and the importance of having the social partners on board for carrying out the reform needed. Others suggested that the degree of reform and its implementation were not satisfactory, and that the search for social consensus could also have paralysing effects.... but there was no agreed recipe for change". This statement suggests that a gap was present between members supporting the welfare system, and others who pleaded for less intervention by the state.

4.3 *The "Outline" (Document 1)*

The outline was drafted in July 1997 and discussed at the first meeting in September 1997. The outline is already clearly structured in the layout, consisting of three points in the beginning, as introduction, and then two main sections: "Present features of the economy", and secondly "lines of action". The genre of a policy paper is visible, the next draft (D2) which we will discuss below takes up these sections (though with different titles) and also adds new sections due to the discussion in the meeting. In the following, I will focus again on the issues dealing with globalization and the introductory statements and leave the lines of action to the comparison in the conclusions, of the resolution of the European parliament and the policy paper (see Chapter 7). As already mentioned above, I will restrict myself to the definition and effects of globalization.

The topics list is recontextualized into 23 points which are devided into four sections, with the numbers following through. First, the introduction contains 3 points, the "present features of the economy" points 4 to 10, the "lines of action" 11–22, and finally point 23 is a summary and outlook, an expression of intent. The reformulated document after the September meeting (D2) where the Outline was discussed elaborates this structure.

> **Outline**
> 1. Employment is the main concern of our public opinion, for which globaliza-tion appears as the principal cause for unemployment and downward pressure on the wages of low-skilled workers.
> 2. It is therefore important rightly to analyze the process of globalization, and to explain what a challenge it is, but also the many opportunities it lends, if Europeans are to be mobilised in support of convincing and effective policies.
> 3. An important part of unemployment in Europe is structural. It results from an insufficient adaptation to economic change. A conjunctural recovery thus can not be counted on for a substantial improvement of the situation.

The introduction starts with the theme of "employment". The impressions and fears of the topics list is taken up and reformulated as "is the main concern of our public opinion". People are dehumanized and nominalized. Globalization as theme in the second clause only "appears" to be the cause of unemployment which implies that there are other causes and that the public opinion might be wrong. Although point 1 is stated in this very hypothetical way, the author decides to discuss globalization, and in a justificatory way legitimizes the neces-sity of globalization and its good sides. The policies are characterized as "con-vincing" and "effective", i.e. good policies follow if one copes with globalization and its challenges in the right way.

The third paragraph introduces another issue, the structural component. This argument serves as juxtaposition to globalization. Unemployment, thus, is not only dependent on changes in the society but also on Europes structures. This argument makes it very clear that growth by itself is not sufficient to change unemployment. Much more would have to happen in Europe. The structural problems are recontextualized in a number of points in the next draft, in the section about "mistakes". The whole introduction serves to differentiate the European situation and also the causes for unemployment. Moreover, it makes clear, that the "public opinion" is too one-sided and badly informed.

In the following part I of the Outline "Present features of the economy", the two introductory propositions are elaborated. Globalization is characterized and evaluated, as well as the European situation and the issues which should be changed. We will just point to some very important points in this argumentative chain:

> 4. The so-called "globalization" is the result of the interaction between two main factors: liberalisation of trade and technological progress in all its forms (innovation in products services management). This makes competition ever fiercer and speeds up the evolution of the economy towards:

The theme of the first clause is "the so-called globalization" with a relational process and a definition as rheme: two factors are the source of globalization, liberalization of trade and the technological process. It is very significant that "globalization" is mitigated by the particle "so-called". This may have different reasons: to distance oneself from the common sense opinions and the "public opinion", to distance oneself from globalization as such or to be able to redefine the process and label the redefinition as "globalization". I assume from the context and intentions of the following that the third interpretation is valid. The next clause is of utmost importance because it introduces competition as rheme, thus as new information. A causal link between globalization, its two characteristics and competition is thus established, a very good example of globalization and competitiveness rhetorics. There is no question or hint that this is a hypothesis or an assumption, the mode is factual. The following rhemes are enumerated as part of competition and the evolution of economy and — through the causal connection — linked back to globalization. We would just like to point the reader to one special statement: "more responsibility given to individuals". This is part of a new economic concept and ideology which are apparent in Great Britains New Labour and also in the "American way". Individuals have to take responsibility for their actions, they can influence economic change.

The next paragraph, which stands out, contains a topos of threat which is characteristic of the whole persuasive document: if nothing is changed, then Europe would lose in the world-wide competition.

> But globalization imposes on all, including industrialized countries, rapid and deep structural adjustments. Any country which proves to be incapable of such adjustment or tries to delay them loses ground in the worldwide competition and condemns itself to decline.

The connector "but" is used as counterargument to the positive characteristics of globalization in the previous paragraph. The positive sides are only to be met if "rapid" and "deep" structural changes occur. The topos of "swiftness" is marked here as well, and — as will be seen — constructs one of the main topoi of the whole document. Not only do deep changes occur, they occur very quickly and this implies the necessity of rapid actions: simply stated, this means that the European Union should stop "thinking" and start "acting" (see also Chapter 5).

The next paragraph continues with the topos of threat. "Yet it would be dangerous blindness to underestimate the difficulty and pains of such an adaptation". This textual chain provides evidence for the argumentative character of the genre of policy papers. The former paragraph is elaborated and differentiated, more evidence is given. As will be shown, this argumentative pattern stays consistent throughout the drafting process, but gets much shorter and more declarative. Then the adaptation which is necessary as argued beforehand, is specified. The adaptations, in the opinion of the author, would be particularly painful for Europe with its history and traditions.

The final paragraph serves as reassurance that the specific European tradition in justice, democracy and welfare would be retained even if the changes are drastic, a specific European way is sought for.

> But this pessimistic view, which leads so many people to see globalization as a deadly threat and wish to take shelter from it, is excessive. There is no insurmountable contradiction between the demands of todays economy and our ideal of security, justice and equality. There is a need to find new ways for reaching it. And the pursuit of this ideal is indeed an asset in the worldwide competition.

Following our analysis up to this point makes very clear that the aim of the policy paper and the globalization rhetoric applied by the employer side constructs a positional argumentation:

1. globalization is linked to unemployment
2. this link is contradicted
3. the positive aspects of globalization are emphasized and common sense beliefs are contradicted
4. European "mistakes" are pointed to
5. the European specific ideals remain untouched
6. these ideals guarantee Europe a very good role in the worldwide competition.
7. the necessity of change is underlined
8. because Europe would otherwise decline in the worldwide competition.

The main persuasive goal therefore, if one takes up this argumentative chain, means understanding the link between unemployment, globalization, and good economy, and competition as the main instrument to reach the goal of reducing unemployment. At the same time, a second aim is exposed: to construct a specific European way, a specific European adaptation to globalization and a new European identity.

5. The meeting from September 19th, 1997

The second meeting of the CAG was held in Brussels, on the 19th of September 1997, from 10:30 am to 13:20 p.m. The following members were present: Jean-Claude Paye (Chairman), M1, M4, M5, M7, M9, M10, F1. Luis Pench, a member from the commission, wrote the minutes. The other members were excused. This means that nobody from the trade unions was present at this meeting, only the employer side and politicians were represented. Numerous statements though had been received by Paye throughout the summer and the previous weeks (see Figure 4 above), which were also summarized by Paye. In the following, it is impossible to analyze the whole meeting in a detailed way because of space restrictions. I will thus restrict myself to some illustrative sequences which discuss issues raised in the previous sections (4.2, 4.3) (5.1, 5.2).

At this point, it makes sense to repeat some of guiding questions, which influenced the following analysis: How are sensitive issues from the drafts discussed, is the draft discussed at all? Which are the main topics of the meeting and how do they relate to the drafts? And, as a last important question, how does this meeting influence the change of the outline into the first document (D2), how is the oral discussion recontextualized into written discourse? (This is the subject of our next Section, 6).

The meeting is held in English and French with simultaneous translation. Elsewhere (Weiss & Wodak 1998; Weiss 1999), the typical structure of meetings inside the European Union are described extensively, the role of the chairperson is analyzed there in detail which should not be repeated here. It just seems to be important to stress the fact that decisions influencing the final decision, the final version of the policy paper, are prepared and taken by the chairperson very directly. The meeting very rarely opens up into a debate and spontaneous discussion, most frequently, one statement follows the next, always directed at the chairperson, he ends and sets the turn taking. He also does not act in a neutral way; much in contrary to this, he comments and evaluates statements, summarizes them and also changes topics (the male gender is not stated by chance; most of the meetings are chaired by a man).

However, this meeting is different then the COREPER meetings studied in Weiss & Wodak (1998) in some important aspects: the members are not delegates of their countries primarily, but experts in their professional roles and functions. Secondly, these meetings do not just consist of a chain of statements, well prepared and not referring to each other, but spontaneous associations and remarks follow each other and the participants also refer to each other. Thirdly, CAG has a very different function then institutionalized other meetings, like COREPER: it prepares policy papers for the European Council and is a quasi "private" consulting group invited by the President Santer ("behind closed doors"). The members are not elected in any official vote and are also not chosen due to their countries but due to their expertise and function. Thus, the CAG is situated very much "inside" the EU, whereas other meetings also have the functions of representing the EU publicly. We will discuss this issue of different public spaces extensively in a next chapter (7) where we compare the resolutions from the European parliament with the CAG policy papers. Fourthly, the CAG could be defined as a "think tank": its task is not to prepare precise recommendations, but to set out the ideological and conceptual frame. Thus, the experts act "politically" and illustrate the claim that the borderlines between the professions do not exist in a clear-cut way. Chapter 7 suggests that the policy papers produced by the CAG and such produced in the European Parliament are significantly different in their genre, they complement each other. This explains, why the document by the CAG is persuasive and argumentative whereas the Van Velzen Report (see Chapters 5 and 6) is imperative and declarative in its mode and much more integrated in the life of the organization by self referencing other sub groups or committees of the EU.

In the following analysis, we will first analyze some turns, structured into phases according to Iedema (1997) and Gregory (1996) and then focus on some arguments which reflect the important issues of the outline analyzed above. The move from one phase to the next is defined by a switch on one of the Hallidayan metafunctions (Thompson 1996; i.e. a switch on the interpersonal, ideational or textual level). We focus primarily on the textual function (theme analysis) and ideational function (transitivity analysis).

Most importantly, we would like to make the recontextualization process (see above) transparent, from monologue to dialogue, from written to spoken to written which occurs in several recursive circles during the drafting process (Figures 2 and 3). Many voices in the Bakhtinian sense (Bahktin 1981) condense to one written and factual voice.

After a first introductory phase mentioning the missing persons and the members who had submitted statements, Paye proceeds to explain the nature of the document, in the second phase (structured by change of topic) (the whole turn is to be found in the Appendix 1): he proposes that the final document should be *"aussi bref, aussi pedagogique eh et aussi concret que possible"*. It is important to note, that the persuasive character of the document is here described as pedagogical, the CAG thus sees itself as instructing the European Council. The document, however, contains many persuasive strategies as was already illustrated. The term "punchy" means convincing and efficient, forceful; the English term is used in the

French statement which is very typical for discourses in the European Union (Born 1999). At the end of this phase, he admits that there will be difficult issues to find a compromise in, but — nevertheless — one should try to cope with these problems: *"Car ça fait evidemment beaucoup de eh d'objectifs eh qui ne sont pas aise à rendre conciliable mais je vois qu'il faut s'efforcer."* This clause makes the power of Payes authority visible. Although there are issues which might not be possible to reconcile, one MUST force oneself to do this. The message is clear, a compromise has to be reached.

In the next phase, he describes the outline, as a checklist that should serve the drafting process, and continues to explain his own motives. In this phase, European identity is constructed, the specific European agenda are stated, with a lot of "mustness" (Iedema 1999). He clearly states that these opinions are his very own and links competitiveness with the still backward European situation: *il faut être alarmiste et optimiste parce que eh la realité fondamentale fait que nous avons en Europe des atouts eh, importants, et qu'il faut savoir exploiter au plus vite.* Both the topoi of danger (*alarmiste*) and of rapidness are explicitly integrated in his utterances from the start. This frames the whole meeting: Europe has to act quickly otherwise it would fall behind. And he repeats an appeal to the members of the CAG in this persuasive and very directive statement:

> La deuxième conviction ou constatation que, que je fais c'est que eh, nous avons les uns et les autres eh, des convictions, des origines, des expériences qui sont différentes. Et qu'il il nous faut essayer de tirer profit de cette diversité mais arriver à quelque chose qui si possible soit eh, la vue commune que eh, nous avons.

One should arrive at a common view in spite of different perspectives. This addresses the members of the CAG personally, Paye uses "nous" to suggest that he himself is meant too. This appeal has the function of forming solidarity in the group and of giving the group a very clear objective. He continues to describe the difficulties of finding a common view and legitimizing his first characteristic of the final document. He paints possible reactions on the wall to enable the members to propose certain very clearcut points as recommendations. Thus, the document should be precise, but also general enough not to allow member states to compete with each other. Exactly this polarity between vagueness and precision characterizes the final document. Paye is very strategic and persuasive in this part of his statement, while using discourse representation and unreal scenarios in an evocation.

> Donc il faut, il faut faire attention à mon avis eh, à à ne pas eh, sortir une liste d'action qui soit simplement une espèce de de d'inventaire et surtout d'inventaire trop long dans lequel finalement personne ne retiendrai les choses parce que certaines actions, les pays diraient, certains pays diraient:"Mais nous les avons déjà faites" et d'autres actions les pays diraient "Elles ne sont pas réalisables chez

nous.".Donc c'est la je crois le, le, la difficulté eh, de de notre tâche, c'est à dire eh, trouver le, le juste, le juste milieu entre ce qui apparaîtra comme de l'affirmation dogmatique ou de l'acte de foie et ce qui a l'opposé apparaîtrai comme des recommandations pratiques mais eh, non-généralisables parce que trop liées à eh, au, aux spécificités de tel ou tel pays. Une fois que nous aurons eh, discuté un petit peu cela je voudrais si vous en êtes d'accord que eh, nous commencions à réfléchir eh, entre nous eh, à, à la suite des opérations après le 21 novembre,

After pointing to all the possible dangers in the drafting process, Paye concludes his statement with a perspective of future work. This is also very strategic in my view, reassuring the members that — whatever they might say- the work will go on. After this introduction where Paye sets the tone of the meeting, he turns to the representative of the commission who is on the one hand consultant, on the other hand controller and asks him if he would like to add something and to introduce some aspects of his own statement which had been distributed. Through this direct address (because otherwise, members raise their hands if they want to contribute) Paye marks the importance of the commission.

M9

Mais effectivement, c'est simplement une reprise eh, d'un certain nombre de propositions eh, C'est vraiment le type de papier sur laquelle on doit tirer eh, l'idée qui se trouve là derrière c'est d'une part on pourrait avoir dans ce papier trois dimensions, trois aspects, points forts et points faibles de l'Europe pour lesquelles il y a déjà eu des contributions des eh, membres du CAG, deuxième eh, élément: les faux messages, là aussi nous avons xxx déjà un certain nombre de contributions ce qui est très important et comme on l'a dit toute à l'heure eh, notre Président, il y aurai dans ce contexte-là du point forts, points faibles et faux messages, une oeuvre de pédagogie a faire. Il est important de faire comprendre à l'opinion publique exactement quelle est la situation. Et cela c'est un appel aussi eh, au pouvoir publiques et nous-mêmes, notre devoir là se sera de substancier eh, ces, ces différents éléments. Donc il faudrait aussi ne pas se contenter d'affirmer la globalisation c'est fantastique, il faudrait avoit quelques indications de type plutôt statistique, pour autre qui permettraient de la donner une base plus solide. Mais si ça doit être relativement bref. Et puis alors le plus délicat et le plus "disputable"ce sont les lignes d'action et de recommandation, les priorités, alors ici j'ai simplement eh, mis une liste de thématiques, de prises au position eh, sans aucune prétention de, de ma part de les soutenir ou de les défendre et pour lesquelles simplement on pourrait voir si il y a une position, un consensus qui se dégage. Le texte est en Anglais et en Français.

M9 emphasizes the weak points of Europe. And he continues that one should not only mention the positive sides of globalization, but also consider the public opinion and fears. The task is, in M9s view, really pedagogical, thus he supports the direction Payee has put forward. In having the commissions support, the authority of Paye stays undisputed.

In the following two turns the notion and concept of globalization is put forward and discussed. We will analyze these clauses carefully and neglect other interesting aspects of the dynamics and discussion.

Paye:

> J'aimerais avoir votre sentiment parce que eh, je, je suis moi-même peut-être un peu, un peu biaisé, eh, a cet égard eh, je me suis battu eh, a l'OECD pendant des années pour essayer de faire reconnaître que, eh, il y avait quelque chose qui était en train de changer dans la manière dont fonctionnait l'économie. Alors qu'on l'appelle globalisation, c'est un, un catchword qui est, qui est commode, mais eh, je crois que eh, il y a vraiment dans la manière dont fonctionne l'économie quelque chose qui a changé c'est à dire une concurrence qui est eh, eh, de plus en plus présente, de plus en plus forte, eh, une concurrence non seulement présente mais potentielle quant on discute avec les chefs d'entreprise, on s'aperçoit que non seulement ils se préoccupent de résister à la concurrence, de concurrent qui existe déjà, mais ils se préoccupent des concurrents qui peuvent naître et surgir, eh, brusquement donc c'est la "contestability of markets" qui, qui est une, une notion nouvelle. Et tout cela je crois a, a changé fondamentalement le paysage parce que ça veut dire que la pression pour eh, le, l'innovation, pour l'adaptation, pour le changement, pour le streamlining etcetera, n'a jamais été aussi forte. Et donc, eh, eh, les effets, eh, perturbateurs eh, de, de l'ajustement structurel que, on les a toujours connus depuis les, les, les débuts de l'activité économique, il y a des métiers qui ont disparus et d'autre qui sont apparus, mais cette destruction créatrice eh, eh, est est, beaucoup plus brutale et beaucoup plus rapide maintenant qu'elle ne l'a été.

Paye starts out with a very personal statement and relativizes his point of view by admitting that he had worked in the OECD and that maybe his view might be biased by his stay in that organization. He had fought for the realization that things were starting to change in the economy. Again, a rhetorical device is used: by marking this statement as a very personal opinion, Paye makes it discussable and also refutable. On the other hand, by using and referring to the outside, to another very important organization, he claims the topos of authority for himself and implicitly indicates that he has a lot of experience and know-how. Paye is a diplomat and diplomats always refer to other organizations, committees and negotiations which they have been involved in (Wodak & Vetter 1999; Wodak et al. 1997). This is the social capital of diplomats, the knowledge of international organizations and their experience with negotiations. Paye continues and switches to impersonal mode, distancing himself from the concept of globalization, something which is "called like that" and which is a catchword. The labeling of globalization as catchword is derogatory, it is even a "comfortable" catchword, something one can use in many situations. However, Paye remarks, there is something true — without defining globalization more precisely, than changes in the economy — , competition has become stronger. This recontextualizes the introduction of the outline, analyzed above. The competition has to be met and to be adapted to, the "contestability of markets". Again Paye introduces an English precise economical term into the discussion. Then follow characteristics of globalization and competition, now set analogous: innovation, adaptation, change, streamlining which are all much swifter and more brutal then it used to be. These notions continue throughout the whole meeting. Paye ends his turn by an optimistic twist: it is possible to discuss much more now then four years ago, thus emphasizing the here and now, the "window of opportunity" which has opened for change and adaptation. This suggests that it is high time to act, NOW! Furthermore, he states that dialogue should be possible between the social partners, "*un effort solidaire*". The notion of solidarity is a most important topos throughout the whole drafting process which seems to contradict the responsibility of the individual which had been proposed beforehand. But they go together: responsible individuals decide to act together, in contrast to the American and Japanese way of economies. This implies the specific European road which should be taken and decided upon.

The next speaker is called upon whose paper had not been distributed, M8, a British employer. M8 characterizes himself as coming from a very narrow sector, telecommunications. He then continues to define two approaches to globalization:

> Ehm and there is one very important point I think we need make about globalization, and that is that you can take two basic approaches to it. One of which is to be defensive and to see it as a threat and there is a tendency I detect within Europe to look at it in that way. And the other is to be offensive, and to see it as an opportunity. Eh, frankly, I think there is only one sensible way of viewing it and that is the latter. Ehm, I detect worries that United States are getting further ahead of Europe, that Japan may be getting further ahead, that other Asian-Pacific countries may be getting further ahead. You will not succeed in a global market unless you aim to do better than the Americans, better than the Japanese, better than the, the Asian Tigers. And I think a key message we need to get over at to the heads of state is that we can.

M8 makes a very general statement about globalization and competitiveness, this statement could be viewed as condensing the employers view into one paragraph. The general claims are embedded into clauses, using the personal pronoun "I" five times, but two of these are in combination with "detect" (which implies that what is "detected" is "there"). The other three are "I think", but these seem less highlighted than Paye's emphasis on his ideas being personal. The theme are the basic approaches to globalization, in an attributional clause he explains the first approach, using "defensive" and "threat" as rhemes. He then continues to state that there are tendencies in Europe that view globalization in this way. This is an insinuation to the public opinion from the outline which is recontextualized as an agentless process. The next clause has "offensive" as rheme and "opportunity", two positively connotated attributes among the business-speak. Then he switches to personal mode and suggests the latter view to be the only one which is sensible, a very evaluative judgement, clearly marking the other approach as the contrary, as insensible and irrational. This is a juxtaposition which we encounter in the next draft, the contrast between insensible and irrational tendencies, i.e. beliefs of many people, and the rational and sensible opinions of the experts. M8 takes this argument further: he "detects worries" which are agentless and anonymous, irrational and without evidence that the Americans and Japanese might get ahead. And then he makes a very general statement that one has to compete and win the competition with the two most eminent competitors. He phrases this as a rhetorical address, using "you" where it is not clear who is actually addressed, the CAG, Europe, the people, or the politicians. The next clause makes the addressee clear and reduces the options, the "heads of state" are the rheme, and the document should be directed at them. In a persuasive way, he continues with a success story as evidence, his own experience with telecommunications. And ends with "it can be done". The story is strategically used as counter argument to the "worries" mentioned beforehand (see Wodak and Reisigl, 2000 for the strategic use of stories in multiple contexts). M8 ends his statement with a very direct, imperative and emphasized appeal: "it[Europe] has to win, it actually has to be best". And the topos of threat continues: "unless you set your sights for that, you will loose". The message which he conveys is taken up by the next speaker, M4, thus M8 has positioned himself and the employer side very well in this meeting.

All these sequences illustrate the impact of globalization and competitiveness rhetorics and the specific argumentation pattern used by the employer side. Paye himself, as diplomat and politician, is more vague about the issue. However, the recontextualization of the outline and topic list in the debates of the meeting are obvious. Moreover, the link between globalization, competitiveness and Europes' new identity is constructed explicitly and the distinction from other economies, the USA and Japan.

6.   The voices of the employers and the conflict with the trade-unions

6.1 *The drafting process*

The outline discussed in the meeting (see above) was redrafted into the first draft of the final document (D2), from October 14th, 1997. The macrostructure of the document recontextualizes the proposals made by Paye and M4 (a turn which we have to neglect here): The title "Ambition for employment" sets the stage for an introduction about the importance of globalization for Europe, the causes of unemployment and the need for competition. The second section "Explaining the stakes; refuting mistaken ideas" is the pedagogical part of the document, refuting the commonsense opinions of "contrary to what many people believe". The third section of the document emphasizes the strong points of Europe, thus constructing the new European identity in contrast to the USA and Japan and aims at a specific European economic policy (see above). Finally, the fourth section contains the recommendations. This macro structures of the document stays throughout the redrafting process and recontextualizes the topic list as well as the outline. It is also rhetorically well constructed. It makes sense to refute mistakes and then juxtapose the positive sides of Europe as legitimation for the recommendations. Thus, this document could serve the politicians as argumentative basis for any decisions they would like to take in their November summit. All the necessary argumentative chains are condensed in this document: the causal chain between globalization, the need for competition in Europe and the need for change in Europe which would also fight unemployment serves as latent structure throughout the document.

The title of the document undergoes several changes which are due to the debates in the meeting about the main focus of the document.

The first suggestion for a title was 'Ambition for Employment'. This became 'Ambition for Employment. Competitiveness as a source of Jobs', and was finally changed to 'Competitiveness for employment'. According to van Dijk (1993), titles function as macro-propositions, i.e. they summarize the content, provide signals for the reader and anticipate what will be said; their additional function is to arouse the addressee's interest. Consequently, titles are predominantly located in the interpersonal metafunction, to use Halliday's terminology. The interpersonal metafunction defines the relational level, in our case between the reader and the text.

At first, the focus was on 'employment'; therefore 'employment' constituted

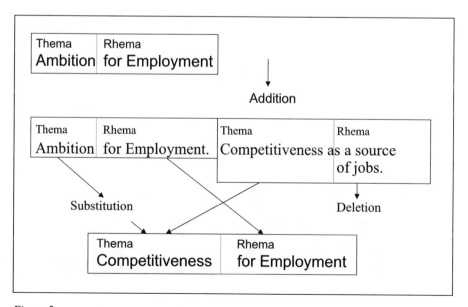

Figure 5

the rheme, the new information, which was to be discussed, without, however narrowing down the number of possible options at this point. At the meeting in September, the participants decided — as befits the name of their own group — to include 'competitiveness' as a subtitle in the title and thus limited possible decisions and options. In the final version, only 'competitiveness' and 'employment' are highlighted, a connection is made between them, although it remains open whether this relation is causal of functional. Throughout the entire policy paper, competition and competitiveness are assumed to be the basis of the new employment policy; therefore the paper includes a discussion of how competitiveness might be increased.

Now let us take a quick look at the third paragraph. This time only two versions, that of October 14th, 1997 and that of October 28th, 1997 will be compared. A third meeting (17th October 1997) took place in between, which was marked by the above-mentioned conflict between the trade unions and the employer side (see below).

1. But it [globalization] is also a demanding one, and often a painful one.
2. Economic progress has always been accompanied with destruction of obsolete activities and creation of new ones.
3. The pace has become swifter and the game has taken on planetary dimensions.
4. It imposes on all countries — including European countries, where industrial civilisation was born — deep and rapid adjustments.
5. The breadth and urgency of the needed adaptations are indistinctly perceived by public opinion, which explains a widespread sense of unease.
6. The duty which falls on governments, trade-unions and employers is to work together
– to describe the stakes and refute a number of mistaken ideas;
– to stress that our countries have the means to sustain high ambitions; and
– to implement, without delay and with consistency, the necessary reforms.

This paragraph is transformed and recontextualised as follows:

1. But it is also a demanding process, and often a painful one.
2. Economic progress has always been accompanied by destruction of obsolete activities and creation of new ones.
3. The pace has become swifter and the game has taken on planetary dimensions.
4. It imposes deep and rapid adjustments on all countries — including European countries, where industrial civilisation was born.
5. Social cohesion is threatened.
6. There is a risk of a disjunct between the hopes and aspirations of people and the demands of a global economy.
7. And yet social cohesion is not only a worthwhile political and social goal; it is also a source of efficiency and adaptability in a knowledge-based economy that increasingly depends on human quality and the ability to work as a team.
8. It has been difficult for people to grasp the breadth aand urgency of necessary adaptations.
9. This explains a widespread sense of unease, inequality and polarisation.
10. It is more than ever the duty of governments, trade-unions and employers to work together

   – to describe the stakes and refute a number of mistakes;
   – to stress that our countries should have high ambitions and they can be realised; and
   – to implement the necessary reforms consistently and without delay.

Failure to move quickly and decisively will result in loss of resources, both human and capital, which will leave for more promising parts of the world if Europe provides less attractive opportunities.

   This is the final version:

   1. But it is also a demanding process, and often a painful one.
   2. Economic progress has always been accompanied by destruction of obsolete activities and creation of new ones.
   3. The pace has become swifter and the game has taken on planetary dimensions.
   4. It imposes deep and rapid adjustments on all countries — including European countries, where industrial civilisation was born.
   5. Social cohesion is threatened by a widespread sense of unease, inequality and polarisation.
   6. There is a risk of a disjunct between the hopes and aspirations of people and the demands of a global economy.
   7. And yet social cohesion is not only a worthwhile political and social goal; it is also a source of efficiency and adaptability in a knowledge-based economy that increasingly depends on human quality and the ability to work as a team.
   8. It is more than ever the duty of governments, trade-unions and employers to work together
   – to describe the stakes and refute a number of mistakes;
   – to stress that our countries should have high ambitions and they can be realised; and
   – to implement the necessary reforms consistently and without delay.

   9. Failure to move quickly and decisively will result in loss of resources, both human and capital, which will leave for more promising parts of the world if Europe provides less attractive opportunities.

What, then, are the transformations? Basically we distinguish between four types of transformation which result from recontextualization: addition of elements, deletion of elements, rearrangement of elements and substitution of elements (van Leeuwen and Wodak 1999). In a textlinguistic framework, these are transformations which refer to the coherence and cohesion of a text in the sense of Beaugrande and Dressler (1981) (see Titscher et al. 1998), i.e. to text syntax and text semantics. Thus, in sentence 4 of the final version we observe a change in word order, which refers to the rheme: Now the emphasis is on 'European countries' and no longer on 'adjustments'. This allows for at least two readings, and an interpretation can only be selected if one is familiar with the entire context: first, it may be interpreted as a purely stylistic change, as a tendency towards making plain English more comprehensible and efficient. Efficiency character-izes the entire document, the content as well as the form. This is business-speak. Or, it can be interpreted as highlighting Europe and its tradition in an attempt to construct a new identity.

Sentence 5 is missing in the initial document. In this sentence, the trade union voice — in the Bakhtinian sense — makes itself heard; therefore this constitutes a concession to the unions, as becomes clear if one looks at the union representative's turn during the meeting (see below). The inclusion of social cohesion as important objective is demanded and it is claimed that the social welfare state is under threat. This topos of danger is further developed and justified in the following two sentences. The trade union argues that social welfare must not be perceived as a burden, but as something intrinsically efficient. Consequently, investment in human capital will improve competitiveness. Moreover, I would like to point out two elements which pervade the entire text like a motto: first, the tension between people's hopes and the implications of globalization; second, the 'knowledge-based economy', which is presented as a European trademark.

The sentence in the initial version of the document is complex and appears as two sentences in the new version, i.e. in a transformed and rearranged form (Figure 6).

At the same time, a shift occurs from the theme to the rheme. Again, this is a case of business-speak, a simplification, but on the other hand the information is transformed. There are further additions, for example in the description of the atmosphere and of the feelings of the people. The transformation of the nominal group 'public opinion' to 'people', i.e. to actors, is also important. Throughout the document, 'people' are consistently described by means of 'sensing processes',

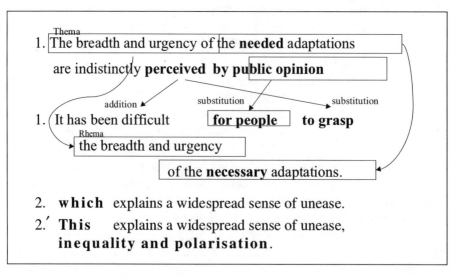

Figure 6

or are characterized by their hopes and beliefs, whereas knowledge and mental processes form the basis of the rational arguments of the experts. Although the distance taken by experts *vis-á-vis* 'ordinary people' is reduced, the group referred to as 'people' remains anonymous. We do not know who is included in this group and who is not. 'Perceive' is replaced by 'grasp', i.e. a mental process is replaced by a physical one, in order to include the element of transitivity as well.

The very last sentence has also been added to the final version: the topos of danger, which is conjured up here, is a rhetorical device used to persuade politicians to act quickly. The topos of speed and urgency also pervades the document, as does the semantic field 'urgent, rapid, quick' etc.; efficient, urgent action is needed. The basic message of this document, then, is that action is required, mere thinking is not enough, otherwise Europe will no longer be able to keep up with competition.

The last example which is of importance to illustrate the recontextualizations and changes in the drafting process is THE one paragraph in the section "Explaining the stakes and refuting the mistakes" where no consensus could be achieved. A footnote in the final version states that "the three trade union leaders in the CAG are not convinced of the evidence of this assertion on the effects of the labour laws. Future work of the CAG could assess these effects". I would like to reconstruct the drafting process of this paragraph in detail, including the correspondence between the meetings, the meeting itself as well as the interview with the chairperson Paye.

> D2: Contrary to what many people believe, laws protecting existing jobs do not serve job creation. They deter entrepreneurs from hiring, out of fear of not being allowed, in case of need, to reduce their staff. This is in particular the case with SMEs, while they are the main potential source for job creation. Such laws, as they are now in force in many member states, undermine the innovation and adaptation capacity of firms and eventually trap in doomed companies the workers they intend to protect. (Figure 7:1)

After the October meeting and due to the debate there, this paragraph changed to the following in D3:

> Contrary to popular belief, laws to protect jobs do not serve job creation. They deter entrepreneurs from hiring, out of fear of not being allowed to reduce their staff if necessary. This is particularly true of smaller enterprises, even though they are the main potential for job creation. The laws in force in many Member States undermine innovation and the capacity of firms to adapt. They eventually trap the workers they intend to protect in doomed countries. (Figure 7:2)

Finally, the version presented to the European Council contains the following paragraph:

> Contrary to the belief of many people, laws to protect existing jobs do not enhance job creation. They serve worthwhile purposes of human dignity and increase the motivation for investing in human capital. But they often deter

entrepreneuers from hiring, out of fear of not being allowed to reduce their staff if necessary. This is particularly true of smaller enterprises, even tough they are the main potential for job creation. When laws hamper firms' capacity to innovate and adapt, they eventually trap the workers they intend to protect in doomed companies. Added is the footnote quoted above. (Figure 7:3)

The whole section about "Explaining the stakes and refuting the mistakes" first contains 6 points and then 7 in the final version. They are all constructed in a similar way, introduced by the same clause or nominal group which is a rhetorical device. In the first draft, we find "*contrary to what many people believe*" which is then changed to "*contrary to popular belief*" and finally expressed as "*contrary to the belief of many people*". A verbal process of sensing is first recontextualized to a more static noun and relates to the more material language of administration (see Iedema 1999). Through this introductory remark, a distinction is made between "us" and "them", the experts and the laypersons. Throughout the whole paper, the laypersons are constructed as believers and irrational, while the experts are the thinkers and rational. As the whole policy paper is formulated as argumentative text, this section is of great importance in the argumentative chain: by refuting "mistakes" which are all due to state intervention and the existing labour laws, the we-group presents itself as knowledgeable, willing to change structural aspects of European economy and above common sense arguments and lays the

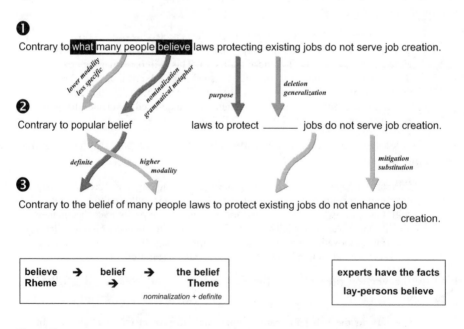

Figure 7

ground for the following section of recommendations which do not have to be justified anymore. Their legitimation is given through the juxtaposition to the enumerated mistakes. The quoted paragraph is the only one where no consensus could be achieved, in all the other issues, even the leaders of the trade unions agreed that changes are necessary and that the status quo was not flexible enough. The conflict of values was too large!

Who are the many people? They stay anonymous and could mean European citizens, non-experts or also experts of different opinion. Popular belief is even stronger, as noun and clearly labels the non-experts, the public opinion which in non informed or misinformed. The compromise of recontextualization in the final version mitigates "popular belief", "many" indicates that not "all people" are meant. Already this recontextualization of the "they-group" illustrates the discussion in the meeting and the debates which occurred, the mitigation in the final version demonstrates that adnministrative language is not aimed at and that the strategy of positive self-presentation and negative other-presentation is formulated in a more indirect way (thus different then in bureaucratic documents!).

As mentioned above, this paragraph is one of the most interesting ones of the whole policy paper. It symbolizes the conflict between the unions and the employers and politicians explicitly because the delegates of the unions insisted that a footnote be added to the final version expressing their opposing position. Thus the paper does manifest a consensus in the CAG, but only after numerous faxes were exchanged to compromise on this paragraph and the footnote (see Section 2 and the quotes by chairperson Paye above). The conflict, which underlies the whole paper — between welfare states and market economy, between the believers in social cohesion and those in favour of efficiency, competitiveness, flexibility and globalization — is symbolically manifested in this one paragraph where no consensus in the wording could be achieved. This is an example of a political compromise.

Already the first sentence manifests the difficulty of achieving consensus. A fax by the President Paye explains why he chose *"enhance"* instead of *"serve"*: more mitigated, less direct, less bureaucratic. Let me quote from his letter to M9 from November 10th, 1997:

> The first and third sentences will read "..laws to protect jobs do not enhance job creation...But they often deter entrepreneurs from hiring". Paye explains this as follows: "TUC proposed "laws to protect jobs may not automatically serve job creation". I consider such a wording would convey the wrong impression that these laws usually contribute to job creation. This could only be conceivable in case of extreme labour shortage, if the level of protection, rather then that of wages, were to become the discriminating factor for choosing among jobs on offer. This is not a frequent situation. Therefore, I retain the original text, with only a change for a less square cut verb.

TUC proposed for the 3rd sentence: "...they sometimes can deter..." In my view, such a wording would not reflect reality. I never heard an entrepreneur saying that laws protecting existing jobs are an inducement to hire. I often heard the opposite, especially from SME or individual entrepreneurs. Again, it would require very special circumstances for protection laws to appear as a boost for job creation. Hence 'often' added to the sentence".

In the second draft, "*existing*" was dropped and then added again, to make the assertion explicit. Not any jobs are meant, only the existing ones. The conflict between unions and employers is about the conditions for losing jobs and firing. There is no problem at all, to fire anybody, the crux is how much this costs. In many countries which have strict labour laws, like Portugal, such laws are illegaly avoided; employees have to sign agreements where they forego such laws (personal communication, Karl Pichelmann). On the other hand, the rigidity of unions makes it difficult for small companies, which are often the focus of this policy paper. If the relationships at work are too rigid, ("*Arbeitsbeziehungen*"), this makes it very difficult to work efficiently and get rid of "bad" workers. Flexibility in some sense is certainly necessary (M3 from the trade unions speaks of "*intelligent flexibility*" in the meeting). In this paragraph, we find the two extreme positions: for and against such laws, no mediating position that argues for some kind of flexibility in these laws is found. The next sentence "*They deter entrepreneurs from hiring, out of fear of not being allowed, in case of need, to reduce their staff*" is changed to — due to Plain English — *They deter entrepreneurs from hiring, out of fear of not being allowed to reduce their staff if necessary.* In the third and forth draft, another sentence is inserted and the sentence above is then connected with the conjunctive "but": *They serve worthwhile purposes of human dignity and increase the motivation for investing in human capital. But they often deter entrepreneurs from hiring, out of fear of not being allowed to reduce their staff if necessary.* The insertion of the first clause juxtaposes the two positions and arguments explicitly. The unions, in any case, have succeeded in making their point explicit. Labor laws are moral and humane (moral legitimation, e.g. van Leeuwen and Wodak 1999), they also imply actions, like training and education as investment in human capital. The entrepreneurs (agents) are then described as irrational, afraid, the material process is dependent on sensing verbs. The entrepreneurs are also described as passive, as agents dependent (on whom?) and not allowed to do what they want. Next follow the arguments about small businesses, which need flexibility: *This is particular the case with SME's while they are the main potential source for job creation.* This sentence is slightly changed, stylistically and emphasizing the argumentation given above to *This is particularly true of smaller enterprises, even though they are the main potential source for job creation.*

Job creation is again the rheme, like in the first sentence of the paragraph which underlines the importance of the issue. The last sentence is obviously the one which was most debated in the meetings and in the correspondence: *Such laws, as they are now in force in many member states, undermine the innovation and adaptation capacity of firms and eventually trap in doomed companies the workers they intend to protect* (Figure 8.1). Instead of having a complex sentence with embeddings, the sentence is changed to two clauses: *The laws in force in many Member States undermine innovation and the capacity of firms to adapt. They eventually trap the workers they intend to protect in doomed companies* (Figure 8.2). Although the two sentences are simpler, this is again recontextualized into a complex sentence, changing the assertions into a coordinated final sentence, with an underlying topos of threat: *When laws hamper firms' capacity to innovate and adapt, they eventually trap the workers they intend to protect in doomed companies* (Figure 8.3). The last sentence is very much mitigated from the first drafts. Instead of the generalizing statement, we have conditional. Instead of "undermine", "hamper" is used which is much weaker and means interfering, disturbing and not destroying. "Eventually" also mitigates as particle the material process in the final clause. Nevertheless, the threat is clear: inefficient companies can not be "cleaned" because of the rigid laws. The laws are counter-productive and contradictory in their effects. This last sentence is non-acceptable for the union-delegates in the CAG, even in its mitigated form (see the footnote above). Also the footnote is a result of many faxes and negotiations. Instead of being assertive, the delegates "are not convinced", they are passive, beneficiaries. They also do not oppose this claim totally but leave it to further discussions and work of

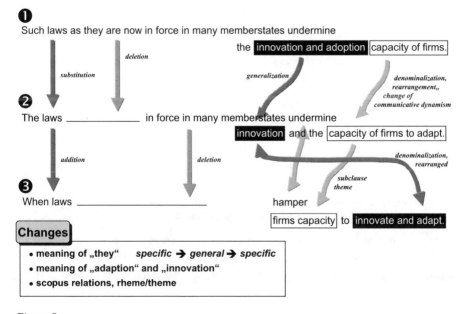

Figure 8

the CAG. This implies that the claims could also be true if there were evidence for them. The indirectness and mitigation in this paragraph are clear indicators of the many negotiations and conflicts in the meetings and the following correspondence and recontextualizes the many voices. But this time, not one voice is the result, but at least two, employers and politicians on the one side, delegates of the trade unions on the other side. Both polar positions are mitigated but they stay explicit in the final version.

In a letter from November 5th from Paye to M9, he comments the conflict about this paragraph in the following way:

> "I know very well that it is difficult for trade-unionists to accept the language about laws that protect existing jobs but do not serve employement creation. But I am convinced that, on balance, this is unfortunately true and entails a risk of polarisation between the insiders (employed and protected) and the "outsiders" (unemployed).

With this comment, Paye touches on a very important aspect of trade-unions policies. Trade unions are -*per definitionem*- only concerned with the employed, not with the unemployed. They aim at labour laws protecting the employed and thus construct a big gap between the insiders and the outsiders. This is a political issue which trade unions are confronted with more and more nowadays.

In the interview with chairperson Paye commented the conflict between trade unions and employers as follows:

```
I:  ja.
P:  and would be criticised — at home by their constituents.
I:                        by      yeah.
P:  and therefore/                      yes. therefore they
I:  THAT was my            interpretation, too.
P:  needed to make reservations someWHERE, and they chose this
I:  ja.                    ja.
P:  öh THIS one.                    yes.
I:  ja.          That's why I asked is this symBOLic. ja?
I:  because I I had the feeling that — they had actually gone very FAR. — %(and)
    % — jumped across
P:  mhm.                            mhm. mhm. —
I:  certain bridges. yah? so
P:  no no. they had killed a number of sacred cows            and
I:                          yeah.   oh absolutely.
P:  they needed to maintain ONE     HALF-living. half aLIVE.
I:  yeah.              one. yeah.        yeah.   yeah.
```

In this sequence Paye uses the paragraph about working time as example of the debate but concludes that the trade unions needed to voice their opposition explicitly because they had given in on other aspects to retain their credibility. "It was a sacred cow". On the other hand, Paye emphasises the goodwill of all the participants of the meeting and also provides evidence that the debate in the meeting had an impact on the drafting process. After the meeting, a number of faxes were exchanged — as mentioned above- and finally, a compromise was achieved.

6.2 *The voices in the meeting of October 14th, 1997*

This meeting is much more formal then the second meeting: the members of the trade-unions are present, a open conflict results between M2 and F2, the most prominent speakers are M6 and M7, due to our analysis of references (Titscher et al. 1998). The draft is explicitly discussed, the confrontation between two models of unemployment policies and two economic ideologies becomes very transparent: the European model supported by the members of the trade-unions requesting state intervention, strict labour laws and high labour taxes, and the alternative model which wants lower taxation and other forms of taxation and a change of the labour laws. Social cohesion is debated, and F2 succeeds in having this issue added to the next draft (D3) as already analyzed above. On the other hand, especially M6 emphasizes competitiveness. Again, the European model is discussed, it is clear for both groups in the meeting that changes are due, but the quality of the changes is different. The draft, which recontextualizes this meeting and has been analyzed above, contains the voices of the two polarized groups. Below, one sequence will provide evidence for the conflict and debate in the meeting, which was only resolved lastly in the footnote, added to the paragraph discussed above. The conflict is manifested in a sequence between F2 and M2:

F2
Thank you Mister Chairman! I was a bit surprised when I got the draft two of the report. It was quiet opposite from the first draft. But Sh — I could see it, it has full, full, full what the discussion that you had on the second meeting. And I hadn't a xxx you can understand to, to make reaction of this draft two, but may the reaction of the xxx from the meeting too. Because it was a long thing I, I disagree with. And I think it's important to, to realise wha/ what's, what is a toast on this group. I mean we shall, we shall contribute to the summit two times here and, and this time to a special job summit. And our, our contribute must be a compliment to, to Commission's work and xxx other prospectives. But the most important thing is that we have a common view. A common view from leading xxx, from the industry, from the (union), from the, the employer side and fro/ from and different eyes of the societies. So, we have to, to think about what's happen if we, if we can't make a, a, a joint report. And I think it's very important that we, we xxx the question that you have on the first meeting. If we talk about competitiveness we also have to talk about social cohesion. And you said it now, xxx Mister Chairman but I'm thinking in the paper I can't say it in, in a, in the same word as you have now. So as the report Sh, is now, it is too much that not acceptable Sh, in my point of view. But I don't think it's — acceptable either if you look at the Commission's guide lines for the job summit or if you listen to, for example, prime minister Junker when he, Junker, when, when he talk about what he think Sh, the, the job summit will, will Sh, talk about. He said when he was at the — I think was xxx

last meeting and he has also been at the, the executive xxx and he said, this job summit, it will not be a meeting about irregulation, not meet about liberalization, it, its must be a meeting about

M2:
La, la der/ le dernier commentaire c'est sur le papier de Madame xxx. Afin, je ne s/ je ne suis pas un fondamentaliste de, de libéralisme, des choses du marche. Je comprends vos préoccupations sur certaines idées qu'on pose ici mais je vous dis très franchement si l'on lit votre papier, vous donnez un message de rigidité, maintenir les choses comme commertant. là, à mon avis c/ c'est pas utile. Ce que vous dites, c'est la, la sécurité sociale c'est bien, on doit continuer avec ça. Le, on doit pas avoir plus d' flexibilité, les choses sont bien comme ça, l'intervention d' l'état c'est bien comme ça, les, la dépense publique c'est bien comme ça. Quand on lit votre papier c'est cette mais/ c'est pas/ peut-être c'est pas si évidement ce que vous voulez dire. Mais ce qu'on vous dites la première fois je parle très franchement, parce que ça c'est utile pour discuter les choses. J/ je pense alors, je ne veux pas détruire la wellfare state, le model social Européen mais je veux accommoder, flexibiliser, ajuster ce model! Mais voir commercial, c'est, tout ça c'est bien, on doit continuer et garder ça. Ma, mon opinion c'est, oui, on doit garder le model sociale mais on doit le discuter et donner une message de flexibilité, d'ajustement et vous donner la une message de rigidité. Excusez-moi, mais ça, c'est mon opinion. Merci bien.

In her turn, F2 first emphasizes that a "common view" has to be reached and that the CAG should complement the work of the commission. This introduction to her strong critic is very strategic because it marks her goodwill and the solidarity, which is aimed at throughout. Then, she explicitly warns the group that a consensus will not be achieved if social cohesion is not added into the draft. She rejects the draft as it stands now, it is not acceptable for her. After her turn, M2, from the employer's side, argues that F2 is too rigid and that flexibility on the side of the trade unions would be necessary. The social achievements should be preserved but also changed. The response to the turn of F2 is not mitigated at all. The conflict is very open and explicit and direct, embedded in meta-linguistic remarks about the possibility of being frank in this group. This sequence is typical for the conflict and debate in this meeting.

7. Conclusions

Die Aufkündigung des sozialstaatlichen Kompromisses hat freilich zur Folge, daß die Krisentendenzen, die er aufgefangen hatte, wieder aufbrechen. Es entstehen soziale Kosten, die die Integrationsfähigkeit einer liberalen Gesellschaft zu über-fordern drohen....Eine solche Desolidarisierung muß jedoch auf längere Sicht eine liberale politische Kultur zerstören, auf deren universalistisches Selbstverständnis demokratisch verfaßte Gesellschaften angewiesen sind (Habermas 1998b: 68–69).

The reconstruction of the drafting process of the policy paper "Competitiveness for Employment" in the CAG has provided evidence for the big debates with which the new European identity and new European employment policies are confronted with: the protection of European values and institutions and, at the same time, the effort to win in the worldwide competition and to make structural changes which would most certainly destroy some of the European traditions of welfare states. We have also gained insight into processes of decision-making, conflicts and achievement of consensus as well as power structures in the European Union. This case study of the CAG illustrates the power of the chairperson and the commission, but it also shows in what way debates in committees influence the drafting and recontextualization process. In regard to our guiding research questions, we can provide some first answers:

The debates in the meetings are concerned with the drafts, the resulting new drafts manifest these debates, the opinions of the committee members are taken into account, and the most prominent speakers and turns have the most impact on the drafting process. Nevertheless, it is the chairperson, together with the representative of the commission who finally decides, sets the dates and proposes compromises. Moreover, globalization and competitiveness rhetorics dominate the debates and the drafting process. The employers win the conflict, the delegates of the trade unions are basically "blown away" except for one footnote in one paragraph. Flexibility and competitiveness mark the discourses, linked to the assumed positive impact of globalization (Weiss and Wodak 2000).

The resulting final draft manifests the voices of the social partners; competitiveness is emphasized, as well as social cohesion, but the priority — as already the name of the group CAG signifies — lies on competitiveness (Krugman 1997; also Chapter 7). The whole paper is an argumentative, persuasive document intended to influence the politicians and to serve as legitimation for their decisions. The new very instable European identity is constructed throughout the paper and opposed to the USA and Japan. The tension lies in the decision to be made how far one would like to adapt to the economic models of these two countries. The search for a new European model is very apparent. Both social partners agree that changes have to occur, but they disagree in the priorities and in the measures, which are to be taken. Globalization is defined as a positive, irreversible phenomenon, and competitiveness is defined as the basic source for job creation and for the fight against unemployment. This naturally illustrates the voice of the employers more then the voice of the trade unions which emphasize that investment in "human capital" is the only way to make the economy more efficient whereas the employers argue for different and less strict labor laws and less state intervention. The individual responsibility of each European citizen is underlined, an ideology which most certainly comes from the USA.

The recontextualization processes, which manifest the debates in the meetings and in the redrafting of the document shows very conflicting tendencies: some clauses are changed into simpler English, some clauses get more complex. Other sequences change to precise wording, whereas some sentences take on vagueness. The argumentative conditional changes into dogmatic declaratives. The detailed analysis on all three metafunctions in the Hallidayan sense illustrates redundancies, from the textual metafunction to the ideational and finally to the interpersonal level. The conflicting tendencies can be explained by the topics discussed and promoted. The topics, which were consensual, get simpler and more precise whereas difficult, sensitive topics, which have to be negotiated at length, get vague and complex. Due to members of the CAG present or absent, whole clusters of clauses get deleted or added or substituted. The textual analysis which illustrates the given and new, the presupposed opinions and beliefs and the causal links to new information illustrates that competitiveness, globalization and job creation are linked into a positive value chain. In contrast to the language of administration (Iedema 1999), the recontextualization from oral to written does not necessarily result in agentless nominalizations and distanciation. This policy paper is a persuasive and political document, thus the genre and also the language are different. The "life of arguments" is not streamlined, it takes various turns and goes into different directions as described above. Recontextualization is thus context dependent!

The recontextualization process and the final document also manifest the consensus achieved inspite of severe conflicts between the views of the trade unions and the employers and politicians. The conflict lastly manifests itself in one footnote, which Paye characterized as "the symbolic sacred cow" (see above). The conflict between the European model of Economy based on Keynesianism and between the neo-liberal economies symbolized by Japan and the USA is not resolved in this document. The search for a new European way is indicated, with some state intervention, a change of labour laws and taxes, however, the welfare models should also not be destroyed. More flexibility is aimed at. We will discuss the recommendations in Chapter 7.

In the interview with the chairperson Paye, I asked about the decision making process and his impressions about it as well as about the impact of such a document:

> I: so — HOW would you actually — I mean from YOUR knowledge in your expertise — WHAT is really — CRUcial for decision-making. — how would you — describe THAT. —
>
> P: it's a %very very [*laughing*]% tough QUEStion.
>
> I: yeah.
>
> P: I 've never been a a — politician. so äh the the the real öh crux of the matter is HOW the politicians DO their — dis/ make their deCIsions. but I 've worked closely with with politicians, AND I 've — been at the (head of) the OECD in contact with an — many many GOvernments of course. — - my my conCERN is that the aMOUNT of öh paraMETers you have to bring into the PICture for making a decision, is — increasing. — I would say (by the DAY) but at least (by the YEAR) — and I think that making a decision NOW, öh is is probably more

difficult than ever, because of the aMOUNT of — information you have access to, and having access to information, if you don't — try to use it, öh öh %you [*laughing*]% you feel öh you feel (xxx) I would say. — - therefore you need to have — a structure a decision-making structure within — (be it your) government or you company or whatever. — which äh äh is able to analyse — in real time — this — inforMATION which is moving FAST and changing — fast, filters THAT for for for YOU, and provides YOU with the öh the — the main öh öh (synthesis) ELements, which — you NEED for — taking the deCIsion. WHERE do they find the time for really öh: leaning BACK, sitting BACK and öh öh devote öh: two hours, to thinkings, and decising, and making a deCISION.

Paye explains the problems of decision making in a complex organization very similar to Niklas Luhmann whose point of view was quoted at the beginning of this chapter. It is a question of space and time in a fast moving world nowadays, a question of choice and selection of relevant information. He emphasizes the necessity of structures, which allow efficient decision-making. This description of the decision making process also serves as legitimation and explanation for his own role in the CAG: he actually decided the content and structure of the drafts and final version, after having heard all the conflicting voices. Lastly, turning back to our thoughts on the nature of conflicts in modern societies, it becomes very clear, that we are dealing with conflicts of values here, and that secondly, the conflict is almost avoided by the most powerful person as well as mediated. The CAG presents an almost perfect example of how conflicts are resolved or almost resolved in organizations, even between such opposing interest groups. The structure is well illustrated in the timeline above. The power is personified in Paye himself.

Another important issue which poses itself after the analysis of the drafting process is the question of readership: who reads the report, what is the impact of this policy paper? There must be important functions of the CAG, because otherwise such busy and influential people would not take the trouble to meet and spend their time together. As already mentioned in the beginning of this chapter, networking is one of the main characteristics of such transnational bodies. The second important function is most certainly legitimation. The policy paper serves as legitimation device for the politicians if they need it. The chairperson himself is well aware of these functions. 'I think that his self-assessment is of interest:

I: WHAT HAPPENS with these reports. who who READS them

P: THIS is this is äh: this is a problem I ähm spoke aBOUT with öh: with the (xxx) président Santer, because — my impression is that öh öh the agenda of öh of öh the (European) Council — according to what I read in — in the [*laughs*] (press communiqué)

I: ja,

P: is so: — HEAVy. so heteROGENEOUS so diVERSE, that they CAN not — devote öh öh much TIME to to every SUBject. — I don't know how it is going NOW, ähm — let me take the example of this äh report in November, [*coughs*] — there were — two reports to the European Council, coming from a wide vaRIETy of öh of institutions and I 've been TOLD that the European PARLiament made

report, the (Hungarian social council) made a rePORT, öh: the — there were —
two or three other reports in addition to OURS. — of COURSE–the the heads of
(State and government) haven't been able to to read all all that STUFF, and not
even their AIDES.

I: ja.

P: %have been able [*low*]% — THEREfore I don't know. — I don't know what
the the real IMpact öh öh IS, — which öh of course is a bit öh: — well
discouraging

As to be seen, Paye himself is very pessimistic about the influence of a group such
as the CAG. Nevertheless, he believes in his work and that the debates are
important. The papers are circulated widely and maybe — as Paye argues —
might have an impact somewhere at sometime.

So, we are left with the question what the functions of such a group are and
why so much work is invested into a policy paper, which is maybe not read by the
audience it addresses. I believe — as mentioned above — that the main function
lies in the establishing of solidarity and networks, of having discussion *fora*
where European citizens meet. Only in such a way, at very many different places
and times, is the construction of a new European identity possible. And at the
same time, only through extended debates between the social partners are new
economic policies to be developed. The CAG provides a stage for such ideological debates, a public space where different ideologies and opinions can meet and
negotiations take place. This, in my view, is the most important function of such
advisory groups.

Chapter 5

A difference that makes no difference?

Decision-making on employment in the European Parliament

Gilbert Weiss

1. Introduction

The European Parliament (EP) holds a special position in European Union (EU) politics. It is the only supra-national body with direct democratic legitimacy, i.e. a mandate from the populations of the member states. It constitutes the public space of political debate within the EU organizational system. The Members of European Parliament (MEPs) serve the task of representing the interests and problems of their electorate in EU decision-making. Although these interests and problems may vary significantly according to regional and local particularities, sometimes they show characteristics common to the bulk of the European population. According to opinion polls, the problem which is most widespread today in all parts of Europe is unemployment (Koch 1997). In other words, the EP has a special responsibility in dealing with this problem which apparently affects European citizens most. The EP's position on un/employment will therefore be critical for the democratic legitimacy of the Union as a whole.

In this chapter I will enquire how the EP contributed to the European Council summit on employment in Luxembourg November 1997. As was described in Chapter 3, the Luxembourg summit, following-up the decision of the Amsterdam summit in June 1997 to establish common employment policy guidelines and annual "action plans" of the member states for the implementation of these guidelines, can be regarded as a culmination of several years development in EU employment policy-making. In Luxembourg, the European Council finally decided on the content and form of the guidelines as well as on the measures to be taken in order to translate them into action.

In July 1997, the EP was asked by Jean-Claude Juncker, Prime Minister of Luxembourg and acting President of the European Council at the time, for its contribution to the summit. The President of the EP at the time, Gil-Robles Gil-Delgado, referred this request to the Committee on Employment and Social Affairs (CESA) as the *committee responsible*. The CESA appointed its member Wim G. van Velzen as rapporteur. In July, the rapporteur produced a first *working document* (tabled on 15 July) which was discussed at the CESA meeting of 3 September. After that meeting van Velzen further elaborated the text and produced a *draft report* (tabled on 11 September) which was then discussed in CESA on 24 September. Subsequently, various members of the committee made amendments to the draft report which were discussed and voted on at the CESA meeting of 6 October and 7 October. At the same time the draft report was also sent to other EP committees concerned for their opinion. Finally, the CESA adopted the *motion for a resolution* by 23 votes to 3, with 2 abstentions (7 October). Having passed the committee, the *Report on the Proposal of the European Parliament to the Extraordinary European Council Summit on Employment (20–21 November 1997)*–tabled on 9 October — was discussed and voted on at the plenary session of the EP on 21 October (Appendix 3). It was then published as *Resolution embodying Parliament's proposal to the Extraordinary European Council meeting on employment* in the *Official Journal of the European Communities* and forwarded to the European Council summit in Luxembourg as well as to the Council of Ministers, the European Commission, the European social partners and the governments and parliaments of the member states (Appendix 4).

The focus in this chapter, however, is not to elaborate the oral negotiating of written texts (as in Chapters 4 and 6); rather it is to examine the organizational, political and social "expectations" and "decision premises" framing the EP's position on unemployment and the corresponding recommendations to the European Council summit in Luxembourg as expressed in the resolution and the preceding report. The chapter aims to investigate how the EP's decision-making in the field of employment policy proceeds, what position it takes on un/employment, what organizational and political characteristics it reveals, and how these characteristics enter into the written "communication of decisions" (Luhmann). In order to do this I will combine linguistic tools from Functional Grammar (Halliday 1994; Thompson 1996) and sociological concepts from Luhmann's organization theory (Luhmann 1984, 1996, 1997). The linguistic perspective on recontextualization (Chapter 1), i.e. reproduction and transformation of information from one text/genre to another, will be linked with the sociological perspective on decision-making as a network of decisions relating to, framing and contextualizing other decisions within one organizational system.

2. Sociological perspectives on decision-making

Before looking at the texts, a few concepts have to be clarified. I define the EP as an organizational part system of the overall EU organizational system. The three organizational part systems most involved in EU decision-making are the EP, the European Commission (EC) and the Council of Ministers (CM). EP, EC and CM are connected with each other through a variety of formal and informal communications. Together, all these communications form the so-called EU decision-making trialogue (see Chapter 3). In this paper, however, I am dealing with one specific communication directed from the EP to the European Council, namely the resolution on employment. Although, as was said above, the resolution was also transmitted to the EC and the CM, its addressee was clearly the European Council. Since the latter is not really part of the decision-making trialogue, but rather its higher authority, which develops the broad guidelines that the EU organs have to follow in their decision-making (Taulègne 1993), I am transcending here the trialogue in a narrow sense. On the other hand, the European Council can never be isolated from the trialogue between EP, EC and CM because — as a higher authority — it intervenes in a variety of ways, and its documents refer to the documents of the EP, EC and CM just as the latter refer to the former. These textual relations almost assume the form of a circle of decisions referring to decisions referring to decisions etc. That decisions "connect" to former as well as future decisions is a precondition for any organization and its reproduction (as well as transformation).

Like any social system, organizations are constituted through communication (Luhmann 1984: 15). More precisely: they constitute and reproduce themselves through the communication of *decisions* (Baecker 1999). The communication of decisions can assume different forms, e.g. oral and written, formal and informal, etc. (see Chapter 3). In other words, when using the notion decision, I do not reproduce the language of lawyers, i.e. I do not limit the notion to its legalistic/functionalistic meaning. Furthermore, my focus in decision-making procedures is not a psychic disposition, nor a thing or an object, but "expectations" as the social frame of decisions (Luhmann 1996: 25ff).

Decisions constitute a twofold difference: on the one hand a difference of options, on the other — and more important — a (temporal) difference between the situation before and the situation after the decision. Even the smallest decision changes the situation, otherwise there would be no need to make a decision. When Peter and Paul decide to go to see a movie and not to play pool, they *draw a distinction* between seeing a movie on the one hand and playing pool on the other — a distinction that *makes a difference* (to the situation before they decided) because playing pool is now excluded. Therefore, we might say that a decision constitutes a "difference that makes a difference" (G. Bateson). Some decisions, of course, constitute differences that make greater differences than other decisions. This depends on the expectations that frame the decision.

How do organizations ensure that decisions are accepted? They do it by institutionalizing expectations; and they institutionalize expectations by establishing decision premises. Decision premises are some sort of meta-decisions; they are decisions about decisions; they contextualize and legitimize decisions. Usually, they represent earlier decisions to which actual decisions have to refer to in order to gain legitimacy. This contextualization of decisions is essential for reducing uncertainty, increasing acceptance of decisions and guaranteeing organizational continuity (Luhmann 1996). For the "absorption of uncertainty" through the contextualization of decisions in former decisions an organization has to develop a kind of "system memory". It has to remember its "history" of decisions (when it decided what); decisions have to be connected to decisions. Of course, the system memory is organized along the lines of specific policies. A decision on employment policy, be it a parliamentary resolution, a directive of the Council or a Commission report — usually refers to the major decisions of the past in that particular field. Very often, the contextualization of decisions in former decisions goes hand in hand with a linguistic "recontextualizing" of the latter, i.e. with reformulations of the content of former decisions in a new situation of decision.

Furthermore, since organizations do not operate beyond society, expectations framing and contextualizing decisions must not be limited to intra-organizational expectations. They rather include societal expectations of various kinds. This is particularly true for political organizations. The EP's resolution from 21 October 1997 is framed not only by former EU decisions on employment (such as the Amsterdam Presidency Conclusions) but also by expectations of the societal environment (media discourses, lobbies, electorate, etc.). It faces a variety of expectations, all of them entering — in one way or another — as decision premises into the decision taken by the EP. A further important point is that organizational texts like the resolution of the EP or the preceding Van Velzen report, *construe* their own decision premises, which may differ from the 'real' decision premises framing the decision. For instance, the Austrian chancellor may mention all kinds of political decision premises that were relevant for the decision taken by the Austrian government on immigration policy, but in fact it might have been primarily the anti-immigrant discourses of boulevard media that served as major decision premise.

In general, the communication of decisions always involves both *self-reference* and *external reference* (Luhmann 1997: 64f) — meaning that decisions, on the one hand, always refer to themselves, i.e. to former decisions and future decisions, and on the other, they refer to their societal environment including the 'problem' or 'question' they decide upon. We could also speak of the form and content of decisions, but this is misleading since the referring of decisions to (former) decisions is part of the content of the decision too.

In the following, we will keep the distinction between self-reference and external reference in mind and systematically elaborate the decision premises of the Van Velzen report which itself served as a decision premise of the EP's resolution from 21 October 1997 which then served as a decision premise of the European Council summit in November 1997. We will ask for which decision premises were construed, and which were hidden. And we will do that by a linguistic analysis of the written texts. Understanding a decision as a "difference that makes a difference", we will finally face the question of what difference the EP's resolution constitutes, and what difference this difference makes — not least with regard to the 'problem' of unemployment. At the end of the paper we shall perhaps know a little more about the characteristics of EP decision-making in general and discourses on unemployment in particular.

3. The construction of decision premises

In the following we will basically analyze two documents: (a) the Van Velzen *Report on the Proposal of the European Parliament to the Extraordinary European Council Summit on Employment* (tabled on 9 October 1997), and (b) the ensuing *Resolution embodying Parliament's proposal to the extraordinary European Council meeting on employment* (tabled on 21 October 1997) (Appendix 3 and 4). Both documents are intimately linked to one another, for the report prepared by Van Velzen and voted on in the CESA served as the basis for the resolution. Like any EP report, the Van Velzen report consists of two parts: a *motion for resolution* ("Part A") and an *explanatory statement* ("Part B") "which provides background information on the problem, and outlines why certain recommendations were made" (Corbett, Jacobs and Shackleton 1995: 131). The explanatory statement "is not put to the vote in the committee, but is drafted by the rapporteur on his or her own responsibility, although it is still supposed to reflect the opinion of a majority within the committee" (ibid: 131). Furthermore, it is no longer part of the final resolution document. It serves primarily the function of explaining to the MEPs — who will vote on the motion for resolution in the plenum — the background and context of the recommendations made in the motion. With regard to what was said above, it is evident that the "background information" given in the explanatory statement shows the premises of the recommendations, i.e. the *decision premises* of the motion for resolution. However, since the explanatory statement is not included in the final resolution document (that is the document transmitted to the European Council), the decision premises also have to shine through in the resolution itself — in one way or another. In the following, we will demonstrate that this is precisely the case. Let us first look at the explanatory statement. Our analysis will show that 4 decision premises construed in this part of the report can be distinguished:

1. former decisions of the European Council
2. aim and purpose of the resolution
3. programmatic EU texts/intertextuality
4. problem to be solved

(1) contextualizes the Luxembourg summit in former summits and the decisions taken at those summits; in so doing, the report signals that the actual decision to be made — the EP resolution as well as the European Council decision in Luxembourg — is framed by an "organizational history", meaning that it is embedded in a sequence of former decisions of the EU organizational system; the reference to an organizational history is important for demonstrating continuity and legitimizing "new" decisions. (2) introduces the aims and goals of the motion for resolution and determines what is regarded as important and what is not. (3) connects the text to be considered here to programmatic EU texts in the field of employment policy. (4) describes what the "problem" is and how it is to be solved.

3.1 Decision premise 1: former European Council decisions as "orienter of the message"

The *Introduction* of the explanatory statement begins with the following paragraph:

> At the Amsterdam European Council, important instruments were adopted for the coordination of European employment policy. At the Essen European Council in December 1994, the foundations had already been laid for a European employment strategy by establishing common priorities. The European Councils in June 1995 in Cannes, December 1995 in Madrid and June 1996 in Florence lent further support to the multiannual program adopted in Essen. However apart from the agreement of declarations, not all that much has yet been achieved, partly because of a lack of specific quantifiable objectives and penalties for Member States which fail to comply.

What is evident in this paragraph is that the decisions that are referred to are entirely decisions of the European Council. It seems as if the text wants to remind the European Council of its own decision-making history. It also signals that the expectations of the EP to the summit in Luxembourg are based on the expectations the European Council itself created through previous decisions. This form of contextualization is important for legitimizing the report as such, since it shows that the report's recommendations to the European Council are based on the knowledge of earlier decisions of the European Council with regard to the relevant topic. The knowledge of these earlier decisions is introduced as a *Given* right at the beginning of the text. It is then — later on in the text — followed by the *new* information about the "idea" of the report. If we go into the single clauses of the first paragraph, we find a similar structure that can be further explicated in Hallidayan terms of Theme/Rheme analysis. For Halliday, the Theme is the given of a message; it is the "starting-point for the message" or "the ground from which the clause is taking off" (Halliday 1994: 38), whereas the Rheme is the new information introduced in the clause. The Theme constitutes the beginning of the clause and is very often identical with the Subject (see Thompson 1996: 119f). It can, however, also be an Adjunct as is the case in the first two sentences of the paragraph. In the third sentence the Theme is the Subject, and in the fourth it is again an Adjunct (Figure 8).

In all four of these sentences the European Council summits, and the decisions taken there, serve as orienter of the message that is about to appear. The rhematic information, on the other hand, contains the newsworthy information, i.e. the information which is in the focus in that message. According to Peter H. Fries, the Rhemes "are likely to contain information which is directly relevant to the goals of the text or text segment" (Fries 1998: 1). The positioning of the former European Council decisions as thematic information at the beginning of the sentence strengthens the character of these decisions as decision premises of the actual decision to be made. In this sense, the signal at the beginning of the text is clear: we take the earlier European Council summits/decisions as given, this is where we start from.

What is now the new information, i.e. the information that is relevant with regard to the "new" decision? It is the following: *important instruments for the*

THEME	RHEME
At the Amsterdam European Council,	important instruments were adopted for the coordination of European employment policy.
At the Essen European Council in December 1994,	the foundations had already been laid for a European employment strategy by establishing common priorities.
The European Councils in June 1995 in Cannes, December 1995 in Madrid and June 1996 in Florence	lent further support to the multiannual program adopted in Essen.
However, apart from the agreement of declarations,	not all too much has yet been achieved, partly because of lack of specific, quantifiable objectives and penalties for Member States which fail to comply.

Figure 8

coordination of European employment policy were adopted (in Amsterdam), *the foundations for a common employment strategy based on common priorities had already been laid* (in Essen), this strategy was then *further supported* (in Cannes, Madrid and Florence), but — and this is the important point — in spite of these declarations *not all that much has yet been achieved because of a lack of specific, quantifiable objectives and penalties for Member States which fail to comply.* This is indeed the information which is not only relevant to the goals of this first paragraph but to the goals of the text as a whole. The subsequent paragraphs describe this new information in more detail.

3.2 Decision premise 2: aims and purposes

This leads us to the second function that is fulfilled by the explanatory statement, namely to specify the aims of the rapporteur. The next paragraph does precisely that:

> This report aims to review the new possibilities created by those provisions and to derive from them a limited number of practical policy proposals for submission to the Luxembourg summit.
> The report is based on the following premises:
> a. At this stage there is no point in working out new ideas. Previous Council, Commission and European Parliament reports already contain enough ideas which have yet to be elaborated in detail.
> b. The main task is to find a strategy geared to a few practical objectives and instruments; a strategy whose implementation, both at European and at national level, can begin without delay and whose deployment and results can be monitored.
> c. Maximum use will be made of proposals which have previously found support within the Council but have not resulted in Community action.
> Apart from EMU, the Member States and the Union must now concentrate on a coordinated, active labor market strategy which will provide training and employment for the more than 18 million unemployed people in the Union. The prime target groups should be the young and the long-term unemployed.

Now, the position of the rapporteur is introduced; and it is introduced in a rather explicit way — as *aims, premises* of the report. In other words, the addressee of the text should immediately recognize these points as decision premises. In contrast to the first type of decision premises, this second type transcends the self-referential circle of organizational decisions and introduces the "idea" behind the actual report, that is, it refers to the content, the *what* of the new information. Since we are now interested in the content of the message, we shall turn from the textual to the experiential metafunction of language in Halliday's sense because it is the latter that shows how the world is represented in language, in a text and, ultimately, in the clause: "From the experiential perspective, language comprises a set of resources for referring to entities in the world and the ways in which those entities act on or relate to each other" (Thompson 1996: 76).

How is the "world" represented in the sentences describing the aims of the report? For this purpose, we will make a brief transitivity analysis of process types. Consider the first sentence, which construes a kind of macro-disposition of what is then further elaborated (Figure 9): *This report aims...*

to review	the new possibilities created by those provisions
Process: Mental (cognition)	*Phenomenon*
to derive	(from them) a limited number of practical policy proposals for submission to the Luxembourg summit
Process: Material	*Goal*

Figure 9

The first process is a cognitive one clearly signalizing the *thinking*-quality in the drafting of the report. The second process, at first sight, is a material one which brings in a certain *doing*-quality. Reviewing, i.e. thinking, alone is not enough; concrete consequences in the form of *practical policy proposals* have to follow from the cognitive undertaking. The *practical* further strengthens the dimension of concrete doing. Nevertheless, *deriving practical policy proposals* like, for instance, *making proposals* can be interpreted as a material process metaphorizing a cognitive process. Indeed, *deriving* in this context means a rather cognitive and — not least — verbal form of doing. Willy-nilly, the deriving of proposals must be a communicative process in one form or another. In this way, this particular metaphor includes a material as well as an intellectual and a communicative connotation, and allows a variety of interpretations of what actually has to be done. It keeps the doing rather vague.

As we will see, the combination of and tension between thinking/talking (mental/verbal processes) on the one hand, and doing/acting (material processes) on the other is constitutive for the whole text. Without making a detailed transitivity analysis let us briefly point out some interesting features of the paragraph. Point (a) starts with an existential process: *At this stage, **there is** no point in working out new ideas*. Existential processes allow definitive statements to be made, they express "the mere existence of an entity without predicating anything else of it" (Thompson 1996: 101). With the anonymous *there* the author creates the image of an unquestionable objectivity; and he does that right at the beginning of the four points — thereby framing the whole paragraph with that definitiveness and objectivity. Furthermore, the phrase *there is no point in* ... is a particular argumentative vehicle to prevent any arguing, i.e. making points, as it were. So, the message is clear: what is going to be presented in the following is not an attempt to develop new ideas because we don't need new ideas — this should be clear to everybody. With regard to the textual organization of this message, we see that *at this stage* functions as Theme, i.e. Given. In other words, it is presupposed that the reader knows what this stage is. What is referred to here, is the stage in the EU organizational history of deciding on employment policy as it was sketched out in the first paragraph. Decision premise 2 is connected with decision premise 1; they are not independent of each other.

However, if there is no point in working out new ideas, what then is the point? The rest of the paragraph informs us precisely about that: Existing ideas in various EU documents *have yet to be elaborated in detail*. Here, we have again a material process (to elaborate) metaphorizing a mental-cognitive one (to elaborate ideas). Note that the reference to other EU documents relates to decision premise 3 (intertextual context) with which we will deal later. Point (b) starts with a relational process: *The main task is to find a strategy geared to a few practical objectives and instruments*; in terms of a Value/Token analysis, *the main task* represents the Value (the general category) and *to find a strategy...* the Token (the specific embodiment). Identifying clauses construing a Value/Token relation are indicators of the "broader concerns and values of the writer" (Thompson 1996: 91). They are linguistic tools for evaluating or ideologizing messages. And indeed, the whole paragraph has a highly evaluative and normative tone. This becomes also clear when we look at the many modal verbs, mood adjuncts and evaluative lexical choices in the paragraph:

> Previous [...] reports contain **enough** ideas which **have** yet **to** be elaborated
>
> The **main** task is [...]; a strategy whose implementation [...] **can** begin **without delay** and whose deployment and results **can** be monitored
>
> **Maximum** use will be made [...]
>
> [...] Member States and the Union **must** now concentrate on [...]. The **prime** target groups **should** be the young and the long-term unemployed.

If we finally look at the participants, i.e. the doers involved in the clauses, we realize that the points remain rather vague with regard to who does what. References to concrete doers and actors are avoided primarily through passivization (*to be elaborated, can be monitored, maximum use will be made*), and also through nominalization (*implementation, deployment*). The vagueness might be explained by the introductory and preliminary character of this part of the text; we will see if the motion for resolution itself will be more concrete. From the perspective of economic or employment policy, it is also interesting that — apart from the notion *active labor market strategy*–no economic-conceptual terms are to be found in the premises. What predominates is institutional vocabulary (*Council, Commission, EP, European/national level, Community action, EMU, Member States, Union*). Summing up, we can say that this part of the text, which is highly evaluative, construes the aim of the whole report. This is the only decision premise which the writer wants to make recognizable as such (by calling it *premise*). Basically, the *aim* is not to develop new ideas but to make something out of the ideas already given. *It is time to act.* Since we do not know much about those ideas yet, the next step of the text seems to be evident: namely the specifying of the ideas through reference to canonical EU texts in the field of employment policy.

3.3 *Decision premise 3: Programmatic EU texts — intertextuality*

Three EU documents are particularly referred to as being *vital to the further development of a European employment strategy*: the new chapter on employment in the Amsterdam Treaty; and the European Council resolution on growth and employment together with the Presidency Conclusions on employment, competitiveness and growth — both of which were adopted at the Amsterdam summit. For one and a half pages the main ideas and concepts of these documents are quoted or paraphrased. Here, the report orients itself indeed very closely to these texts; almost each sentence starts with the respective document or parts/ points of the document as Theme, i.e. as orienter for the message. Let us take as an example the paragraphs on the new employment chapter in the Amsterdam Treaty:

> *In the new chapter on employment policy*, four points are of particular importance...
> *Firstly*, ...
> *In addition to this requirement of coordination*, it is also important to note that...
> *A third important point* is that the Council, [...], may each year draw up employment guidelines...
> *A further important point* is that the Council may adopt...

Beside the specific form of Thematic information, the overall use of relational processes is significant here. The first two clauses present an attributive relational process (construing something which carries the quality *important*), whereas the last two clauses show identifying processes with Value/Token structure (Figure 10):

A third important point	Is	that the Council may each year draw up employment guidelines...
A further important point	Is	that the Council may adopt...
Value/Identified	*Process: Relational (Identifying)*	*Token/Identifier*

Figure 10

As was said above, identifying relational processes are linguistic tools for evaluation — particularly when they have a Value/Token structure. The same counts of course for relational processes attributing specific qualities to specific Carriers. With regard to the construction of intertextual relations, this means that the question of which other texts a particular text refers to is a question of selection and evaluation. Certain texts have to be *identified as important* against the background of others which seem to be less important; and within the *important texts* points have to be identified that show this importance. This is exactly what happens here.

The references to the three documents mentioned, however, are only the *marked* part of the report's construction of intertextual relations. There is a variety of unmarked or less marked intertextual relations established in the fourth part of the Explanatory Statement which is entitled *Notes on the Resolution on the Employment summit*. Partly, the intertextual links to other EU documents are mentioned within the text, partly they are hidden. Documents explicitly mentioned are, for instance, the *European Social Charter*, several Commission reports and EP resolutions, and the Delors *White Paper*. I cannot pursue the question of intertextuality in detail here. What is important, however, is that intertextuality is clearly a decision premise in organizational text production; a "new" text referring to former texts (which are commonly accepted as relevant texts) increases its chances of being accepted, and therefore helps to allay uncertainty. It "sells" itself better. To be sure, intertextuality is not only a characteristic of organizational texts; on the contrary, texts are always embedded in a network of other texts:

> All meaning is intertextual. No text is complete or autonomous in itself; it needs to be read, and it is read, in relation to other texts. *Which* other texts? Each community, each discourse tradition, has its own canons of intertextuality, its own principles and customs regarding which texts are most relevant to the interpretation of any one text. In our own community, texts are more relevant for one another's interpretation the more they share the same patterns of presentational meaning. (Lemke 1995: 41)

What counts for any text, counts even more for EU texts. As a huge political organization, the EU necessarily involves enormous intertextual complexity. Any document produced within the decision-making trialogue between EP, CM and EC is intertextually linked — in one way or another — to documents of the partners in decision-making. Furthermore, there is not only intra-organizational intertextuality; EU texts also refer to texts beyond the border-lines of the organizational system; they may link to national documents of various kinds, documents of other supranational organizations (e.g. OECD reports), scientific studies, etc. In our specific case of employment policy, the intra-organizational "canon of intertextuality" mainly consists of "soft" legal documents such as the White Paper, Presidency Conclusions of the European Council, reports from the Commission, etc. "Strong" legislation at the Union-level ("primary law") is still largely missing in employment policy, although, with the inclusion of an employment title in the Amsterdam Treaty, this has slightly changed.

3.4 *Decision premise 4: What is the problem and how is it to be "solved"?*

The Explanatory Statement ends with *Notes on the resolution*. There, the "problem in the world" which has to be solved by EU policies and on which the various points of the resolution's recommendations are based is further established. Four "problematic" areas are pointed out: (a) *training,* (b) *organization of working time,* (c) *financial measures,* and (d) *co-ordination of European economic policy.* At the same time, solutions for these problematic areas are suggested. The two aspects are intimately related to each other in the text, as the following example — a paragraph taken from area (c) — shows:

> **c. Financial measures**. In Europe, unskilled work in particular is too costly. Reducing *labor costs* (without cutting net disposable income) could both preserve and create jobs. A start must be made as soon as possible on shifting *taxation* from employment to the environment and capital-intensive production. The analysis and recommendations contained in the Delors White Paper are still relevant. SMEs, especially in the services sector, have a key role to play in the job creation strategy, but this is being underexploited because labor-intensive services are relatively expensive. This results in much work being carried out in the black or grey economy. Reducing the disparity between gross and net wages is the appropriate way of reducing pressure on labor. This can primarily be done at national level. In addition, however, there is an instrument which could be adopted *immediately* at Union level: *reducing VAT on labor-intensive services to the lowest rate.* Following the decisions taken in Amsterdam, the European Council ought at the very least to allow Member States to carry out trials in certain designated sectors. These should also extend to the *'third system'*.

With this final part of the *Explanatory Statement*, the report gets down to business, so to speak. Now the terminology changes. According to the categories of political vocabulary developed by Klein (1988), it is no longer the "institutional vocabulary" (European Council, EC, CM, EP, etc.) that predominates but the vocabulary of a special policy sector, namely employment and economic policy. We might also call this vocabulary "conceptual". In the above paragraph it includes the following notions: *unskilled work, labor costs, net disposable income, jobs, taxation, employment, capital-intensive production, SMEs, services sector, job creation strategy, labor-intensive services, black or grey economy, gross and net wages, labor, VAT, third system.* From a grammatical point of view, it is interesting how the "world" is presented here, i.e. how the description of the "problem" as well as its solution is linguistically realized, namely through relational processes (The problem *is...*) which are closely linked to modalized material processes (this or that *should* be *done...*). The structure seems to be simple: one or more clauses constructing the "problematic" status quo through relational processes (*unskilled work is too costly*) followed by one or more clauses indicating what can or should be done — modality plus material processes (*Reducing labor costs **could** both **preserve** and **create** jobs/A start **must** be **made*** *as soon as possible...*). Partly, the solution is also represented through attributive or identifying relational processes (*Reducing the disparity between gross and net wages is the appropriate way of reducing pressure...*); nevertheless it is then again mostly concretized by modality plus material process (*This can primarily be done at the national level*). Very often, the identifying processes — as in the last example — assume the Value/Token-form. As was said, this serves to introduce evaluations as objectified declaratives. The actors of the material processes, however, are rarely mentioned; mostly they are "hidden" in passive-constructions (*A start must be made/This can be done at national level/There is an instrument which could be adopted immediately...*). It is not clear who *makes the start*, etc. I will return to this point below. Another significant tool is the performance indicators specifying the temporal frame of the problem solution: *A start must be made as soon as possible/instruments could be adopted immediately...* This signals: the problems have to be solved quickly; it is time to act now. The pressure of time which the report puts on the European Council also becomes evident in the sentences framing the *Notes on the resolution* at the beginning and at the end: The *Notes* start with the sentences:

> At the Luxembourg summit, heads of government will have the opportunity to show the public that they are just as serious about combating (sic) employment as they are about EMU. This cannot be achieved by means of yet another ministerial declaration but only by concluding specific, verifiable and enforceable agreements which enter into force *immediately*.

And — again referring to verifiable convergence criteria based on quantitative objectives that should permit a comparison of the member states' employment policies through benchmarking — the *Notes* end:

> [...] the results of such a comparison cannot be used immediately in the design of concrete measures without taking into account the real socio-economic situation prevailing in each Member State.

So, at the beginning as well as at the end of the *Notes* the temporal performance indicator *immediately* appears — in the first case it is even put in italics. The statement at the beginning informs us about the background and reason for this pressure of time: it is the *public* to which the EU must prove that it is serious about combating employment; and to do this, it needs not only words but results that come into force immediately. In other words, what is required by the report is *concrete* and *immediate* measures for solving the problem.[1] This is the overall frame of the *Notes*. Temporal performance indicators occur throughout this part of the text.

Coming back to the paragraph on *Financial Measures* for one moment, all the characteristics elaborated there — conceptual vocabulary, representation of

---

1. On the use of the fight-metaphor *combating unemployment* which further strengthens the claim for action and is significant in EU discourses on unemployment, see Straehle, Weiss, Wodak, Muntigl and Sedlak (1999).

problem and problem solution via relational processes linked to/followed by modalized material processes, passive-construction of material processes, temporal performance indicators — are representative of the description of all four problem areas in the *Notes* (Appendix). In addition, what is interesting in this last part of the Explanatory Statement is that the decision premises 1, 2 and 3 re-enter into the *Notes*–and they do that in the same grammatical form. Former decisions of the European Council and references to other EU texts re-enter as Thematic information: *Following the decisions taken in Amsterdam, the European Council ought ...* (decision premise 1), *The analysis and recommendations contained in the Delors White Paper are still relevant* (decision premise 3); the aims of the report re-enter primarily through modalization and Value/Token clauses (decision premise 2). This clearly shows that decision premises have to be repeated again and again to legitimize decisions; in particular, the decision premises 1 and 3 function as tools for continuous "authorization legitimation" (van Leeuwen/ Wodak 1999). We shall see in which form they enter into the resolution itself.

Before we move on to the resolution, let us make some brief conceptual remarks on the results so far. We distinguished 4 decision premises of the report framing the resolution. The Explanatory Statement is an institutionalized way of introducing and construing decision premises. As described above, every organizational decision has to be contextualized, on the one hand, in the organizational system itself (former decisions, canonical organizational texts), and, on the other, in the "outer world", i.e. the societal environment, i.e. the "problem" it decides upon. Decision premises construe expectations — intra-organizational as well as extra-organizational. The communication of decisions always has to communicate two things at the same time in order to legitimize itself: (a) its context within the organizational system, and (b) its context in the outer world (e.g. labor markets, unemployment, economic development, etc). The Explanatory Statement obligatory to EP reports serves the function of establishing these two forms of context as decision premises of the motion for resolution. In other words, the communication of decisions always presupposes two "references": *self-reference* and *external reference* (Luhmann 1997: 754f).

Slightly modifying J. Lemke's terms, we can identify three constitutive meanings of decisions which can be grouped around the difference of self-reference and external reference: (a) *presentational,* (b) *orientational* and (c) *organizational* meaning. Lemke defines (a) as "the construction of how things are in the natural and social worlds by their explicit description as participants, processes, relations and circumstances in particular semantic relations" (1995: 41). This is what we — following Luhmann — call external reference of decisions; it can be linguistically elaborated through Transitivity analysis explicating the ideational metafunction of grammmar. What is crucial here is the content of the message, i.e how the world is represented in the message, what the "problem" is that the decision decides upon. (b) and (c) correspond to the self-reference of decisions. Here, the communication of decisions constructs an orientational frame allowing a specific decision to be connected to earlier and future decisions, establishing expectations of what *shall* be done by whom (b) (in Hallidayan terms: interpersonal relations come into focus); and (c): the communication of decisions constructs "relations between elements of the discourse itself, so that it is interpretable as having structure [...], texture [...], and informational organization and relative prominence across meaningful stretches of text and from text to text" (Lemke 1995: 41). These two dimensions of self-reference of organizational communication can be linguistically explicated through the tools Halliday provides for the interpersonal and textual metafunction (Thompson 1996: 38f and 147f). As Lemke points out, it is important to see that all three kinds of meaning have a constructive character, i.e. are constructed through communication. Furthermore, they are "intimately interdependent" and therefore must never be separated from each other; and, with regard to the ideational, interpersonal and textual "resources" of language, "all three kinds of resources contribute to all three kinds of meaning-making" (Lemke 1995: 41).

The van Velzen report can be described as the communication of a decision. As such, it refers to former and future decisions within the EU organizational system (self-reference) but it also presents new information about *what is going on in the world* (unemployment, employment, economics, etc. — external reference). Of course, there is a close interdependency between self-reference and external reference, between orientational and organizational resources on the one hand, and presentational resources on the other, but nevertheless the distinction is important for understanding the structure and unfolding of EU communications of decisions. In the following when analyzing the resolution itself, we will pay special attention to the presentational patterns, i.e. how the topic of unemployment is talked about, how it is "problematized", what "solution" is suggested; but, as will shortly become clear, we must not forget the orientational and organizational patterns.

4.   The resolution

The core of the resolution are the recommendations from the EP to the European Council summit in Luxembourg. In more analytical terms, the resolution communicates a decision taken by the EP and to be considered by the European Council when making *its* decision at the summit. It represents the EP's *expectations* of the summit and is intended to serve as *decision premise*. The final version, that is the version which was adopted by the plenary of the EP on 21 October 1997, can be separated into five parts: (1) formal frame of the decision, (2) brief sketch of general problem (status quo), (3) position of the EP with regard to what the problem is (problematization), (4) recommendations on what has to be done (solution), and (5) formal conclusion.

Part 1:

The European Parliament,

– having regard to the decision of the Amsterdam European Council of 16–17 June 1997 to call for an extraordinary meeting of the European Council under the Luxembourg Presidency to review progress in the creation of employment opportunities (SN 150/97),

– having regard to the letter of Mr. Juncker, President-in-Office of the European Council, to Mr. Gil-Robles Gil-Delgado, President of the European Parliament, asking for Parliament's contribution to the extraordinary summit (C4–0389/97),

– having regard to the report by the Committee on Employment and Social Affairs and the opinions of the Committee on Economic and Monetary Affairs and Industrial Policy, the Committee Research, Technological Development and Energy, the Committee on the Environment, Public Health and Consumer Protection, the Committee on Women's Rights, the Committee on Culture, Youth, Education and the Media, the Committee on Regional Policy and the Committee on External Economic Relations (A4–0307/97),

Part 2 (which immediately follows Part 1):

A. whereas the portents of economic recovery in Europe, though faint, are undeniable and forecasts of growth have been revised upwards everywhere; whereas GDP will rise by an average of 2% in 1997, and growth will be between 2,5 and 3% in 1998; whereas in view of the structural improvement in the relationship between GDP growth and job creation, the return to normal growth will be reflected in the creation of more employment than at the time of previous economic recoveries, but whereas it will not be enough to reduce employment to a tolerable level,

Part 3 (which immediately follows Part 2):

1. Considers that, in the light of decisions taken by the Amsterdam European Council on employment, definite agreements should be reached at the Luxembourg employment summit concerning the creation of employment in the form of verifiable convergence criteria with quantitative objectives based on benchmarking and best practices; also believes that the combined efforts of the Member States and the EU must aim to increase the current employment rate of 60,4% to 65% within five years and to cut the unemployment rate to 7%; youth unemployment should be reduced to 50% of its current level;

2. Stresses the fact that despite the progress made with the free movement of goods and services, which has created new jobs and business opportunities, there is still much to be done to transform the fifteen national markets into a single large and homogenous market; [...] too many Directives are poorly transposed into national law; all these make the case for supporting the Monti proposals regarding the internal market;

3. Favours the adoption of a norm for the inactive/active ratio which reflects the ratio between the active population and the total population aged between 15 and 65 in the three best performing Member States, [...]; considers that this norm

should include criteria for underrepresented groups and be linked to social criteria such as the provisions of the European Social Charter and the Community Charter of the Fundamental Social Rights of Workers;

4. Emphasizes the need for European economic, financial, income and monetary policies to be coordinated in order to achieve an appropriate policy mix in the EU that is capable of contributing to growth, investment and employment; emphasizes the need for this co-ordination to be consolidated by means of an economic, investment and tax pact;

With point 4, the 3rd part of the resolution is finished. Before we go to Part 4, which represents the explicit recommendations, let us look at what happened up to this point. What is interesting from the point of view of textual organization is that the first finite verb is to be found at the beginning of Part 3 (*considers*). Everything that comes before that is the Theme, i.e. the orienter of the following message. In other words, Parts 1 and 2 serve as an orientational frame for what starts only with point 1/Part 3. What kind of orientation is that? It is both an orientation to the intra-organizational context (Amsterdam summit, Juncker's letter, Van Velzen report, opinions of various EP committees) and to the extra-organizational context (economic status quo, recovery, GDP growth) of the resolution. The extremely long Theme (Part 1 and 2) serves the purpose of showing the decision premises — *circumstance*–of what follows. But we will see that these premises do not remain limited to the Thematic information given at the beginning of the text, they also re-enter continuously into the Rhematic information. However, the Theme (Subject: *The European Parliament* and Circumstance) remains the same throughout the text, meaning that each clause introducing a paragraph/point has Parts 1 and 2 as Theme.

The *whereas*-paragraph of Part 2 introduces the "world"; it sketches out the economic disposition and the employment status quo: although there is clear evidence for *economic recovery* in Europe, and the increasing GDP growth *will be reflected in the creation of more employment*, these economic circumstances *won't be enough to reduce unemployment to a tolerable level*. This implicitly signals that something has to be done politically in order to reach this goal. Economic recovery and growth alone are not enough. In this way, a constitutive difference is already drawn at the very beginning of the text, namely between economic disposition and political action. In terms of Transitivity analysis, what has to be done is expressed through material process plus goal (*to reduce unemployment*). Who is the actor to do this? Is it the European Council? When we look at the first paragraph of Part 1, we see that — according to the decision taken in Amsterdam — the European Council's task at the Luxembourg summit is something different: *to review progress in the creation of employment opportunities*. Reviewing progress in employment policy is clearly something different from *making* employment policy in the form of *reducing unemployment*. In the first case, it is a cognitive/mental process that is required, in the second case it is a material process, i.e. a process of *real* doing, as it were. We shall keep this contradiction in mind for it will prove to be relevant for the whole resolution.

Let us now look at Part 3, i.e. what the EP considers/stresses/favors/emphasizes. This part presents the EP to us as Senser with mental-cognitive processes and a Phenomenon (Figure 11):

The EP	Considers	that [...] definite agreements should be reached at the Luxembourg employment summit [...]
The EP	Stresses	the fact that despite the progress made with the free movement of goods and services [...] there is still much to be done [...]
The EP	Favours	the adoption of a norm for the inactive/active ratio which reflects the ratio [...] in the best performing Member States [...]
The EP	Emphasizes	the need for European economic, financial, income and monetary policies to be coordinated [...]
Senser	*Process: Mental (cognitive)*	*Phenomenon*

Figure 11

In all these clauses the Phenomenon is quite complex and involves sub-clauses. Although, in this part of the text, the EP is still *thinking* (mental processes), recommendations are already made in a more implicit way. Modality plays an important role from the interpersonal point of view (*agreements* **should** *be reached, there* **is** *still much* **to** *be done,* **must** *aim,* **should** *include, the* **need** *for*). Former decisions and other EU texts enter again as orientational frame into the clauses (*in the light of decisions taken by the Amsterdam EC, Monti-Proposal, the European Social Charter, the Community Charter of the Fundamental Social Rights of Workers*). Actors are widely missing. They are hidden in passive-constructions. It is not clear who should reach definite agreements and who must do much in order to transform the fifteen national markets fully into one single market. Obviously, these claims refer to the European Council who is confronted here with concrete goals and numbers (*to increase the employment rate of 60,4% to 65%, to cut the unemployment rate to 7%, to reduce youth unemployment to 50% of current level*). This is the first and last time in the whole resolution that the goals assume the concrete form of numbers and percentage.

Point 3 construes a linkage between employment policy and social policy (*the i/a norm should include criteria for underrepresented groups and to be linked to social criteria [...]*). Since these two policy fields are institutionally linked in the EP (e.g. *Committee on Employment and Social Affairs*), it is not surprising that this connection is created here. Point 4 presents a notion which is very popular in EU discourses on unemployment, namely the notion *policy mix*; this notion indeed reflects the central problem of coordinating different policies, mainly economic, financial, income, monetary and labor market policies, in order to change the unemployment situation effectively (Chapter 2). How this policy mix should look like, however, is not so clear. We will see if the following recommendations tell us more about this.

4.1 *The recommendations*

Part 4 is separated along the lines of the four "problem areas" already sketched out in the Explanatory Statement of the report: *training, organization of working time, financial measures* and *co-ordination of economic policy*. In the following I will quote one or more paragraphs of each area in full and summarize the others:

> Training
> 5. Calls upon all parties, in future, to link programs of training and high-quality education aimed at developing market-relevant skills of the unemployed to a guarantee that the retrained unemployed will be given paid employment for at least a year; special attention should be devoted to groups which are particularly badly affected by unemployment;

Point 5 is followed by 3 further points giving recommendations with regard to training. All of them start with *(the EP) calls on ...*, that is with verbal processes. The EP occurs as Sayer; the Receiver, however, changes; it is not the European Council as one might expect but *all parties* (point 5), *the Member States* (point 6) and *the two sides of industry* (points 7 and 8; appendix). In other words, the Receiver remains rather vague, and, what is particularly interesting in view of the fact that we are facing EU policy-making, it is not EU organs in the narrow sense. The transitivity structure — EP as Sayer, verbal process, different Receivers — stays the same through all points of the four areas (there are only two exceptions). Accordingly, the EP first considers (Part 3) and then recommends (Part 4), *it thinks before it talks*.

From a content-related perspective, it is mainly the following points that are recommended with regard to *training*:

a. better training and education for developing "market-relevant skills"
b. paid employment for retrained unemployed (for at least a year)
c. increasing member states' spending on education and training
d. active labor market policy instead of passive
e. not putting social protection systems at risk
f. lifelong learning

The text does not argue why these measures should be taken, it takes their sense and necessity as given. It does not build argumentative chains often found in present-day economic and political discourses like, for instance: globalization requires international competitiveness requires flexible labor markets requires market-relevant skills requires lifelong learning. This kind of globalization rhetoric (see Chapter 2 and 4) does not appear. Incidentally, the notion of globalization does not once occur in the resolution. This non-argumentative character remains throughout all recommendations.

In principle, the recommendations on training do not bring anything really new; they reproduce what was already articulated in the White Paper and the various declarations on employment from the Essen summit up to the Amsterdam summit. This corresponds well with what was already stated in the Explanatory Statement of the report, namely that *there is no point in working out new ideas. Previous Council, Commission and European Parliament reports already contain enough ideas which have yet to be elaborated in detail.* It is time to act now, to "really" implement measures. With regard to this point, it is interesting, that the central process types in the training-part are indeed material processes, and not mental or verbal ones:

> ... **gearing** national budgets ...
> ... **increase** average **spending** on education ...
> ... progressively **use** resources to **alleviate** the consequences of unemployment ...
> ... **finance** active employment measures
> ... **raise** employment without **putting** social protection systems at risk ...
> ... **creating** jobs ...
> ... **assist** SME's ...
> ... **make** *training of staff part of strategic and investment planning* ...

In this way, the doing/acting-quality is strengthened. Furthermore, these doings are closely related to budgetary and financial matters. Since the latter are usually the main obstacle when it comes to the implementation of measures, this is not surprising. In any case, it demonstrates the EP's will not only to *think* about employment measures but really to enact them.

The second problem area explicitly mentioned in the resolution refers to the *organization of working time*. It includes only two points:

> Organization of working time
> 9. Believes that Member States need to address the issue of promoting flexibility in the labor market with regard to working hours, working time and working patterns (such as career breaks, sabbaticals, etc.) through a non-legislative, non-compulsory process based on social dialogue at the level of the individual enterprise, in particular having regard to the vital role of SME's in job creation; notes the importance of enhancing labor market mobility through improved mutual recognition of diplomas, and through the portability of pensions, insurance and social insurance;
> 10. Calls on the Commission and the two sides of industry to make proposals concerning "atypical" employment to ensure that the irregular work which is prevalent in it is accompanied by adequate social security and employees' rights which are equivalent to those for full working-time;

The organization of working time is of course a crucial point in the discussion on unemployment (see Chapter 5). There are those who say that a reduction in working hours is a necessary — some would even say, the only — effective measure to increase employment; this position is combated by those who say that it is not the reduction that helps but only the increasing flexibility of working time. The first position is usually represented by trade unions, the second position by employers' organizations. The EP resolution clearly takes the position of the employers and *promotes flexibility*. It furthermore emphasizes *a non-legislative, non-compulsory process based on social dialogue at the level of the individual enterprise*. From the point of view of social security, this formula is rather dubious because the adjectives *non-legislative* and *non-compulsory* attributed to the *process* can only mean less legal security for employees. Needless to say, trade unions become particularly sceptical when the *level of the individual enterprise* is emphasized as an adequate level for negotiations of working time. Commentators such as P. Bourdieu (1998) would even say that this kind of deregulation of labor markets opens every door for the capriciousness of employers (Chapter 2). However, although the EP promotes deregulation and flexibility, it seems to be cautious in its formulations. First of all, it only **believes** that *Member States need to address the issue of promoting flexibility*. Note that here the EP does not *call on* (verbal process) the member states to do something (as in most of the other recommendations), it limits itself to *believing* (mental/cognitive process) that the member states should do something. What should they do? They *need to address the issue* (mixture of mental and verbal process). In other words, the EP does not demand immediate implementation of measures (material processes, acting/making/doing) as in the training-area, but only discussion. So the claim is quite different here. The EP also only *notes the importance of enhancing labor market mobility*. Concrete consequences or measures do not follow. The same cautiousness occurs again in point 10. Although the EP now *calls on* the Commission (note that this is the first time that an EU organ is called on) and the two sides of industry, it demands only the *making of proposals* (material process metaphorizing a cognitive/verbal process). What is demanded, therefore, is again discussion rather than the implementation of concrete measures.

Another controversial point is named by the notion "atypical employment". For critics of the deregulation of labor markets, this is only a "nice" formula which helps to "hide" the existential hardship of badly paid part-timers. At least here the EP wants to make sure that this form of employment *is accompanied by adequate social security and employees' rights which are equivalent to those for full working-time*. Nevertheless, it is the topic of the organization of working time that brings in the flexibility discourse into the EP resolution.

Let us turn to the *financial measures* — definitely an area that is no less "problematic" than the organization of working time. In the following, we quote points/paragraphs 11, 12, 13, 18 and 19:

Financial Measures

11. Calls for a social or minimum VAT rate to be introduced for labor-intensive services, particularly in the case of work experience and training places and the "Third System"; the European Council should immediately permit trials of reduced VAT rates;

12. Urges that decisions be taken without delay to reduce taxation of labor by means of European agreements on transferring taxation to the environment, natural resources, energy and capital-intensive production, as proposed in the White Paper on Growth, Competitiveness and Employment.

13. Urges a shift towards reducing the overall tax burden for individuals and companies.

[...]

18. Calls on the Commission and Council in future to assess all relevant policy measures in the light of their impact on employment; also calls on the Commission to undertake a review of the employment impact of all sections of the EU budget and in the same framework to gear more significantly the Structural Funds towards the prevention of long-term unemployment, the promotion of higher skills, entrepreneurship and adaptability; urges also Member States to increase the efficiency of Structural Fund programs with greater emphasis on employment.

19. Calls on Ecofin to devote its next meeting primarily to support for and elaboration of the measures decided at the employment European Council.

[...]

What is significant in this section is that in half of the *calls* the receivers are EU organs (see points 16, 18, 19, 20, 21). This is surprising at first sight since the financing of employment policies and measures is to large extent still a matter for the member states. When we look more closely, however, at the issue that is crucial for concrete financial measures, namely taxation, the picture changes. It is primarily the first 3 points that deal with questions of taxation. As we see, in these paragraphs the receivers of the EP's calling/urging are completely missing. Let us go into detail: in all three points, the calling/urging is accompanied by one or more material processes:

> ... calls for a social or minimum VAT rate to be **introduced** ...
> ... urges that decisions be **taken** without delay to **reduce** taxation ...
> ... *urges a **shift** towards **reducing** the overall tax burden* ...

These material processes strengthen the making/doing-quality of the proposed measures. Nevertheless, what is missing is the actors. Who is supposed to do all that? The actors are "deconstructed" through passive construction and nominalization. In other words, not only the receivers of the EP's call are missing but also the actors of the *doing*-measures proposed by the call. Point 12 is most extreme in this sense: (The EP) *Urges that decisions be taken without delay to reduce taxation of labor by means of European agreements on transferring taxation to* ... Here, it is not clear who takes the decision, who reduces taxation of labor, who agrees on transferring taxation, and who actually does the transferring. Accordingly, the EP's recommendation remains very vague with regard to the crucial issue of taxation and changes in taxation.

In those points where the receivers occur again and assume the form of EU organs, the proposed measures seem to be only indirect actions of financing:

> ... urges the Commission and the Member States to **exercise** increased **vigilance** when **granting aid** to **undertakings** by **monitoring** the **use made** of it so as to **ensure** that it **contributes** [...] to **creating** jobs ...

> ... calls on the Commission and Council in future to **assess** all relevant **policy measures** in the light of their **impact on employment** ...

> ... calls on the Commission **to undertake review** of the **employment impac**t of ...

> ... calls on Ecofin to **devote** its next **meeting** to [...] **elaboration** of the measures ...

> ... calls on the European Council to **make it possible** for under-utilized EU budget headings to be **used** for **action** to **enhance employment** ...

> ... *calls on the European Council to **take the initiative** of **bringing forward** the remaining appropriations entered in the ECSC budget to **fund operating budgets** and [...] use them for **job-creation measures** ...*

Several things are interesting here. First, what the EP calls on/urges are measures of monitoring, discussing or initiating financial actions. Second, the critical part of actually *using/funding* money/budget for *creating jobs (impact on employment, action to enhance employment, job-creation measures)* is deeply embedded in the clauses. So, the real financial activities take a secondary position in the clause. They are foregrounded (straightened out, as it were) by mediating activities. With reference to Van Leeuwen and Wodak (1999), we might call this a "secondary activation". For instance, in the last example above: *to take the initiative of bringing forward appropriations to fund operating budgets and use them for job-creation measures* is a highly complex construction. The European Council is not called on to fund operating budgets ("real" financial activity), it is not even called on to bring forward appropriations to fund budgets (secondary "financial activation"); what it is called on, is only to take initiative of bringing forward appropriations to fund budgets; since there are two mediating activities (taking initiative, bringing forward) of the real financial activity, we might call this a "secondary secondary financial activation". We could also do the same sort of detailed analysis with the other examples and the result would be similar: the EU organs are widely limited to mediating activities (mainly monitoring, reviewing, discussing) in respect of financing *job-creation measures*.

To be sure, the EU organs are indeed very seriously restricted in the area of financing employment policies. The competence in this area still lies most widely with the governments of member states — which, of course, makes the proclamation of an effective union-wide employment policy rather dubious. In any case, the part of the resolution on financial measures clearly shows these tensions between

EU competences on the one hand and member states' competences on the other, and it "solves" them through "secondary activation", that is through "mediating" activities such as monitoring, discussing, initiating, etc. The general position of the EP as expressed in this part of the text more or less follows the Commission's proposal for employment guidelines: it emphasizes — although without going into detail — the need for reducing taxation of labor, eliminating bureaucratic obstacles to investment, gearing Structural Funds towards the prevention of long-term unemployment and promoting entrepreneurship and adaptability (see Chapter 3). Particular attention should be drawn to one aspect, however: the resolution urges all these political measures in order to *create* employment/jobs; it speaks of job-*creation* measures/*action* to *enhance* employment. In so doing, it makes clear that it is political action that creates employment. This position contradicts the neo-liberal argument widely used by today's economists that employment cannot be created by politics but only by the market itself. In other words, the overall tone of the resolution is not "economistic" but one that follows the *primacy of politics* (see Chapter 2). The only problem, however, is that the EU's scope for political action is rather limited in the field of employment policy.

The last part of recommendations refers to the *co-ordination of economic policy*. This brings up the issue of "policy-mix" again. I quote the first two paragraphs:

> Co-ordination of economic policy
>
> 22. Calls on the European Council meeting in Luxembourg to determine the procedures for coordinating economic policy, drawing up the employment guide-lines, carrying out monitoring and drawing up annual reports, so that the Amsterdam conclusions in the field of employment can be put into practice immediately and so that lasting economic growth and ecology, sustainable em-ployment, and social security become the top priorities of the economic policy of the Union and the Member States; calls on the European Council to declare that the Monti proposals on the internal market should be adopted as soon as possible given the very positive effect they are expected to have on employment.
>
> 23. Calls on the European Council to take greater account of the economic interdependence of the Member States that has emerged with the transformation of fifteen national markets into a single large and homogenous market and increasingly limits the effectiveness of purely national economic policies; consid-ers it absolutely essential, therefore, that further progress be made towards greater complementarity of the Member States' economic policies so that synergies may be achieved in the stimulation and promotion of innovation, research and techno-logical development by means of appropriate tax concessions for SME's, the facilitation of access to and availability of venture capital for SME's operating in R&D sectors, the promotion of efficient research infrastructure and close cross-border co-operation between undertakings, universities and research institutions.
>
> [...]

These paragraphs are quite complex; many different aspects and topics are packed into them. The Receiver is in both cases the European Council. In the first paragraph, we face again a form of secondary activation: the European Council is not asked to co-ordinate economic policy. Instead it is asked to *determine the procedures for coordinating economic policy*. This grammatical structure reflects the fact that the European Council's main task is to establish overall guidelines for Union policies. It is not part of the "real" EU decision-making trialogue (EP, Commission, Council); it is the task of the latter actually to co-ordinate policies. Consequently, the European Council appears also at the end of the first and the beginning of the second paragraph as a body which only *declares/takes greater account of*.

As the *top priorities* of EU economic policy, *lasting economic growth and ecology, sustainable employment and social security* are named. With this, the policy-mix assumes a visible form: it should combine economic, employment and social policies; and it should combine these policies under the heading of economic policy itself. In other words, employment and social policies have to be integrated into economic policy, and not the other way round. This widely corresponds with the idea already developed in the White Paper that employment policy should be an *integral part of economic policy* (see European Commission 1994: 53f). That such an integration is the only effective way to increase employment can be considered as common sense among economic and employment experts. What is not so clear, however, is how the orientation to employment is supposed to fit together with the other "orientations" dominating present-day economic policies in the Western world (Todd 1999). How does the focus on financial markets, stock exchanges and speculative capital fit together with employment goals? How should capital-intensive production suddenly be transformed into employment-intensive production? How can the *sine qua non* of economic policy in the 1990s, namely the "war against inflation" (L. Thurow), lead to increasing employment? Is a "Shareholder-Capitalism" compatible with something like "Employment-Capitalism" (see Chapter 2)? The resolution does not give answers to these crucial questions. It calls for *a binding "European Pact for Employment, Sustainability and Solidarity" as a compliment to the Stability Pact concluded in Amsterdam* (paragraph 24), but it does not say if these pacts are compatible with each other at all. There are good arguments to be made that the exclusive orientation to price and monetary stability as expressed in the Stability Pact is not only incompatible with the aim of increasing employment, but even contradicts the latter (see Thurow 1996; Krugman 1994; BEIGEWUM 1997, 1998). In other words, a truly employment-oriented economic policy would require some drastic changes of "heart" in 1990s' capitalism. The EP's resolution, however, does not tell us about that. As was said above, it is not an argumentative text, it limits itself to stating or noticing things as given. This is also evident when, in paragraph 23, it states that *interdependence of the Member States has emerged with the transformation of fifteen national markets into a single large and homogenous market*. Does such a single large and homogenous market really exist already? It might be true for the financial market, but it is most probably not true for the production market, and it is definitely not true for the labor market. With regard to the latter, there are still enormous structural differences between the individual member states (see, for instance, the *Employment Rates Report 1998. Employment Performance in the Member States*). It is therefore not surprising that, in the remaining part of paragraph 23, particular emphasis is given to *further progress towards greater complementarity of the Member States' economic policies* and *cross-border co-operation* (note again the secondary activation: the EP does not directly emphasize *greater complementarity* but *further progress towards greater complementarity*). Here, the EP returns to the "soft" position of thinking instead of urging/requesting/demanding. It does not request further progress, it only *considers it absolutely essential that further progress be made*. All in all, as in the area of financial measures, the EP's position on the co-ordination of economic policy remains rather soft and vague. That the EP puts temporal pressure on the European Council through introducing the temporal performance indicators *immediately* and *as soon as possible* does not greatly alter this fact.

The last part of the resolution which formally concludes the text brings us back to the circle of decisions referring to decisions referring to decisions — which is crucial for the continuity and reproduction of organizational systems. It once more shows that decisions are always simultaneously communications of decisions, and they have to make this clear. The resolution ends with the following paragraph:

> 27. Instructs its President to forward this resolution to the extraordinary European Council on employment, the Council, the Commission, the European social partners and the governments and parliaments of the Member States.

5. Conclusions

In the preceding analysis I have pointed to some major *presentational, orientational* and *organizational* resources of language used in the resolution of the EP and the preceding report. The use of these resources can be understood only against the background of EU decision-making and the characteristics of its organizational system. I have therefore elaborated a conceptual apparatus for applying tools from organization and systems theory to a socio-linguistic approach to organizational discourses. Certainly this application must be considered a first attempt. Accordingly, the model is still quite rudimentary. On the other hand, it was not and is not my purpose to construe a monistic, universal model; the idea rather was to take tools from different theoretical strands — sociological as well as linguistic — and see how their use helps us to understand a phenomenon as complex as EU decision-making and its discourses. I followed a kind of "conceptual pragmatism" which — according to N. Mouzelis — "has as its major task to clarify conceptual tools and to construct new ones by following criteria of utility rather than truth" (Mouzelis 1995: 9). What I have presented in this chapter is only a first step in this direction. Further steps have to follow.

The linguistic operationalization of decision premises, as well as the further differentiation of self-referential and external-referential decision premises turned out to be an adequate frame for analyzing the EP's contribution to the European Council summit on employment in Luxembourg. The first step in understanding the complex network of EU communications of decisions is to see how decisions relate to other decisions as well as to the "world" they decide upon. What are the intra- and extra-organizational expectations framing decisions? What aims do they construe? What intertextual relations do they reveal? In what way do decision premises enter into texts?

In this chapter I have at least partly answered these questions with regard to the EP's resolution. I have elaborated the decision premises construed in the Explanatory Statement of the Van Velzen report and in the resolution itself; and I have shown how they are linguistically realized in the documents. In the second part of the paper I focused on the presentational language patterns revealed in the resolution, i.e. on how the "world" is construed/presented in the text, or what the EP's position on employment is. Let us finally summarize this position as it revealed itself in the text: employment, for the EP, is definitely an area where political action has to take place. Throughout the resolution, the need for political measures for the *creation* of employment is emphasized. Furthermore, these measures must be realized *immediately* or at least *as soon as possible*. It is time to act! No more words but concrete measures! The EP seems to be aware of the societal pressure put on politics finally to do something after all these years of declarations without any "real" consequences in the labor markets, as it were. Particularly Part 2 of the resolution signals: Employment is not created by the market alone, it requires political actions. The resolution emphasizes the *primacy of politics*; in an era in which the market is more and more regarded as the universal force in the world, such a position is by no means a matter of course. Nevertheless, the EP is caught in a difficult situation which is mainly due to a lack of legal competence in the field of employment policy. It is still the individual member states who are the primary employment policy-makers. The situation is indeed ambivalent: on the one hand, the EP demands political action at the Union level, while on the other, the possibilities for effective action are quite limited. This ambivalence is definitely a major reason why the resolution largely remains rather vague and "soft" — especially when it comes to the crucial point of financial measures. From a programmatic point of view, the EP seems to be caught in another ambivalence: on the one hand , it understands employment policy mainly as structural labor market policy, in the sense that training, education, development of market-relevant skills, flexibility are the focus of improving employment; on the other hand, it appeals for an integration of employment policy into economic policy. How such an employment-oriented economic policy should look, is not elaborated. Macro-economic indicators are widely missing. What the proposed policy mix might effectively mean, remains unclear; monetary and wage policies are not mentioned at all.

The EP considers, stresses, favors, calls, urges — and it connects decisions to decisions to decisions. This is not meant to sound cynical; as the only truly democratically legitimized part of a supranational organization that still lacks a real democratic basis in the form of a constitution, the EP moves slowly; and in the field of employment policy it moves even more slowly than in other fields. At the beginning of this chapter we said that a decision can be described as a difference that makes a difference. The EP resolution on employment clearly constitutes a difference: employment is becoming a *top priority* of EU politics. But what difference does this difference make? Maybe this question should be directed to the 18 million people still unemployed in the EU.

Chapter 6

Dilemmas of Individualism and Social Necessity

Peter Muntigl

1. Introduction

In their 1998 Employment Guidelines, the EC made employability, entrepreneur-ship, adaptability, and equal opportunities — what the EC refers to as the four *pillars* — the central employment issues for the EU. Each of these may easily be linked to liberalism in which the individual is foregrounded. Here, the four pillars recommend aiding individuals in becoming entrepreneurs, providing them with attributes of employability and adaptability and creating more chances for equal opportunities for employment. The pillars, then, seem to foster a strong form of individualism in the sense that 'government' is merely there to provide the right conditions so that individuals can economically flourish. At this point, it is tempting to view the pillars as non-dilemmatic and as a 'pure' construction of liberalism. The four pillars, however, are not the EU policies. When the contents of the policies are examined and the pillars are related to what the EU, the MSs, industry, and the social partners must do, a slightly different picture emerges. That is, the EU policies of employability, entrepreneurship, adaptability, and equal opportunities also consist of themes contrary to individualism such as social necessity and authoritarianism. In this paper, I attempt to flesh out these contrary themes by examining the policy making process of the EP. Here, I will show how issues of individualism stemming from the four pillars are met with the opposing tendency of social necessity. What is being claimed is that policy makers are faced with the task of shaping policy to conform to issues of both individualism and social necessity.

I gratefully acknowledge the support of the Social Sciences and Humanities Research Council of Canada Doctoral Fellowship #752–95–1442 during my tenure at the Research Centre for Discourse, Politics, and Identity. Many thanks go also to Aaron Cicourel and Glenn Stillar for providing me with many helpful comments on an earlier version of this chapter.

By associating liberalism with contrary themes, I am not suggesting that liberalism devotes equal attention to issues of individualism and social necessity. Liberalist policies will most surely endorse individualism over social necessity. Rather, the track I am following is in line with the proposals made by Billig et al. (1988) and Billig (1991) that ideologies are paradoxical. Because of this, themes of individualism, whether liberalist or something else, will encounter themes of social necessity in much the same way that more social oriented themes will encounter themes of individualism. So, although liberalist policy may attempt to obscure the paradox between individual and social, the potential for a contrary theme to surface is always there. My interest, therefore, is to expose those instances in policy making where the dilemmas of ideology are present and oriented to and to examine the discursive and rhetorical practices used to present the dilemmas or, conversely, to obscure them. In order to analyze the discursive and rhetorical practices used in policy making that relate to ideological dilemmas, I use resources from Functional Grammar (Halliday 1994) and from rhetorical theory (Burke 1969).

1.1 *Functional Grammar (FG)*

Policies, in general terms, get people to do things. Someone, therefore, proposes what is to be done and who should go about doing it. In addition to directing someone, information needs to be provided concerning *what* needs to done, *how* to go about doing it, and *why* it needs to be done. Of course, other bits of information also enter into policy such as when, where, for how long, who with, etc., but, from the policies that were analyzed in this paper, the what, how, and why appeared most frequently. In order to examine these various aspects of policy discourse analytically, I use a transitivity analysis that is based on FG. Halliday (1994: 107) proposes that clauses have a transitivity structure made up of a *process*, *participants* in the process, and *circumstances* associated with the process (Table 1). Processes represent the 'goings-on' in the clause and are typically realized by a verbal group. Participants are most centrally involved with the process, are associated with a participant role (e.g., actor, goal, sensor, beneficiary) and appear as a nominal group. Circumstances are less centrally involved with the process and are typically realized by a prepositional phrase. To give an example of how a clause may be divided up into these three components, consider the following example taken from the EP Report's Explanatory Statement:

Table 1

Process	Participants	Circumstance
were adopted	important instruments	– At the Amsterdam European Council – for the coordination of European employment policy

> At the Amsterdam European Council, important instruments were adopted for the coordination of European employment policy.

The process in this clause is passivized and appears in the form *were adopted*. Only one participant, *important instruments*, is present. The other participant, the ones who adopted the important instruments, has been — as is often the case in passivized constructions — deleted. Two circumstances, one expressing location (*at the ...*) and the other expressing purpose (*for the ...*) begin and end the clause.

Taking a close look at transitivity structure is important for examining dilemmas of ideology because it is within and across the various components of clause structure that aspects of individualism or social necessity are constituted. Also, in examining drafts of policy papers, it can be shown when or if aspects of individualism or social necessity become promoted (e.g., placed within the participant role or process) or demoted (e.g., placed within the circumstance) within the clause. Especially in regard to policy is it important to consider the role that circumstances play since it is often here that the purpose of an action or the manner in which an action is to be executed is expressed. The types of circum-

Table 2

Circumstance Type	Example
Extent (distance, duration)	within 5 years
Location (place, time)	at the Amsterdam European Council
Manner (means, quality, comparison)	in the form of time off for vouchers
Cause (reason, purpose, behalf)	for the coordination of European employment policy
Accompaniment (comitation, addition)	including flexible working arrangements
Role (turn something into something else)	to 50% of its current level
Matter (what about)	concerning the creation of employment
Angle (from what point of view)	on the basis of the Commission study

stances that most often appear in the policies analyzed are listed in Table 2 (see Halliday 1994: 151 for the list of all nine different types of circumstances):

The various kinds of semantic roles such as purpose or manner that are expressed by circumstances do not always appear within the clause. As Martin, Mattiessen & Painter (1997) point out, these roles may also be expressed across clauses. So, in the following clause:

> to support proposals involving the collective shortening of working hours by lowering social security contributions

although *by lowering social security contributions* expresses the manner in which working hours are to be shortened, it is not a circumstance of the process *to support*. Instead, manner is expressed in a separate clause. Circumstances and their clausal variants will be referred to as circumstance roles.

1.2 *Burkean Rhetoric*

It is also possible to probe the action orientation of policies from a rhetorical perspective. For instance, many of the clause functions expressed in the catego-ries of process, participant, and circumstance have rhetorical correlates. In order to tease out these rhetorical functions, Stillar (1998) suggests using a *pentadic* analysis developed by Burke (1969). This translates into an examination of how a series of grammatical-rhetorical resources — represented by the five terms **act**, **agent**, **scene**, **agency**, and **purpose** — form clusters or what Burke terms ratios. It is the way in which these resources are clustered or organized in social actions that provide an insight into human relations and motives. Put simply, *act* refers to the 'goings-on' of a text (i.e., usually embodied in the verb), *agent* refers to those actors implicated in the act, *scene* refers to where the act takes place or the situation in which the act occurs, *agency* refers to with what instrument or by what means the act was performed, and *purpose* refers to the end or the aim of the act. To illustrate how these terms may be represented in a text, take the example from the EP resolution (see Appendix 4) shown in Table 3.

Table 3

Pentadic Units	EP Resolution
Agent	The European Parliament
Act	Urges that decisions be taken without delay
Purpose	to reduce taxation of labour
Agency	by means of European agreements on transferring taxation to the environment, natural resources, energy and capital-intensive production
Scene	as proposed in the White Paper on Growth, Competitiveness and Employment

In this example, the EP (agent/proposer) directs an unspecified agent/proposee to take decisions (act) so that taxation of labor gets reduced (purpose) by means of European agreements on various issues (agency) in the context of what is stated in the White Paper on Growth, Competitiveness and Employment (scene).

At this point, it might appear that I am merely introducing a rhetorical variant of an FG transitivity analysis. Although it is possible to link the pentadic terms to a grammatical vocabulary such as FG, Stillar (1998: 89, fn. 1) argues against attempting to reduce the pentadic units to linguistic terms since they both have differing scopes and aims when used in an analysis:

> Lining up the two vocabularies, we could arrive at: act/*process;* agent/*partici-pant;* scene/*circumstance:place* or *time;* agency/*circumstance:manner;* purpose/ *circumstance:purpose.* I would, however, resist reducing the pentad to these terms. The two vocabularies, ideational structure and the pentad, have different scopes and purposes in analysis.

So, while the great strength of a transitivity analysis resides in detecting, at the level of the grammar, where ideological dilemmas are made explicit or where one side of the ideology is abstracted or generalized, the pentadic analysis' strength lies in another direction. In my view, Burke's important contribution to ideology lies in what he terms *ratios*. In other words, different arrangements or ratios of the pentadic units offer different ways of constructing and interpreting the world. Ratios relate to ideologies in the sense that one type of ratio may highlight one side of the dilemma while a different ratio may highlight the other. This point is reinforced in an example provided by Stillar (1998: 92) in which the unemployed's inability to find work (act) may be cast in terms of individual or societal constraints. Ratios play a major part in this construction since by positioning the scene (i.e., recession) as causing an action (i.e., the unemployed are unable to find work), societal constraints are invoked. Whereas by positioning the agent as causing the action, focus is placed on the individual's shortcomings:

> ...a news report that characterizes the unemployed in a **scene:act** ratio where the attributes of the unemployed (e.g., their inability to find work) are understood as a reasonable consequence of the scene they are in (e.g., a recession) constructs a particular version of the social and predisposes us to act accordingly. By contrast, another report (say, of the opinions of a conservative politician) may characterize the unemployed in an **agent:act** ratio that attributes their inability to find work (the act) to their characteristics as particular types of agents (e.g., unmotivated, lazy, waiting for "handouts," and so on).

This is particularly important for employment policy-making because the way in which employment or unemployment is characterized (i.e., unemployment due to recession, lack of worker flexibility, too many immigrant workers) may effect the kinds of measures that EU members will place into employment policy. Burke (1966) sees these various clusterings (e.g., different ways of characterizing the unemployed's situation) as a *selection* and therefore a *deflection* of reality. In other words, a particular ratio makes us, the readers or listeners, see things in its terms rather than in terms of another ratio. The selected ratio, therefore, deflects from other ways of construing a situation or event. In addition to seeing the ratios as selecting different reality constructions, different ratios may also be constitutive of paradoxes. One such paradox referred to by Burke (1969: 26) is the *paradox of contextual definition*. Burke provides an example of an art historian who, when focusing mainly on the social context surrounding an artist's work, is castigated by critics because not enough attention was placed on the artist's individual technique. Similarly, when focus is placed only on the work of art in itself, it is countered that the period in which the artist lived contributed significantly to the style. Therefore, when highlighting the scene, questions concerning the agent's role become salient and vice versa. Here again, the dilemma between individual and society — or, more generally, figure and ground — is made manifest.

The analysis is based on written and spoken texts. The former includes documents from the EP, the EC, and the European Council. The latter includes an English translation of the audio recordings of the European parliamentary debate held in Strasbourg in October 1997 on a parliamentary report that was to be sent to the "European Council on Employment." The Council Summit was held at a later date in Luxembourg in November 1997. In the debate, Members of the European Parliament (MEPs), a member of the European Council (Mr. Juncker), and two members of the European Commission (Mr. Santer and Mr. Flynn) gave their views on a report written by the MEP, Wim van Velzen. Each speaker contribution was given in the official language of the speaker's country. All contributions were then translated into English.

2.   Background to the EP and the report

The EP differs significantly from National Parliaments. Unlike National Parliaments, the EP may not introduce legislation (Corbett, Jacobs, & Shackleton 1995). Instead, the EP can only, through the consultation procedure, co-operation procedure, co-decision procedure, and the assent procedure influence Commission or Council proposals. Other functions of the EP include drawing up and monitoring its budget, scrutinizing the executive, making appointments, and providing a forum for discussions of political importance. MEPs generally belong to a Political Group[1] and each MEP is a full member of at least 1 of the 20 specialized standing committees. Much of the detailed work of Parliament is carried out within these committees (Corbett et al. 1995).

> "When Parliament receives a formal Commission or Council request for an opinion or advice on a particular proposal it is then referred to the appropriate committee as *"the committee responsible"*, and to one or more of the other committees for their "opinion". The decision as to where to refer the proposal is prepared by officials in Parliament's legislative co-ordination unit and is then announced by the President of Parliament in the subsequent plenary session." (Corbett et al. 1995: 123).

The committee responsible selects a rapporteur to write up a report and the committees concerned for their opinions select a draftsman to write up an opinion. In this case, the EP was requested by the European Council to contribute a report for the European Council Summit to be held in Luxembourg. The parlia-

---

1. In 1997, there were 9 different groups. Below, in decreasing order of size, is the list of groups of the EP: **PSE** = Group of the Party of European; **PPE** = Group of the European People's Party; **UPE** = Group Union for Europe; **ELDR** = Group of the European, Liberal, Democratic and Reformist Party; **GUE/NGL** = Conferderal Group of the European United Left — Nordic Green Left; **V** = The Green Group in the European Parliament; **ARE** = Group of the European Radical Alliance; **I-EDN** = Group of Independents for a Europe of Nations; **NI** = Non-attached Members

mentary report serves as recommendations to the European Council and suggests what employment-related issues should be addressed in the Presidency Conclusions. A specific time is then given in Parliament to debate the committee report. The debate on the van Velzen report adhered to the following format:

a. 7 minute statement by the rapporteur (i.e., Mr. van Velzen);
b. Unlimited time for the President-in-office of the Council (i.e., Mr. Juncker);
c. Unlimited time for the President of the Commission (i.e., Mr. Santer)
d. Shorter time for draftsmen of opinions from other committees (draftsmen did not speak in this debate)
e. The main Group spokespersons for the issue then spoke in descending order of size of Groups. (varying from 1 to 5 minutes)
f. Reply from the Council (i.e., Mr. Juncker — given unlimited amount of time)
g. Reply from the Commission (i.e., Commissioner Flynn — given unlimited amount of time)

Since the working languages of the EP include Danish, Dutch, English, Finnish, French, German, Greek, Italian, Portuguese, Spanish, and Swedish, speakers are at liberty to present their speeches in their language of choice. Speakers generally present in the official language of their country. All speaker contributions, during the debate, are simultaneously translated in all the EU official languages. Following the debate, the proposed amendments are voted on and incorporated in the final resolution that then proceeds to the Luxembourg Summit.

The list below illustrates some of the more important texts that are considered in this analysis. The Presidency Conclusions were tabled by the European Council, the other two written documents were tabled by MEPs and the debate was conducted in Parliament. Those texts that are primarily 'Parliamentary' (i.e., 2 written documents and the debate) are given most attention in the analysis.

–   Van Velzen Report (drafted on Oct. 9, 1997)
–   EP Parliamentary Debate (held on Oct. 21, 1997)
–   EP Resolution for the European Council on Employment (drafted on Oct. 21, 1997)
–   Presidency Conclusions (drafted on Nov. 24, 1997)

3. The van Velzen Report

The report debated on in Parliament was the van Velzen report and it is to the contents and structure of the overall report that we now turn to — please see the Appendix for the entire report and also the Resolution that followed the debate. The van Velzen report is a policy report and policies have to do with directing others to do things. More specifically, the report is about employment policy and so part of the subset of those that are directed are the unemployed. The report is divided up into two parts: a motion for a resolution and an explanatory statement. The first part, the resolution, provides a list of directives for MSs, social partners, industry, etc. whereas the second part 'explains' or legitimates the contents of the motion for a resolution. I will analyze only the first part, the actual policy. The explanatory statement is discussed in Chapter 5.

3.1 *Motion for a Resolution*

The report begins with the EP as theme. Following this is a list of three inserted clauses (*having regard to*) that provide a context for or a reference to what is about to follow. Each of these points, therefore, can be interpreted as the clausal variants of Matter circumstances. Here, a step-by-step account is given for why the rapporteur came to write up a report in the first place. This part, therefore, grounds the report in and reproduces the EP's institutionalized history of how reports generally come to be written (i.e., by a request from the Council or Commission to the EP and then the EP requesting a contribution to the various committees producing reports or opinions and so on). Grounding the report in an institutionalized process of report writing associates the report with a number of other actors (e.g., European Council, Mr. Gil-Robles, Committees) and documents (i.e., A4–0307/97, SN 150/97). These associations are similar to the kinds of discursive practices mentioned by Latour (1987) in which referents are positioned around a claim in order to strengthen it and make it more fact like. In this way, the report no longer stands on its own and therefore becomes fortified through its links to and embeddings within other claims. Following the inserted clauses is a list of points that specify what is to be done. The report, up to and including the first point, is shown below:

> The European Parliament ,
>
> – having regard to the decision of the Amsterdam European Council of 16–17 June 1997 to call for an extraordinary meeting of the European Council under the Luxembourg Presidency to review progress in the creation of employment opportunities (SN 150/97),
>
> – having regard to the letter of Mr Juncker, acting President of the European Council, to Mr Gil-Robles Gil-Delgado, President of the European Parliament, asking for Parliament's contribution to the extraordinary summit (C4–0389/97),
>
> – having regard to the report by the Committee on Employment and Social Affairs and the opinions by the Committees on Economic and Monetary Affairs and Industrial Policy; on Research, Technological Development and Energy; on the Environment, Public Health and Consumer Protection; on Women's Rights; on Culture, Youth, Education and the Media; on Regional Policy; and on External Economic Relations (A4–0307/97),

1. Considers that, in the light of decisions taken by the Amsterdam European Council on employment, definite agreements should be reached at the Luxembourg Employment Summit concerning the creation of employment in the form of verifiable convergence criteria with quantitative objectives based on benchmarking and best practices. The combined effort of the Member states and the EU must aim to increase the current employment rate of 60,4% to 65% within 5 years and a reduction of the unemployment rate to 7%; youth unemployment should be reduced to 50% of its current level within three years;

Point 1 provides an outline of what is to be done. Clear targets concerning employment and unemployment rates are given and the focus of policy is on creating employment. Employment, therefore, is constructed mainly in relation to targets, rates, or numbers. This way of seeing employment parallels the EC's pillars of employability, entrepreneurship, etc. What is advocated here is getting individuals more employable so that employment rates can increase. A breakdown of the first point's transitivity structure in terms of participants, processes, and circumstances is shown in Table 4.

Notice first of all that the whole content of Point 1 is embedded within a series of projected clauses of the process *considers*. This process may be taken as a weaker form of believe and therefore as a weak commitment to the information contained within the projected clauses. The clauses contain a series of directives in which the implicit proposer (i.e., the EP) directs others (proposees) to perform specific actions. These are *should be reached, must aim to increase, must aim to* and *should be reduced*. The proposee is only explicitly mentioned for the second and third directive (*The combined effort of the Member states and the EU*). But

Table 4

Process	Participant	Circumstance
Considers	EP	in the light of ... (matter)
should be reached	definite agreements	at the Luxembourg Employment Summit (location) concerning the creation of employment (matter) in the form of verifiable convergence criteria with quantitative objectives based on bench-marking and best practices. (manner)
must aim to increase	The combined effort of the Member states and the EU the current employment rate of 60,4%	to 65% (role) within 5 years (extent)
(must aim to ...)	a reduction of the unemployment rate	to 7% (role)
should be reduced	youth unemployment	to 50% of its current level (role) within three years (extent)

here, the proposee is contained within an abstracted nominal form. It is only by the attached prepositional phrase, *of the Member states and the EU*, that we can infer that polities are to be the agents who should increase employment and decrease unemployment. The other two directives occur in passivized form without the inclusion of the proposees. Although the proposees are not made explicit or are abstracted the 'goals' of the actions — that which is affected by the doing — is, for the most part, made explicit. This is summarized in Table 5:

Table 5

Process	Participant
should be reached	definite agreements
must aim to increase	the current employment rate of 60,4%
(must aim to)	a reduction of the unemployment rate
should be reduced	youth unemployment

In this sample, all of the participants are goals: *definite agreements, the current employment rate of 60,4%, a reduction of the unemployment rate* and *youth unemployment*. Extra information, realized in circumstances, is expressed in the first directive. What the agreement is about is expressed in a *matter* circumstance, where the agreements are to take place in a *location* circumstance, and by what means the agreements are to be reached in a *manner* circumstance. The other clauses contain circumstantial information of role and extent. The roles of each clause express what the employment rates and unemployment are to be increased or decreased to — 65% and 7% respectively. The extent circumstances convey the time frames in which the increased and decreased rates must be achieved.

So, the matter and manner circumstances express what the policy is about — *the creation of employment* — and the means to go about creating employment: *convergence criteria and quantitative objectives*. What I am suggesting here is that the main action of policy is not, as expressed in the first process, reaching agreements but creating employment. Creating employment, since it has been nominalized and embedded within a matter circumstance, has grammatically been given a more peripheral status. The next clauses build upon employment creation by quantifying some objectives (e.g., employment rate of 65%). Lowering unemployment also deals with employment because one of the aims of employment policy is to create jobs for the unemployed. Although not expressed as a circ:purpose (purpose circumstance), I would argue that the latter three clauses express the purpose behind job creation. This is the case because the processes are cast in terms of *aims* and aims relate to what one plans or intends to do. Put differently, the aims or purpose of creating jobs is to reach the proposed targets set out in the policy.

At this point, it is also relevant to consider some of the rhetorical implications of the way in which Point 1 is discursively constructed. So far, I have analyzed creation of employment as the main act, verifiable convergence criteria with quantitative objectives as the means to creating jobs and achieving a 65% employment rate, 7% unemployment rate and a halved youth unemployment rate as the purpose behind creating jobs. Rhetorically then, a **purpose:act** ratio is constructed: Job creation is seen in terms of reaching the EP's targeted employment and unemployment rates.

Purpose	:	**Act**
65% employment rate		
7% unemployment rate	$\Rightarrow$	creation of employment
halved youth unemployment		

At least two points are worth mentioning here. First, the purpose chosen by the EP is not the only (possible) purpose for framing or providing legitimation for employment creation. Other possible purposes could also have been referred to such as improving living conditions, alleviating poverty or offering other disadvantaged groups more chances at gaining employment. Instead, EP employment policy is cast in terms of what the Amsterdam European Council has already decided and in terms of employment and unemployment as rates or quantities. The second point is that another pentadic term could have been used to provide reasons for focusing on job creation: *scene*. That is, the EP could have cited social situations of poverty and gender inequality as the reason for creating more jobs. So, rather than a **purpose:act** ratio, the EP could also have constructed a **scene:act** ratio. Note also that purpose may imply scene. For instance, a *purpose* of improving living conditions implies a *scene* in which living conditions are improved. Purposes often relate to an end product of an action and this end product can relate to a scene. However, by relating this back to the van Velzen Report, it is not entirely obvious how reaching set employment and unemployment targets imply a scene. That is, what kind of scene, aside from a situation in which more people are working, is being created? It could be suggested that jobs for more implies better living conditions for more but this claim is not grounded in the data. Rather, the targets seem to support themes of individualism in which individuals are seen in terms of their employability and adaptability and success is measured in terms of improving these qualities. I am not suggesting that job creation is Neo-liberalist. Job creation can certainly be linked to, for instance, improving working and living conditions. However, when a 'social' purpose is not given for creating employment and when job creation is seen in terms of rates, then it is Neo-liberalist themes of employability and adaptability that are being constructed and not themes of social necessity.

Following the two points in the report are a list of 17 points that outline the instruments to be used in creating employment. These instruments are divided into four sections: Training; Organization of working time; Financial measures; and Coordination of economic policy. Each of these sections can broadly be viewed as

Table 6

Participant1	Process1	Participant2	Process2	Participant3
Proposer	*Directive*	*Proposee*		
The EP	Calls upon	all parties	to link	the training of unemployed young people and the long-term unemployed to a guarantee that the retrained unemployed will be given paid employment for at least a year
The EP	Calls on	the Member States	to align	their efforts
The EP	Calls on	the Member States, in conjunction with the two sides of industry, instructors and training institutes	to develop	a system of training, employment, and work experience
The EP	Calls on	the two sides of industry	to conclude	agreements
The EP	Calls on	the Member States and the two sides of industry	to remunerate	overtime
The EP	Calls on	the Commission and the two sides of industry	to make	proposals
The EP	Calls for		to be introduced	a social or minimum VAT rate
The EP	Urges		be taken	decisions

the means to increase employment and decrease unemployment. These 17 points are directives given by the EP to various proposees that provide instructions on what to do, how to do it, and for what purpose. Although not all points contain circumstances of purpose and manner, all contain the same basic transitivity structure. Consider the first 8 'instruments' of the document (Points 3–10) shown in Table 6.

In the first column, the EP is positioned as the proposer throughout the document. The second column, Process1, is consistently a directive. The directive takes the shape of *calls on/for* with the three exceptions: *urges*, *asks*, and *instructs* (the latter two not shown in the table; see Appendix 3). The third column, Participant2, contains the proposee and varies from directive to directive. The proposee is generally made explicit but is sometimes vague, as the first example shows with *all parties,* or is unmentioned as is the case in the last two examples when Process2 is passivized. What the proposee is required to do is found in the fourth column under Process2. These processes, such as *to link, align, develop, conclude,* etc. are generalized processes. Generalization, as can be recalled from Chapter 1, refers to terms that 'collect' meaning. For instance, the verb *to develop* implies a number of social processes such as taking something in one state, altering it in some form and having some (vague or explicit) notion about how something is to be altered. Now, to be sure, all terms have a degree of generality to them and it is only when placed in a context of social action that terms come to acquire specific meanings. The point, however, is that some terms such as *develop, align,* and *introduce* retain certain collected meanings even when placed in a context of use. Some processes have, in addition to being generalized, taken on abstract features. Here I am referring specifically to *conclude agreements, make proposals,* and *take decisions.* These are examples of generalized processes that have been nominalized and turned into participants. So, instead of appearing as agreeing, proposing, and deciding, they appear as conclude/make/take + [nominalized verb].

Assigning a second participant to a generalized process — although it answers the important question of what is to be developed, aligned, and introduced — does not rid the process of its generality. Part of the reason for this is that participants, especially in EU reports, also contain a significant amount of generality. Consider the third point in the table: *to develop a system of training, employment, and work experience.* The participant, *a system ...,* is also a generalized term that collects meaning. For instance, a system of training implies that some individuals will be trained in some manner for some purpose. In order to unpack generalizations, it is therefore necessary to include circumstance roles that explain the how and why.

The EP directives tend to include purpose and manner roles — expressed in circumstances or a separate clause — when directing others. Table 7 shows 5 examples of processes that include manner and/or purpose.

In the report, manner roles tend to be preceded by the prepositions *by* and *in the form of* and answer the questions 'how' or 'in what way'? Purpose roles tend to be preceded by the prepositions/conjunctions *to, such that, thus,* and *for* and answer the questions 'why' and 'for what reason'? Including both manner and purpose in a directive alleviates some of the generality surrounding the act to be performed. For instance, in Pt. 4, MSs are being directed to align their efforts. If the directive were to end here, the action required of the MSs would be too opaque and generalized to be executable. Adding a purpose, such as *to promote training,* provides the necessary direction that aligning one's efforts should take. What is still missing, however, is how to go about doing it. This information is then provided by the manner (i.e., *by gearing their national budgets ...*). That is, the instruments are mentioned by which the MSs are to go about aligning their efforts to promote training. Pt. 5, in contrast, mentions the purpose for developing a system of training, etc., but it does not provide the tools for developing this

Table 7. Processes that include manner and/or purpose (Van Velzen Report)

Pt.#	Process	Participant	Manner	Purpose
4	to align	their efforts	by gearing their national budgets to the mean of the three best-performing Member States and undertaking to increase average spending on the education, professional training of adults and RTD by 5% of GDP	to promote training
5	to develop	a system of training, employment, and work experience		such that no person aged under 25 need draw unemployment benefit
7	to remunerate	overtime	in the form of time off of vouchers (for services or courses) or longer career breaks or sabbaticals	
	to support	proposals involving the collective shortening of working hours	by lowering social security contributions	thus enabling (partial) compensation for workers' loss of income to be guaranteed
8	to make	the Commission,.. proposals		to ensure that the irregular work which is prevalent in it is accompanied by adequate social security and employees' rights equivalent to those for full working-time
12	Calls for	the elimination of bureaucratic obstacles to investment		for the review and simplification of the administrative burdens on SME's

system. On the other hand, the first process in Pt.7 states the means in which overtime is to be remunerated but no hint is given as to why this should be done.

Having now gone through a step-by-step illustration of the grammatical make-up of the tools listed in the report, focus will now be placed on the two points (7 & 8) in the report that express the ideological dilemma of individualism and social necessity: *Organization of working time.*

3.1.1 *Organization of working time*

So far, the discursive and rhetorical analysis of the report has shown that EP employment policy has made the creation of employment the central act, increasing employment rates and decreasing unemployment rates the purpose of this act and the four 'headings' (i.e., Training, Organization of working time, Financial measures and Coordination of economic policy) the instruments or means to create employment. Furthermore, the report casts employment in terms of a **purpose:act** ratio in which reaching targeted employment and unemployment rates is the reason for creating employment. As implied above, linking employment with rates and numbers coincides with individualism since the focus is on making individuals more employable and adaptable so that they can participate in increasing employment rates. Since employability and adaptability highlights the individualist side of employment the contrary side, social interests, may be evoked. It is to the social purpose of working time that I turn to first.

Purpose:act — *purpose is social*

Relating social interests to employment in the EU goes back to, at the very least, 'The Community Charter of the Fundamental Social Rights of Workers, 1989' (in Field 1995: 105–109). In Pt. 7 of this Charter, it is stated that:

> The completion of the internal market *must lead to an improvement in the living and working conditions of workers in the European Community*. This process must result from an approximation of these conditions while the improvement is being maintained, as regards in particular the *duration and organisation of working times* and *forms of employment other than open-ended contracts, such as fixed-term contracts, part-time working, temporary work and seasonal work.* (italics mine)

At the very beginning of this excerpt, *an improvement in the living and working conditions of workers in the European Community* is claimed to be a necessary result of the internal market's (i.e., free movement of goods, people, services, capital) completion. Associating the latter with obligation (i.e., must), I would argue, constructs purpose. That is, the internal market's completion and working conditions are not merely being relationally associated (i.e., 'x' leads to 'y'); Inserting *must* before *leads* establishes obligation and makes what follows the reason for — and therefore purpose for — the internal market's completion. The instruments that will yield improved living and working conditions include the nominalized processes '*organisation* of working time' and '*forms* of employment other than open-ended contracts'. The Charter, therefore, contains a **purpose:act** ratio in which improving EU workers' living and working conditions through the instruments *organisation of working time* and *forms of employment* ... is understood as the reason behind completing the internal market (act).

Purpose	:	**Act**
an improvement in the living and working conditions of workers in the European Community	$\Rightarrow$	The completion of the internal market

In this way, social interests are given a dominant role in issues concerning the free movement of people and services and the organization of working time is positioned as a means to ensure that social interests are maintained. Note also that this purpose relates directly to a scene in which living and working conditions are improved. That is, the purpose, when realized, will construct the targeted scene, which, in this case, are the improved conditions.

Purpose:act ratio — purpose is job creation
Since then, however, the discourse on the organization of working time has changed significantly. In 1994, the Commission appointed an expert group to address work organization. The expert group based much of their recommendations on the 1993 Commission White Paper on Growth, Competitiveness, and Employment. One of the main foci of this Commission document was on improving flexibility and adaptability in the workplace. The Commission described the working group's task as follows (in Field 1995: 126):

> Based on the guidelines set out in the White Paper and the Conclusions of the European Council in Brussels, *to examine the action taken or proposed* within and outside the European Union, at different levels, *on flexibility and work organisation* with a view to preparing an evaluation of the extent to which *such action might be beneficial for the creation or retention of employment*, taking into account implications for competitiveness and productivity, and *to make recommmendations on practical steps that can be taken to increase employment through improved flexibility and work organisation.* (italics mine)

In this excerpt, I focus on the various grammatical positionings of the nominalizations employment, flexibility and work organization. The terms flexibility and work organization are initially represented in a circ:*matter* but, at the end of the excerpt, end up as the *manner* through which employment is to be increased. This recontextualization of flexibility and work organization is shown in Table 8.

To begin, *the action taken or proposed* is expressed as being about flexibility and work organization and is, in a later clause, associated with a circ:behalf — *for the creation or retention of employment*. Towards the end, two transformations occur. First, employment creation shifts from being the beneficiary of an action to the purpose of an action. Second, flexibility and work organization are shifted from being what the action is about to the means by which employment is to be increased — note that this manner circumstance is embedded within the prior matter circumstance. Rhetorically, the Commission uses a **purpose:act** ratio in

Table 8

Process	Participant	Circumstance roles
to examine	the action taken or proposed	on flexibility and work organisation (matter)
might be	such action beneficial	for the creation or retention of employment (behalf)
make	recommendations	on practical steps (matter)
can be taken	(practical steps)	to increase employment (purpose) through improved flexibility and work organisation (manner)

which increasing employment is seen as the reason behind recommending practical steps and taking or proposing actions.

Purpose	:	**Act**
increase employment	$\Rightarrow$	recommending practical steps the action taken or proposed

Flexibility and work organization contributes to this ratio by being cast as a tool in which the EC may increase employment. Removed is the social dimension of work organization and in its stead is placed a more economic one. The shift to more economic concerns is highlighted in the expert group's summary of their recommendations in a document entitled: List of recommendations, Report of Expert Working Group on Flexibility and Work Organization, Social Europe, Supplement 1/1995 (in Field 1995: 126–129):

> Variable working hours are an important source of flexibility for firms, which they have to use in order to deal with short-term market fluctuation or disruption. Overtime is a traditional way of coping with such instability. The massive difference in the level of overtime worked between countries and between firms shows that there is considerable scope for the redistribution of work. A strict ban on overtime would be damaging, since it would undermine firms' flexibility.

Working hours and overtime are cast in relation to the interests of business. They are tools for dealing with fluctuation, disruption, and instability so that firms may remain flexible, and therefore competitive and profitable. Although it is perhaps not surprising that a Commission appointed an expert group — most probably consisting of mainly business leaders and ex-politicians — to promote this view, it nevertheless indexes the economic, management focus that the organization of working time has come under.

3.1.2 *van Velzen Report on Organization of Working Time*
The van Velzen Report's contribution to the organization of working time re-introduced some of the social dimensions that were found in the 1989 Charter of

the Fundamental Social Rights of Workers. Consider the transitivity structure of Pt. 7 of the van Velzen Report, which is analyzed in Table 9.

> 7. Calls on the Member States and the two sides of industry to remunerate overtime in the form of time off or of vouchers (for services or courses) or longer career breaks or sabbaticals, and to conclude agreements for flexible working time on the basis of the Commission study and to support proposals involving the collective shortening of working hours by lowering social security contributions, thus enabling (partial) compensation for workers' loss of income to be guaranteed; such proposals should principally be a matter for collective agreement between the social partners, and stresses that fundamental working time standards should be governed by national and European legislation;

Table 9. Van Velzen Report, Point 7

Process	Participant	Circumstance roles
Calls on	The European Parliament the Member States and the two sides of industry	
to remunerate	overtime	in the form of time off of vouchers (for services or courses) or longer career breaks or sabbaticals (manner1)
to conclude	agreements	– for flexible working time (matter1) – on the basis of the Commission study (angle1)
to support	proposals involving the collective shortening of working hours	– by lowering social security contributions (manner2) – thus enabling (partial) compensation for workers' loss of income to be guaranteed; (purpose1)
should principally be	such proposals a matter for collective agreement	between the social partners; (behalf1)
stresses		
should be governed	fundamental working time standards by national and European legislation	

The organization of working time consists of a number of ways in which working time is *organized*. van Velzen includes remunerating overtime, agreements on flexible working time, the collective shortening of working hours, and national and European legislation on fundamental working time standards in this organizing. Moreover it is stated how overtime is to be remunerated (i.e., time off of vouchers), from what point of view agreements on flexible working time are to be concluded (i.e., on the basis of the Commission study) and how and to what end proposals on the collective shortening of working hours are to be supported (i.e., by lowering social security contributions and to guarantee compensation for workers' loss of income). Additional information is also given on the collective shortening of working time. Through a relational process it is indicated who should agree on the proposals (i.e., collective agreement between the *social partners*) and, finally, that working time standards should be governed by national and European legislation. The acts, means, and ends proposed in this report seem less directed at creating employment and more at maintaining or improving living and working conditions. Remunerating overtime, guaranteeing workers' loss of income to be guaranteed if working hours are shortened does not focus on the flexibility of firms and the adaptability of employees. Rather, it places the workers and their working conditions as the prime target of EP policy. What is being emphasized are the social interests of workers and not their employability or adaptability. I would argue that it is at this point that the ideological dilemma of employment creation becomes manifest. In Point 1, employment creation and employment rates were presented as the central actions of employment policy. The quantified rates, in turn, can be linked to liberalist notions of individuals' employability and adaptability since by adopting these qualities, individuals help to bring about the desired statistics. Similarly, the focus of work organization can be on getting more individuals into jobs. This focus, however, may raise the question as to what kind of working and living environment an employment-oriented organization will bring about. And, as seen in the EP policy on work organization, it is the working/living environment, not employee's flexibility and adaptability that receives the main emphasis. So, while the purpose of job creation was related to increasing employment rates at the beginning of the report, improving working and living conditions become the main reasons behind organizing work.

Purpose	:	**Act**
improve working and living conditions (time off, sabbaticals, compensating workers' loss of income)	⇒	remunerate overtime make working time flexible shorten working hours

Although policy's overall purpose is to increase employment rates, social aspects such as improving working and living conditions can sneak their way into other sections of the text. The tools for generating employment, as the report shows, are one place in which this is possible. Let us turn now to Pt. 8 (Table 10).

> 8. Calls on the Commission and the two sides of industry to make proposals concerning 'atypical' employment to ensure that the irregular work which is prevalent in it is accompanied by adequate social security and employees' rights equivalent to those for full working-time;

Table 10. van Velzen Report, Point 8

Process	Participant	Circumstance roles
Calls on (directive)	The European Parliament the Commission and the two sides of industry	
to make proposals	concerning 'atypical' employment	to ensure that the irregular work which is prevalent in it is accompanied by adequate social security and employees' rights equivalent to those for full working-time (purpose1)

This point (the one appearing in the EP Resolution) was analyzed back in Chapter 1. Recall that this directive concerns forms of work that are not full-time. It was argued that the report constructs an 'uncommon sense' taxonomy by classifying working time as irregular, atypical, or full. Here, an incompatible set of oppositions is constructed in which atypical and irregular is on one end of the spectrum and full on the other. That is, we do not have atypical-typical, irregular-regular, or full-part but atypical/irregular-full. Constructing this kind of uncommon sense opposition is rhetorical in that, by categorizing not full-time work as irregular and atypical, it makes us see full-time work as regular and typical. What is being suggested here is that a commonsense taxonomy of atypical-typical and irregular-regular will be read into part-full time work. What this piece of policy does provide, however, is a directive to ensure that individuals who do not have full-time work also receive the same social security and rights as full-time workers. So, as in point 7, point 8 provides a social purpose as the reason behind addressing diverse forms of work and does not position non-fulltime workers in relation to worker attributes such as employability or adaptability.

4.   EP Debate on the Organization of Working Time

EP debates are institutionalized practices in which the speakers, speaker turn orders, and speaker turn length are pre-assigned (except Commission or Council members who may speak for an 'unlimited' amount of time). Moreover, speeches are, for the most part, read out from written texts leaving little room for spontaneous discussion. Speaker turn orders are assigned from largest to smallest party. That is, a member of the largest party speaks first then a member of the second largest then third, with the cycle repeating itself when the member of the smallest party has spoken. Since smaller parties generally do not have enough members to provide a speaker for each cycle, the larger parties tend to dominate the debate. Here is the breakdown of the number of members from each party (not including

Commission and Council members) that spoke in the debate:

- PSE=17 (turns)
- PPE=10
- ELDR=4
- GUE/NGL=5
- UPE=4
- V=2
- ARE=2
- I-EDN=2
- NI=2

The largest parties are PSE and PPE and these members account for over 50% of the turns taken. PSE is characterized as a 'socialist' party whereas PPE is 'conservative'. Fifty-two speaker turns (not including intervening turns by the President=presiding officer who briefly introduced each speaker) were taken in the debate. Although many aspects of the report were discussed by the speakers, only those contributions involving the organization of working time are discussed here. Two points will be considered: What was said concerning overtime and the collective shortening of the working week. Since the EP, the EC, and the European Council all make arguments in favor of or against various aspects of the van Velzen Report and since all three bodies attempt to influence and decide (the Council being the most influential since they end up writing up the Presidency Conclusions) what will go into the final Presidency Conclusions, it is important to examine how they position themselves to the Report. The analysis will therefore trace the paradoxical themes surrounding issues of overtime and the reduction of the working week. At issue is the tension between liberalist claims concerning the adaptability and flexibility of individuals and businesses for the purpose of job creation and more social views of employment creation that consider workers' living and working conditions.

4.1 *Overtime*

Since overtime is the first issue addressed in the report's section on organizing working time and since the report was written by a member of the largest EP party (PSE), one might have expected overtime to have been extensively discussed and debated. This was not so. Only five speakers spoke on this issue, the first being the rapporteur of the report, Mr. van Velzen:

Van Velzen (PSE)
Structureel overwerk dient naar mijn mening te worden uitgebannen en waar het voorkomt, te worden uitbetaald in vrije tijd of dienstenbonnen. Het is een schande dat tegenover de bijna 30 miljoen werklozen, als je alles meetelt, zo'n 9 miljoen mensen in Europa overwerken, structureel overwerken

'Structural overtime has to be stamped out, in my view, and whenever it occurs it has to be remunerated in extra free-time or service-vouchers. It is shameful towards the almost 30 million unemployed, if you take everything in account, that approximately 9 million people are doing overtime, structural overtime.'

Here, van Velzen recontextualizes the point expressed in the Report that overtime be remunerated in extra free-time (sabbatical, career breaks) or service-cheques (vouchers). As in the report, he highlights the means or instruments used to compensate workers for doing overtime (Table 11):

Table 11.

Process	Participant	Circumstance roles
worden uitbetaald 'has to be remunerated'	te (structureel overwerk) 'it (structural overtime)'	in vrije tijd of dienstenbonnen 'in extra free-time or service-vouchers'

These instruments do not merely supply the how but also have an ideological component. That is, overtime is to be remunerated by free-time or service vouchers rather than money. In this way, the incentives for doing overtime are not to increase one's income but to take a longer holiday or to receive additional training. Therefore, one does more work in order to take more time off from work or to improve one's skills at work. Rhetorically, van Velzen constructs a **scene:act** ratio[2] in which improved living or working conditions (scene) result from doing overtime (act). The other speakers, while in favor of reducing overtime, did not express support for remunerating overtime. Instead, the focus was placed on reducing overtime so that more jobs may be created. Consider Schiedermeier's use of a 'causal' relational clause to express job-creation as the outcome of working time reduction:

Schiedermeier (PPE)
Der Abbau von Überstunden wird von uns schon lange und zu Recht gefordert, dies führt zweifellos zu mehr Beschäftigung. Das gilt in Deutschland auch für die 610 DM-Beschäftigungsverhältnisse. Der Missbrauch dieser Ausnahmeregelung vernichtet in ungeheurem Ausmaß Beschäftigungsverhältnisse in der Bundesrepublik Deutschland. Die rechtliche Gleichstellung der atypischen Arbeitsverhältnisse entsprechend der Vollzeitarbeit wird von mir uneingeschränkt unterstützt.
The reduction of overtime has been demanded by us, rightly so, for some time, and this undoubtedly leads to more employment. That is also valid in Germany for the 610 DM-employment-condition. The abuse of this exceptional arrangement destroys to a tremendous extent the employment conditions in the Federal Republic of Germany. The legal harmonization of atypical labor-conditions with respect to full-time labor carries my unrestricted support.

---

2. An **agency:act** ratio is also constructed here in which remuneration (act) is seen in terms of extra free-time or service-vouchers (agency). However, the result of this act and the tools used to execute the act is a 'scene' in which workers' living or working conditions can be improved.

Table 12.

Process	Participant	Circumstance roles
führt	dies (der Abbau von Überstunden)	zu mehr Beschäftigung
'leads'	'this (The reduction of overtime)'	'to more employment'

This relational process treats employment creation as a natural and result of reducing overtime. What is backgrounded is the purpose, manner, and even action (i.e., processes) undertaken to bring about reducing overtime or creating employment. Schiedermeier's use of abstracted nominalized processes (i.e., reduction, more employment) and high positive modality expressed in the relational clause construct the view that the information expressed to the left of the relation is, in some natural or universal way, related to the information expressed to the right. As van Velzen, Schiedermeier constructs a **scence:act** ratio. The scene related to reducing overtime, however, differs greatly for Schiedermeier. Instead of relating overtime to a scene of improved living or working conditions, Scheidermeier constructs a scene in which more jobs are available; that is, *mehr Beschäftigung* is not a process nor a purpose nor a means but simply the end result of the action of reducing overtime. Here, organizing working time relates to more job opportunities and to increasing the employment rate. In this way, overtime becomes a liberal concern in that individuals are seen as filling up job vacancies that, in turn, helps to achieve the targeted employment rate set by the EU. At this point, it appears that the differences between remuneration and job-creation may be differences in 'party ideology.' Since van Velzen is a member of PSE and Schiedermeier of PPE this may reasonably correspond to social and conservative views on overtime. This, however, is not the case because Alonso, also a member of PSE, is against remuneration and for reducing overtime to create jobs (Table 13):

Alonso (PSE)
Los interlocutores sociales deben ofrecer acuerdos concretos orientados a crear empleo, por ejemplo convirtiendo las horas extraordinarias en puestos de trabajo -en mi país, el año pasado se han hecho 65 millones de horas extraordinarias-, convirtiendo esas horas extraordinarias en puestos de trabajo y no en remuneraciones, mediante fórmulas de trabajo flexible, por ejemplo acordando reducciones de jornada a cambio de empleo, salvaguardando siempre la productividad de las empresas, apostando por acuerdos sobre nuevas formas de organización del trabajo
'The social partners must offer concrete proposals designed to create employment, for example by converting overtime hours into regular jobs: last year, in my country, 65 million hours of overtime were recorded. By converting these hours of overtime into actual jobs and not simply remuneration or by putting into place more flexible working hours, for example by reducing the working day instead of assigning new jobs, while at the same time continuing to safeguard corporate productivity and reinforcing it through agreements on new forms of work organization, the situation would be helped.'

Table 13.

Process	Participant	Circumstance roles
deben ofrecer 'must offer'	Los interlocutores sociales 'The social partners'	por ejemplo convirtiendo las horas extraordinarias en puestos de trabajo 'for example by converting overtime hours into regular jobs'
	acuerdos concretos orientados a crear empleo 'concrete proposals designed to create employment'	

Here, Alonso expresses the means to create employment in a manner clause (*convirtiendo las horas extraordinarias en puestos de trabajo*). Later on, he emphasizes that the focus on overtime should be on job creation and not remuneration (*y no en remuneraciones*). Here, he positions himself specifically against van Velzen, a member of his own party, and therefore against the Report. Alonso's opposing view suggests that Parties cannot be treated as siding with only one side of the ideological dilemma. As shown here, more social ways of dealing with overtime (i.e., van Velzen) and liberalist views of seeing overtime as a means to job creation may and do exist within parties. More importantly, though, these opposing views on overtime index a shift in view from seeing overtime primarily in terms of a social objective in which the living and working conditions of workers are improved to seeing it in terms of a quantitative objective: an increased employment rate.

4.2 Shorter Working Hours

That aspect of the organization of working time that was most hotly debated concerned shortening the working week. Much of EU policy centers on 'organizing' the working week and employment. As evidenced in the Commission's Joint Employment Report 1997, reducing working time is claimed to play a potential role in job creation. A case in point was the Volkswagen agreement of 1994. Here it was argued that Volkswagen was able to continue the job contracts of 100,000 workers by shortening the working week to 28.8 hours. The debate over negotiating new working time arrangements also came at a time when national governments such as France and Italy were seeking to collectively reduce the working week to 35 hours — France, in the mean time, has already reduced the working week to 35 hours. Although many MEPs voiced agreement with working time reduction, opposition arose as to whether or not the shortening of working hours should be governed by legislation (national or European). Recall Pt. 7 of the van Velzen report in which it was mentioned that *fundamental working time standards should be governed by national and European legislation*. This proved to be a contentious point in the debate. Those that were most vehemently against working time reduction, such as Hermange, came from the UPE (Table 14):

Hermange (UPE)

Deuxième initiative importante, il faut favoriser l'émergence d'une nouvelle organisation du travail. Mais la par rapport à ce qui est dit dans le rapport je voudrais faire quelques observations. Car dans le rapport il est indique que cette réorganisation ne pourra se faire que dans une réduction systématique du temps de travail. Moi j'ai vraiment peur qu'aujourd'hui, l'expression "réduction du temps de travail" soit à la mode dans certains pays européens et qu'elle se révèle quelque part à terme, peut-être pas a court terme, mais à terme, antinomique et antisociale si elle est appliquée selon des modalités contraignantes à toutes les entreprises, et j'ai peur aussi que la réduction automatique du temps de travail risque au contraire de générer le développement d'heures supplémentaires, voire du travail au noir, ainsi qu'un recours accru a la mécanisation. Alors, plutôt que de réduction systématiquement, je préférais, pour la compétitivité des entreprises européennes, que nous puissions réfléchir à une organisation flexible et judicieuse du temps de travail, adaptée aux réalités économiques et humaines de l'entreprise et de son environnement.

'Second important initiative, the emergence of a new work organization it is to be favored. But the per-report what's said in the report I'd like to make a few observations. For in this report it is stated that this reorganization couldn't be done but within a systematic working time reduction. I really fear that today, the expression "working time reduction" is only in fashion in certain European countries and that it will reveal in time, maybe not in the short term, but in time, to be antinomical and antisocial if it is applied, by way of obligatory methods, to all enterprises, and I also fear that an automatic working time reduction risks, on the contrary, to generate the development of supplementary hours, the appearance of moonlighting, and also an increased resorting to mechanization. So, rather than a systematic reduction, I'd prefer, for the competitiveness of the European enterprises, that we could reflect on a flexible and judicious working time organization, adapted to the economic and human realities in the enterprise and it's surroundings.'

Hermange uses two relational clauses to point out the negative attributes of working time reduction (*à la mode, antinomique et antisociale*). Arguing that *l'expression "réduction du temps de travail"* is merely an expression and in fashion suggests that, as all fashions, they will not remain fashionable. Hermange, therefore, argues against the universality of working time reduction by implying that if it does not last it cannot be of any use. This argument supports the notion that only universal attributes should be advocated. Furthermore, the enforcement of working time reduction is argued to be antinomical and antisocial. Here, a liberalist view in which the freedom of the individual is of paramount importance is being asserted against authority by way of legislation. So, by implication, the freedom of individuals is identified with being social whereas legislating individuals restricts their freedom and is therefore antisocial. Finally, she identifies the consequences of supporting legisled working time reduction: *le développement d' heures supplémentaires, voire du travail au noir, ainsi qu'un recours accru a la mécanisation*. These consequences — the development of

Table 14.

Process	Participant	Circumstance roles
soit 'is'	l'expression "réduction du temps de travail" 'the expression "working time reduction"' à la mode 'in fashion'	dans certains pays européens 'in certain European countries'
se révèle 'will reveal'	elle 'it' antinomique et antisociale 'antinomical and antisocial'	quelque part à terme, peut-être pas a court terme, mais à terme 'in time, maybe not in the short term, but in time'
est appliquée 'is applied'	elle 'it'	selon des modalités contraignantes à toutes les entreprises 'by way of obligatory methods to all enterprises'
risque de générer 'risks to generate'	la réduction automatique du temps de travail 'an automatic working time reduction' le développement d'heures supplémentaires, voire du travail au noir, ainsi qu'un recours accru a la mécanisation 'the development of supplementary hours, the appearance of moonlighting, and also an increased resorting to mechanization'	

supplementary hours, moonlighting, and increased mechanization — are seen as naturally following from legislated working time reduction. Working time reduction is being constructed in terms of a **scene:act** ratio. The act, working time reduction, is seen in terms of antisocial working situations (scene).

Scene	:	**Act**
antinomique et antisociale	⟹	réduction du temps de travail

Note that Moreau's use of a **scene:act** ratio is different from the **scene:act** ratios used regarding overtime. In the latter, a scene (i.e., improved living/working conditions or more job positions) was cast as the driving force behind reducing overtime. These scenes were used as positive reasons for doing an action. In contrast, Moreau constructed a **scene:act** ratio in order to highlight the negative scenes that result from an act. In this way, working time reduction is not seen in terms of positive reasons for doing the act, but in terms its negative consequences (i.e., antisocial conditions). So, one way of countering views that support, in this case, social interests, is to claim that those acts that profess to be social in nature actually lead to the opposite scene. That is, not to a more social conditions but to antisocial conditions.

Two turns later in the debate, Moreau challenged Hermange's assertion that legislated working time reduction brings negative social consequences. In addition, Moreau argues that the van Velzen report should include concrete figures for working time reduction and follow the lead of France and Italy (Table 15):

> **Moreau (GUE/NGL)**
>
> C'est si vrai que, traitant de l'emploi, le rapport van Velzen ne dit pas un mot de la réduction du temps de travail, et ce au moment même où deux gouvernements de l'Union européenne viennent de décider de s'orienter vers les 35 heures hebdomadaires dans les toutes prochaines années. Ce n'est pas une mode, Madame Hermange, les 35 heures, c'est un grand objectif de civilisation pour vivre mieux et pour créer des emplois. Notre groupe apprécie donc positivement la décision des gouvernements français et italien d'aller dans cette voie de progrès, amorçant une rupture avec les politiques menées jusqu'à présent. Les 35 heures ont fait irruption en Europe, titrait récemment le journal El Pais. Le secrétaire général de la CES ne s'y est pas trompé en déclarant: "Les lignes directrices pour l'emploi qui seront décidées à Luxembourg devraient inclure d'une façon explicite la perspective de la réorganisation et de la diminution du temps de travail comme des priorités essentielles de la lutte contre le chômage."
>
> 'It's so true, that in dealing with employment, the report van Velzen doesn't say one word about working time reduction, and this at the exact moment where two governments in the European Union decide to turn towards the 35-hour working week in the next coming years. This is not in fashion, Madam Hermange, these 35 hours, it's a big objective of civilization for better living and to create jobs. Our group thus appreciates positively the decision of the French and Italian governments to progress in this direction, initiating a break with the policies carried out until now. The 35 hours have flooded Europe, recently headlined in the paper El Pais. The Secretary-General of the ECS wasn't mistaken by declaring: "The employment guidelines, decided upon in Luxembourg, should include in an explicit way the perspective of the reorganization and the reduction of working time as an essential priority in the fight against unemployment."'

As Moreau, Hermange also uses relational processes to make her point. Moreau recontextualizes parts of Hermange's speech by addition, substitution, and deletion (see also Chapter 1). That is, addition occurs by negating the verb *soit* to *n'est*, and deletion/substitution occurs by deleting *réduction du temps de travail* and substituting it with *les 35 heures*. This recontextualization marks a shift from reduction of working time as an abstracted process to an abstracted, nominalized number. Notice that in *les 35 heures*, reduction of working time cannot even be inferred. In this way, a 35 hour working week is constructed as an already established organization of work rather than as a number of hours that needs to be

Table 15.

Process	Participant	Circumstance roles
n'est pas 'is not'	Ce 'This'	
	une mode 'in fashion'	
	les 35 heures 'these 35 hours'	
est 'is'	c' 'it'	pour vivre mieux et pour créer des emplois 'for better living and to create jobs'
	un grand objectif de civilisation 'a big objective of civilization'	
apprécie 'appreciates'	Notre groupe 'Our group'	
	la décision des gouvernements français et italien d'aller dans cette voie de progrès 'the decision of the French and Italian governments to progress in this direction'	

negotiated and decided upon. *Les 35 heures*, therefore, black-boxes the social processes that must be set in motion to establish its existence and therefore serves as a useful rhetorical device to gain its acceptance. Moreau also challenges Hermange's claim that working time reduction is anti-social by asserting that it is *un grand objectif de civilisation*. Moreau strengthens her claim by providing working time reduction with a dual purpose: it affords better living and it creates jobs. In this way the economic purpose of working time reduction (i.e., job creation) is fused with the social concern of improving living conditions. So, in a way, the paradox between working time reduction's individualist/egalitarian and social/authoritarian themes are momentarily dissolved. According to Moreau, imposed working time reduction attends to both the social need of improving quality of life and ensuring that people are able to find jobs and the need to raise employment rates. Nonetheless, the social aspects are given priority. It is work organization/reduction as a social concern that is the central act with the purpose of improving social conditions and creating jobs and not work organization as merely the means to achieve employment.

Other groups, such as V, PSE, and ARE also supported reducing working hours. But, as Mollar pointed out in the debate, group internal conflicts on working time reduction were the rule rather than the exception:

Mollar (PPE)

Y qué decir del gran tema estrella que es la reducción del tiempo de trabajo. Cuándo va la Comisión a presentar los estudios que se le han requerido para hacer un examen comparativo allí donde se está aplicando? No hay unanimidad en la aplicación de esta solución. Hay diversidad de opiniones. Incluso dentro del Grupo del Grupo Socialista hay quienes se manifiestan en contra de que sean los Gobiernos quienes a golpe de decreto la impongan.

'And what about the key issue, which is that of reducing the working hours? When is the Commission going to present the studies which it was asked to do in order to make a comparative examination of the areas in which they are being applied? There is no unanimity in the application of this solution. Opinions vary greatly: even within the Socialist Party there are those who are opposed to the idea that the governments should be those to impose this solution with a single Act of Parliament.'

Here again, liberal themes of non-state intervention continue to surface. Although reduction of working time is supported in general, the possibility of legislating it is considered anathema, especially to the other EU sub-organizations. Consider here what Commissioner Flynn said in the debate:

I would like to say is that the Commission has not dodged under the issue of the proposed guidelines the question of working time. Under the adaptability heading, the Commission acknowledges that reductions in working time may be appropriate in some sectors or situations but that such reductions should be negotiated by the social partners. The overall aim must be however, to make enterprise productive and competitive and to achieve the necessary balance between flexibility for the enterprise and security for the individual worker.

Table 16

Process	Participant	Circumstance roles
has not dodged	the Commission the question of working time	under the issue of the proposed guidelines
acknowledges	the Commission	Under the adaptability heading
may be	reductions in working time	
appropriate	in some sectors or situations	
should be negotiated	such reductions by the social partners	
must be	The overall aim to make enterprise productive and competitive and to achieve the necessary balance	between flexibility for the enterprise and security for the individual worker

Flynn asserts that reductions are to be negotiated by the social partners. His position on working time argues for a considerably weaker role played by government than expressed in the report. Flynn uses two kinds of lower strength modal verbs (i.e., may, and should) when referring to who should address working time reduction (i.e., *may be appropriate in some sectors or situations* and *reductions should be negotiated by the social partners*). Note that Flynn's recommendations of who deals with working time reduction is different from van Velzen. In the report it was the MSs and the two sides of industry whereas with the Commission it is the Social Partners. In this way, Flynn steers clear of the possibility of national legislation. Flynn then switches to a stronger modal form (i.e., must) when discussing the aims of working time reduction. It is consistent with Neo-liberal arguments by highlighting productivity, flexibility, and competitiveness of enterprises. Moreover, these attributes of enterprises are implied to lead to the security of individual workers. Workers' wants, needs, and security are therefore tied up with enterprises' productivity. The social aspects of working time are completely left out of Flynn's arguments.

5.   The EP Resolution

Following the debate, the points of and amendments to the van Velzen report were voted on. The amended Report became the official EP Resolution and it was this version that was sent off to the Luxembourg Summit. As with all EP Resolutions, part B (i.e., the Explanatory Statement) is excluded. In this way, the Resolution is left without its legitimation for the contents of the policy. 8 points were added to the Resolution increasing the total to 27. Some points remained virtually unchanged whereas others underwent significant recontextualizations. Point 7 of the van Velzen Report became Point 9 of the Resolution and Point 8 became Point 10. Since Point 8 remained virtually unchanged (see Appendix), the analysis focuses only on the recontextualizations of the transitivity structure of Point 7 of the Report (Table 17):

> 9. Believes that Member States need to address the issue of promoting flexibility in the labour market with regard to working hours, working time and working patterns (such as career breaks, sabbaticals, etc.) through a non-legislative, non-compulsory process based on social dialogue at the level of the individual enterprise, in particular having regard to the vital role of SMEs in job creation; notes the importance of enhancing labour market mobility through improved mutual recognition of diplomas, and through the portability of pensions, insurance and social insurance;

Table 17. EP Resolution, Point 9

Process	Participant	Circumstance roles
Believes	The EP	
need to address	that Member States the issue of promoting flexibility in the labour market	with regard to working hours, working time and working patterns (such as career breaks, sabbaticals, etc.) (matter1) through a non-legislative, non-compulsory process based on social dialogue (manner1) at the level of the individual enterprise (location1) in particular having regard to the vital role of SMEs in job creation (matter2)
notes	the importance of enhancing labour market mobility	through improved mutual recognition of diplomas, and through the portability of pensions, insurance and social insurance (manner2)

The first change occurred at the very beginning. Whereas the Report began with the EP issuing a command (i.e., calls on the Member States and the two sides of industry), the Resolution positions the EP as a senser who expresses a belief (i.e., believes that Member States). The directive is shifted further down into the next clause (i.e., need to …). This is a clear example of backgrounding obligation. By shifting the directive deeper into the next clause, it is made less explicit. Note also that it is no longer the MSs and the two sides of industry that are to be directed. The latter group has been deleted leaving the MSs with the sole responsibility of organizing working time.

A second change relates to the types of processes used. In the Resolution, a shift occurs in what the MSs are to do. In the first sentence of the report, they are *to remunerate*, *conclude* and *support* whereas in the Resolution, the MSs are *to address*. The former processes (i.e., what is to be done concerning the organization of working time) are taken away and one is merely left with the inference something, some process, will be done to working hours, time, and patterns. The recontextualizations of the processes in this section have thus resulted in an increased generalization of what is to be done. It has gone from a variety of actions (i.e., remunerating, concluding agreements, and supporting) to a single action (i.e., addressing) that presumably has collected some of the former actions expressed in the Report.

The third change occurs at the Participant level. Not only are MSs' actions made more explicit in the Report, but what these actions involve is also included. That is the doings and what the doings are to impact upon are provided. In the Report, the MSs are to remunerate *overtime*, conclude *agreements for flexible working time*, and support *proposals involving the collective shortening of working time* whereas in the Resolution they are to address *the issue of promoting flexibility in the labour market*. In other words, the participants of processes such as overtime and the collective shortening of working time are removed from the Resolution and are substituted by the Participant: *the issue of ...* . So, instead of having the components that make up the organization of working time as participants, the Resolution makes labor market flexibility the main participant. The recontextualization, therefore, moves towards Neo-liberalist issues of flexibility, leaving the ways of organizing working time as merely adjuncts to Neo-liberalist concerns. Furthermore, much of the information in the Report that was contained in Participants is now moved into the circumstances of the Resolution. The Participants — overtime and the collective shortening of working time — are recontextualized into a matter circumstance: *with regard to working hours, working time and working patterns (such as career breaks, sabbaticals, etc.).*

The fourth change involves making the taxonomy of working time more general by removing the classifiers of 'working time' nominal groups. So, instead of *over*time, *flexible* working time or *collective shortening* of working hours, the Resolution contains only the bare nominal groups working hours, working time, and working patterns. Aside from claiming that working hours needs to be addressed in regards to labor market flexibility, the Resolution does not make clear what should be done to working hours. Deleted are the specific connections between working time, collective shortening and overtime. The only trace that remains from overtime is a recontextualization of how overtime is to be remunerated (i.e., as a manner clause in the Report) into a parenthetical mention of career breaks and sabbaticals.

The final major change that occurred concerns the Report's position on legislating working time standards. Now, instead of advocating national and European legislation on working time standards, the Resolution advocates that the issue of working time be addressed ... *through a non-legislative, non-compulsory process based on social dialogue at the level of the individual enterprise*. The MSs' role is reduced to that of a facilitator in which the individual enterprise decides on issues of working time organization. Note also that the two sides of industry are no longer included in this social dialogue — or at least not explicitly mentioned as such. So, instead of MSs playing an active legislative role in working time reduction and the two sides of industry negotiating what these working time standards should be, it is the individual enterprise (i.e., management) that is the main decision-maker. Here, issues of working time move from one of authority to one of equality. By claiming that working time is to be addressed through **social dialogue** implies that those affected will take part as

Table 18. The Discursive Transformations occurring in Point 7 of the van Velzen Report to Point 9 of the EP Resolution

Transformations:	Van Velzen Report ⇒	Resolution
Modulation: background directive	EP calls on MSs	EP believes that MSs need to
Generalization: verb collects more meanings	remunerate conclude support	address
Abstraction: information formerly contained within participants is moved into a circumstance	overtime proposals involving the collective shortening of working hours	address the issue … with regard to working hours working time working patterns
Abstraction: classifiers of working time nominal groups are deleted	*over*time *flexible* working time *collective shortening* of working hours	working hours working time working patterns
Abstraction: participants involved in setting working time standards are backgrounded in a circ:location and directive is nominalized and backgrounded in a circ:manner.	fundamental working time standards should be governed by national and European legislation	address the issue … through a non-legislative, non-compulsory process based on social dialogue at the level of the individual enterprise

equals in the decision making process. These five transformations are summarized in Table 18.

As was shown by these transformations, the information contained within the van Velzen Report's section on organization of working time was recontextualized into a more abstract and generalized Resolution. Two other differences between these documents are worth pointing out here. First, purpose has vanished from the organization of working time. From the Report's perspective, a purpose of organizing working time is to maintain or improve workers' living and working conditions. For this reason, a separate purpose-clause is included in the van Velzen report that guarantees compensation for workers' loss of income if working hours are to be shortened. In the Resolution, this part has been deleted. This brings us to the second difference. Rhetorically, these two documents construct different pentadic ratios. While the Report constructed a **purpose:act** ratio by selecting working and living conditions (i.e., time off, service vouchers, compensating workers' loss of income) as the purpose behind organizing working time, the Resolution associates promoting and enhancing labor market flexibility and mobility with the means to do so. In this way, an **agency:act** ratio is constructed in which making labor markets more flexible and mobile is seen in terms of how it is to be done:

Agency	:	Act
a non-legislative, non-compulsory process		promoting flexibility in the labour market
improved mutual recognition of diplomas	⇒	enhancing labour market mobility
portability of pensions		

The Report's inclusion of more 'social' purposes for organizing working time makes the Report more oriented to the effect this organizing will have on workers. In contrast, the Resolution, with emphasis on labor market flexibility, the vital role of SMEs in job creation, and enhancing labor market mobility, places economic and management concerns at the center of working time organization. Hence, the recontextualizations helps to place job creation and the flexibility and mobility of labor markets at the heart of organizing work. So, in effect, EP policy has gone from a pre-dominantly social/authoritative view of organizing work to an economic/individualist-egalitarian view of organizing work.

Those that expressed support in remunerating overtime (e.g., van Velzen and groups such as the PSE, V, and GUE/NGL), in laying down concrete figures for reducing working time, and for legislating working time reduction clearly lost in the final resolution. The Report, which began as a directive to the MSs and the two sides of industry on what to do about organizing working time and how to do it, became a considerably 'weakened' final resolution that expressed a 'belief' on the need to do something about working hours, working time, and working patterns. Although the recontextualization of the Report through deletion, rearrangement, generalization, abstraction, etc. of its contents implies the existence of divergent, alternative, or evolving views, the Resolution obscures this. That is, the Resolution leaves little trace of prior conflict and opposition to those who were not involved or who have no knowledge of the prior process. The various lines of conflict on overtime and working time expressed in the debate are also effaced. What is left in the Resolution are merely a set of weak directives on working time organization that refrain from making specific proposals on what and how. This does not mean, however, that what was written in the final resolution conveys nothing. The Resolution constructs a Neo-liberalist view in which working time is seen in terms of labor market flexibility and mobility. Effaced is the social frame of work organization. Because of this, there's a greater chance that, at the MS level, working time will be interpreted as increasing jobs through increased flexibility and mobility rather than as increasing jobs while improving working and living conditions.

6.   The Presidency Conclusions

The Resolution was not the last word on working time organization. As can be recalled, the Luxembourg Summit produced Presidency Conclusions that serve as guidelines for Member State employment policy was the end of the line on EU employment policy. It is worth examining what aspects of the Resolution had been incorporated into the Presidency Conclusions. In order to do this, a comparison of the transitivity structures of each are made. The Presidency Conclusions are shown below and Point 70 is then analyzed in Table 19.

> Presidency Conclusions: Extraordinary European Council Meeting on Employment Luxembourg (20–21/11/97)
>
> **69.   Modernizing work organization**
>
> In order to promote the modernization of work organization and forms of work:
>
> 70.
>
>   – the social partners are invited to negotiate, at the appropriate levels, in particular at sectoral and enterprise levels, agreements to modernize the organization of work, including flexible working arrangements, with the aim of making undertakings productive and competitive and achieving the required balance between flexibility and security. Such agreements may, for example, cover the expression of working time as an annual figure, the reduction of working hours, the reduction of overtime, the development of part-time working, lifelong training and career breaks;
>
> 71.
>
>   – for its part, each Member State will examine the possibility of incorporating in its law more adaptable types of contract, taking into account the fact that forms of employment are increasingly diverse. Those working under contracts of this kind should at the same time enjoy adequate security and higher occupational status, compatible with the needs of business.

Table 19. Presidency Conclusions Point 70

Process	Participant	Circumstance roles
are invited	the European Council (implicit proposer) the social partners	
to negotiate	agreements	to modernize the organization of work (purpose1) including flexible working arrangements (accompaniment1) at the appropriate levels, in particular at sectoral and enterprise levels (location1) with the aim of making undertakings productive and competitive and achieving the required balance between flexi- and security (purpose2)
may, for example, cover	Such agreements the expression of working time as an annual figure, the reduction of working hours, the reduction of overtime, the development of part-time working, lifelong training and career breaks	

The first difference is seen in the very first process: *are invited*. Recall that the Resolution positions the EP as a senser who expresses a belief that the MSs need to address an issue. In the Presidency Conclusions (PCs), the social partners are invited to negotiate agreements. While the Resolution shifts the directive further down into the next clause (i.e., need to ...), the PCs make use of a weak directive (i.e., invite). In both documents, backgrounding the directive weakens modulation. Note also that in the PCs it is not the MSs but the social partners that are being directed. This quite clearly removes any involvement from the MSs on issues of organizing working time.

The second difference involves the processes. Both documents used generalized verbs to state what the proposees are to do. In the Resolution it is *address* and in the PCs it is *negotiate*. However, the verb negotiate, unlike *to address*, carries the additional implication that more than one party is to be involved in coming to an agreement and that an outcome is expected. Although address does not have this specific implication it may nonetheless still be implied. That is, addressing an issue may mean negotiating an issue, doing a study on an issue, introducing an issue, supporting an issue, etc. In other words, addressing something is more generalized than negotiate since *to negotiate* may fall under the list of activities that constitute *to address* but not vice versa. One can, for instance, address an issue by negotiating it with someone but one cannot really negotiate an issue with someone simply by addressing it.

The third difference involves the way in which 'working time' terms are grammatically constructed. Recall that the Resolution referred to organizing working time in the abstracted forms: working hours, working time, and working patterns. Although the PCs also contain abstracted forms, these abstracted forms express more information — meaning the information is recoverable from the nominal group itself and not merely implied — since a host of descriptive terms are used to classify the types of work organization that should be negotiated. These include *flexible* working arrangements, the expression of working time *as an annual figure*, the *reduction* of working hours, the *reduction* of *over*time, the development of *part*-time working, lifelong training and career breaks. These descriptive terms tend to unpack some of the numerous bits of information contained within such abstracted, generalized forms as working hours, working time, and working patterns.

The fourth difference is found at the level of circumstance. The PCs contain two purposes whereas the Resolution does not. The PCs' purpose of organizing working time is most compatible with Neo-liberal arguments. That is, making sectors and enterprises productive, competitive, flexible, and secure. In both documents, however, the social aspects of working time are excluded while job creation is highlighted.

The final difference involves the groups that are to negotiate or address the organization of working time. The Resolution directs the MSs to address issues of working time with individual enterprises. In contrast, the PCs direct the social partners to negotiate with sectors and enterprises. The Resolution explicitly states that the organization of working time is to be non-legislative and non-compulsory. While the PCs are not explicit about this it is nonetheless implied. Since the PCs do not make mention of the MSs in regard to modernizing work organization, it may be assumed that any agreements made will be non-legislative. This is because the social partners or enterprises do not have the ability to legislate these matters. The differences between the Resolution and the PCs are summarized below. These differences should not be viewed as recontextualizations from the Resolution to the PCs because the EC did not directly take information from the Resolution. The EC had a number of documents from the EP, EC, social partners, expert groups, etc. that were all taken into consideration when tabling the PCs. The differences, therefore, should be regarded more in terms of intertextuality; that is, what components of the transitivity structure are similar or different. An intertextual comparison of the two documents is given below in Table 20.

Table 20. An intertextual comparison of the EP Resolution and the Presidency Conclusions

Transformations	Resolution	Presidency Conclusions
Modulation: both documents background the command	EP believes that MSs need to	social partners are invited to
Generalization: both processes are generalized but address may subsume negotiate and is therefore more generalized	to address	to negotiate
Abstraction & Generalization: nominal groups of PCs are less generalized since they contain more descriptive information	working hours working time working patterns	working time as an annual figure the reduction of working hours the reduction of overtime the development of part-time working, lifelong training and career breaks
Purpose is not mentioned in the EP Resolution and is provided in the Presidency Conclusions.	(purpose is not mentioned)	to modernize the organization of work with the aim of making undertakings productive and competitive and achieving the required balance between flexibility and security
Abstraction: in both documents, participants involved in organizing working time are backgrounded in a circ:location	address the issue ... through a non-legislative, non-compulsory process based on social dialogue at the level of the individual enterprise	negotiate agreements ... at the appropriate levels, in particular at sectoral and enterprise levels

In sum then, the transitivity structure of the PCs on modernizing work organization contains a less generalized process, less abstracted and generalized nominalizations, and an explicit purpose. With this purpose, the PCs are able to construct a **purpose:act** ratio in which modernizing the organization of work and making undertakings productive and competitive are seen as the reason behind organizing working time (i.e., negotiating agreements on the expression of working time as an annual figure, the reduction of working hours, the reduction of overtime, the development of part-time working, lifelong training and career breaks).

Purpose	:	**Act**
modernizing the organization of work	$\Rightarrow$	organizing working time
making undertakings productive and competitive		

What both share in common, however, is a liberalist view that supports the creation of an environment of productivity, competitiveness, and flexibility. Consider the next Point in the PCs as analyzed in Table 21:

Table 21. Presidency Conclusions, Point 71

Process	Participant	Circumstance roles
	the European Council (implicit proposer) each Member State (implicit proposee)	
will examine	each Member State the possibility of incorporating in its law more adaptable types of contract	
taking into account	the fact that forms of employment are increasingly diverse	
should ... enjoy	Those working under contracts of this kind adequate security and higher occupational status, compatible with the needs of business	

Three differences are worth pointing out here. First, the MSs are directed to deal with employment contracts. This is in stark contrast to the Resolution that directed the Commission and the two sides of industry to deal with this issue. In addition the PCs also suggest introducing legislation on the matter. It may therefore be implied that the shift from the Commission to the MSs suggests that legislation remain in the domain of the MSs and not of the Commission. What is being advocated is national rather than European standards on employment contracts. Second, the uncommon sense taxonomies of the Resolution (i.e., atypical, irregular, full-time) are deleted in the PCs. Instead, we find descriptions referring to non-full-time and full-time work as *diverse* forms of employment and *adaptable* types of contract. The final difference involves a renewed economic focus concerning diverse forms of employment. The Resolution grounded the focus on non-full time forms of employment in issues of social security and employees' rights. This part is not only missing from the PCs but the renewed focus is on the needs of business: *Those working under contracts of this kind should at the same time enjoy adequate security and higher occupational status, compatible with the needs of business.* So, the point is that workers may enjoy adequate social security and higher occupational status *as long as* this security and status does not interfere with the needs of business.

Based on this comparison, the PCs seem to bear very little resemblance to the Resolution adopted by the EP (at least that part on organization of working time). Paradoxically, the PCs have more in common with the van Velzen report. Overtime, which was the first issue in the report and taken out of the final resolution, found its way back into the organization of working time when it was placed into the PCs. Although it is difficult to say with certainty what impact the EP had concerning the PCs, a comparison of the final resolution and the PCs shows that few elements from the Resolution bear much intertextual resemblance to the Council document. The main commonality between the two was their economic, enterprise focus.

7.   Discussion

The ideological dilemma depicted in this chapter involved, at one end, the maintaining or improving of workers' living and working conditions as the motivation behind working time organization. On the other end are the discursive practices that construct the organization of working time in terms of enterprise and worker productivity, security, flexibility, adaptability and competitiveness or increased employment rates. In the latter instance, changes in work organization are always seen with respect to, in terms of, and in accordance with, enterprise flexibility, productivity, and security; in other words, the survival (i.e., profitability) of business.

Employment policy, I would argue, always meets up with these opposing themes in which either the social conditions or the job-getting skills of workers are highlighted. In relation to job creation, policies that aim only to improve workers' working conditions will run into problems in terms of how improving these conditions beget more jobs and the individual worker's role in procuring employment. Or, policies that focus only on employees' attributes of flexibility, competitiveness and adaptability will raise questions about how the worker's working conditions or organized work environment can contribute to job creation. The EP Report found an interesting balance between these contrary themes by focusing the whole report on job creation and un/employment rates and by aligning organization of working time with social concerns. In this way, both sides of the dilemma were made explicit. The emphasis, however, was still mainly on the employability side of job creation. The policies following the Report — the Resolution and the PCs — increased their emphasis of the employability side of job creation by (1) making labor market flexibility and mobility the purpose behind organizing work and (2) obscuring the social side of the dilemma through the discursive practices of abstraction and generalization. So, in the end, the final word in EU policy was more focused on making individuals more employable than on their working and living situations. Although, for an unemployed person, getting a job may improve his or her living situation, it does not necessarily have this effect. Jobs, for instance, may be poorly paid and in this way contribute little to a person's financial well-being. Employment policy, therefore, should be explicit about its social aims with respect to job creation. If it does not, job creation becomes, at best, the concern of 'business' or, at worst, merely a statistic that, when rising, is celebrated by governments.

Chapter 7

Discussion: The EU Committee Regime and the Problem of Public Space

Strategies of Depoliticizing Unemployment and Ideologizing Employment Policies

Gilbert Weiss and Ruth Wodak

1. Introduction

In the preceding chapters different organizational spaces, genres and flows of arguments in EU policy making have been analyzed. In particular, it has been shown how arguments change from one genre to another, from one organizational space to another; how information is construed and transformed through practices of recontextualization; how decisions assume the form of decision premises for further decisions and thereby continuously contextualize and recontextualize organizational processes in a system as complex as the EU. It was no accident that we chose the field of employment policies for approaching the "innards" of this organizational system. Employment is clearly one of those fields of political activity that reveal the manifold problems and difficulties accompanying the process of European integration and supranational institutionalization. What becomes manifest in this realm in particular is not only the conflict between supranationalists and intergovernmentalists, between closer and looser political cooperation of the member states, between the different EU organizational part systems (e.g. the Commission representing "European interests", the Council representing member states interests), but also the tensions and gaps between supranational strategies, national "action plans" and local measures. Furthermore, the question of how efficient employment policies have to be like still evokes ideological answers. Quite often, Neo-liberal positions and Keynesian positions stand diametrically opposed to each other; trade unions have quite different answers to the problem of unemployment than employer representatives; French social democrats have different "solutions" compared to British social democrats. Finally, the *fight against unemployment* is embedded in the more general debate about the relationship between economy and politics on the whole in the *age of late capitalism*, between welfare and market, between (global) economic freedom and (nation state) government regulations. In the chapters of this book we have dealt with these different aspects of employment discourse, conflict and decision-making in the EU organizational system. In the following we will summarize the major results of the study by pointing to crucial problems in the emergence of a supranational political union.

2.   Organization, bureaucracy and politics

With the Commission's Competitiveness Advisory Group (CAG) and the European Parliament (EP) two different organizational spaces representing two different dimensions of public space were analyzed. The CAG, a group of high level experts, works and decides "behind closed doors", so to speak, beyond any public-democratic legitimacy or control. In contrast, the EP represents the only supranational EU body with direct democratic legitimacy, i.e. a mandate of the populations of member states. It constitutes public space in the traditional western-parliamentarian sense. The EP's decision-making is largely transparent and observable from the outside, while the decision-making in committees set up by the Commission is not. Along the lines of the traditional division of powers in the nation state, we might also say that the Commission constitutes the bureaucratic-administrative space, whereas the EP represents the space of political debate. But, as we will see below, this separation — although often applied to the EU political system (see, e.g., Greenwood 1997; George 1996) — is not or only partly true, because the organization of EU decision-making cannot be simply compared with the division of power at the level of nation states. In order to determine the 'new' characteristics of the EU political and organizational system we have to outline briefly what we mean when speaking of bureaucracy, public space and politics in the context of EU institutions.[1]

In Max Weber's *Herrschaftslehre (Domination Theory)*, bureaucracy represents the overall organizational type of rational, i.e. modern, *Herrschaft* (domination). Bureaucratic organization, for Weber, was based on the following characteristics: hierarchical chain of authorities; civil servant status of personnel; exact delimitation of functions, responsibilities and competences; legitimation by virtue of procedure and legal statutes; the bureaucratic actor as executive agent of political decisions; normative separation of administration and politics (Weber

---

1. Of course this does not mean that this classical separation of powers is not to be changed more and more at the national levels too (see Bach 1999).

1976: 126f; Bach 1999: 34; Breuer 1991: 208f; also Chapter 1 in this book). The representative figure of modern bureaucracy was the *"menschlich unbeteiligte, daher streng 'sachliche' Fachmann"* [humanly impartial, therefore strictly objective specialist] (Weber 1976: 563). Although Weber used this ideal type of bureaucracy primarily to describe the modern state and its administration, it was clear to him that bureaucratization had to be regarded as a universal phenomenon absorbing all realms of modern societies. He expected a general expansion of the bureaucratic habitus through advanced Capitalism and the division of labor, i.e. an *"Entwicklung zur rationalen 'Sachlichkeit', zum 'Berufs'- und 'Fachmenschentum'"* [a development to rational objectivity, to professional and specialist humanity] (Weber 1976: 576).

3.   The committee regime and the policy-entrepreneur

If we take Weber's model of bureaucracy and apply it to today's EU organizational system, we face several problems. Weber's model presupposes the differentiation and relative balance of legislative and executive powers as developed in the democracies of the Western nation states. The supranational EU system, however, is different mainly because of the constitutional preponderance of the Commission in the policy-making process. The Commission serves not only as administrator and "guardian of the Treaties" but also monopolizes the right of initiative in the legislative procedure of the Community (Cini 1996). It is truly the initiator and driving force of the decision-making process — not only in a formal but also in a material sense of developing political ideas, concepts and strategies. This structural superiority of the Commission is at the expense of democratic participation in general, and the role of the EP in particular (Corbett, Jacobs and Shackleton 1995). With the Commission taking over not only the *political-administrative* function of the EU organizational system but also an important part of the *political-strategic* function, Weber's concept of the normative separation between politics and administration is no longer valid. The removal of differentiation between the executive and the legislative procedure evokes two interdependent tendencies: (a) the *bureaucratization* of political decision-making processes, and (b) the *politicization* of the administration (Bach 1999: 32). As a result, the bureaucrat is no longer an executive agent of the political system (as in Weber) but becomes him/herself a kind of political actor or, as P. Krugman calls it, a *policy-entrepreneur* (Krugman 1994: 10). Such a policy-entrepreneur is both a *Fachmensch* in Weber's sense, i.e. an expert, and a political strategist. The dominance of policy-entrepreneurs in the EU organizational system goes hand in hand with the emergence of what is called the "committee regime" of EU policy-making — meaning the many highly specialized expert groups developing programs, concepts, strategies in their respective policy fields (Pedler and Schaefer 1996; Schaefer 1996; Bach 1999). It is this network of hundreds of expert groups that shapes EU policy-making and creates a new type of "bureaucratic-expertocratic politics" based on a transnational elite of functionaries (Bach 1999: 99). Political legitimacy in the traditional sense is increasingly being replaced by functional legitimacy by virtue of administrative efficiency and technocratic expertise. As a consequence, the 'real' politicians, i.e. the MEPs, feel more and more excluded from policy-making. Accordingly, conflicts between the EP and the Commission, between parliamentary committees and the Commission's committee regime, are continuously growing. M. Bach summarizes the problem as follows:

> Mit der bemerkenswerten Entdifferenzierung von Legislativ- und Exekutiv-kompetenzen im institutionellen Kernbereich der Europäischen Gemeinschaft sind zweifelsohne optimale Voraussetzungen gegeben für eine funktionalistische Effizienz des Zweckverbandes. Damit ist aber zugleich auch eine Dynamik in Gang gekommen, die in die Richtung der Begründung eines neuen techno-kratischen Herrschaftsgebildes weist. Diese mag den Steuerungsanforderungen der europäisierten und globalisierten Marktgesellschaften entsprechen; die nor-mativen Legitimationsbedingungen der westlichen Demokratien erfüllt es indes-sen nicht. Unter diesen Gesichtspunkten stellt sich das Problem des sogenannten Legitimationsdefizits der Europäischen Gemeinschaft nicht allein als ein Problem der unzureichenden Kompetenzen des Europäischen Parlaments dar. Es stellt sich darüber hinaus die Frage, welche Instanzen die sich instrumentell gebenden Einzelentscheidungen der von den politischen und rechtlichen Kontrollverfahren der Einzelstaaten weitgehend freigesetzten expertokratischen Eliten der suprana-tionalen Fusionsbürokratie kontrollieren, wer deren Voraussetzungen prüft und die Folgen abschätzt. (Bach 1999: 36)

> [With the remarkable removal of differentiation between legislative and execu-tive competences in the core institutional area of the European Community, optimal conditions are undoubtedly created for a functional efficiency in the expert group. But this has also set in motion a dynamic that points in the direction of establishing a new technocratic domination. This may correspond to the control requirements of the Europeanized and globalized market companies, but it does not fulfill the normative conditions of legitimation of Western democracies. In these respects the problem of so-called legitimation-deficit of the European Community appears not only as a problem of the inadequate competence of the European Parliament. It asks the additional question of what bodies control the expertocratic elite of the supra-national fusion-bureaucracy, who are largely freed from the political and legal control procedures of individual states by separately taken empowering decisions; and who examines their rationale and assesses the consequences.]

In Chapter 4 of this book, R. Wodak presented an example of this "expertocratic elite", the CAG. There, policy-entrepreneurs at work were analyzed. U. Beck, although not using the word policy-entrepreneur, gives a good description of what such policy-entrepreneurs generally do: mostly organized in "epistemic communities", i.e. "transnational knowledge and expertise communities", they "process, possess and provide common definitions of problems, assumptions of causes and policy recommendations" (Beck 1998: 39). Typically, this becomes articulated in so-called *policy papers*. And indeed, the aim of the CAG meetings analyzed was to produce a policy paper for the European Council. Wodak elaborated how this policy-paper developed, how the discussions in the group were recontextualized in the various drafts up to the final paper. It was shown what argumentation chains were created, how the problem of unemployment was defined, and what causes and what solutions to the problem were construed. The results make clear that what Beck draws attention to in the above quotation is precisely what happened in the committee.

Against the background of this new type of *bureaucratic-expertocratic politics*, the borderline between technocratic expertise on the one hand and political action on the other is becoming blurred. It can no longer be determined without ambiguity who is a politician or diplomat and who is an expert, and what actually separates the former from the latter (also Wodak et al. 1998; Wodak and Vetter 1999). In order to demonstrate the politicization of the administrative-bureaucratic complex of the Commission through the committee regime — which, at the same time, means a depoliticization of policy-making in the traditional sense — we will quote the beginning of the "Recommendations" section from the CAG's policy paper. The section starts with the following paragraph:

To subject any government policy to two criteria. Both are necessary, but the first ranks first:
–   to contribute to making the national economy more competitive, which is key to spur sustainable growth and employment;
–   to maintain and improve social cohesion, which increases adaptability and the willingness to change. But measures designed to enhance social cohesion will hurt, over time, the very people they intend to help if they actually impair competitiveness.

The recommendation section which represents the third and last part of the policy paper is preceded by what Beck called *definitions of problems and assumptions of causes* (Chapter 4). Now comes the point when recommendations of what should be done in order to create employment are made. What is immediately evident in this text is that it does not deal with specific questions or problems but with nothing less than overall *political strategies*. There are not just certain elements or parts of government policies that should be subjected to certain criteria; it is rather *any* government policy that has to be subjected to *two* criteria. The experts take a strict position here. Note that *government policy* is positioned as an object in the clause. Since it is the CAG as the recommending subject that positions government policy as an object, it automatically positions itself higher than governments. The expert committee seems to be superior to governmental policy. This fits very well the label of an *advisory* committee: the committee advises, counsels, instructs politicians. Someone who advises somebody apparently must know more than the one who is advised. Since the advice is not about technical details but general political strategies, the experts seem to be the 'real' political strategists behind the official politicians. The cover of P. Krugman's book on "Pop Internationalism" (1998) showing a photomontage of some technocrat-like figure whispering something into US President Bill Clinton's ear emphasizes precisely this point. It is this whispering that epigrammatically describes the main business of the policy-entrepreneur. The committee regime is by constitution a regime of advisers.

The recommendation example of the CAG policy paper illustrates very well the political-strategic function that is increasingly being taken over by the Commission's expert committees within the EU organizational system. What the policy paper offers is not some technical expertise in the narrow sense but a political program — a program that stands above the low points of everyday institutional procedures. Consequently, in the whole recommendation section we find almost no *institutional vocabulary* (see Klein 1988) like, for instance, Commission, Council, EC, EP, Ecofin, Luxembourg Presidency, EMU, etc; no references to previous decisions and texts of EU institutions like, for instance, Amsterdam European Council, European Social Charter, White Paper on Growth, Competitiveness and Employment, etc (Chapter 5). Instead, what dominates the text might be called economic-programmatic vocabulary accompanied by a specific interactional vocabulary (*making economy more competitive, spur sustainable growth, maintain and improve social cohesion, increase adaptability, impair competitiveness*). This vocabulary almost assumes the form of *jargon* of a specific economic position that puts all the emphasis on competitiveness, flexibility and liberalization of labor markets. We will return to this economic position below. At this point, it is important to see that the "expertise" of the CAG is not free of evaluation and ideology. The evaluative and ideological character of the text becomes evident by looking at some of the grammatical resources used: the *two criteria* are introduced by the clause: *Both **are** necessary, but the first ranks first*. Here, we have a relational clause with a Value/Token construction; the same is true for the description of the first of the two criteria (*making the national economy more competitive **is** key to spur sustainable growth and employment*). And identifying clauses construing a Value/Token relation are linguistic tools of evaluating and ideologizing messages (Thompson 1996: 91; Chapter 5). The whole recommendation section is full of such constructions and of modal verbs, mood adjuncts and evaluative lexical choices — all of them strengthening the ideological tone (see appendix). This is indeed a crucial aspect: the expertocratic undertaking is not a neutral enterprise in the sense of the *Dienst an der Sache* ('service of the matter in hand') of the Weberian *Fachmensch*, it rather evaluates and ideologizes. In Chapter 4, it was shown what interests, values and ideological positions were involved in the CAG debate and how the conflicts between them were solved in the written policy paper through practices of recontextualization. Of course, the ideological character of the "expertise" is not surprising, once it turns out that the expertise is *de facto* a political program — and a political program evaluates and ideologizes *per se*. The linguistic analysis, however, proves this point. Furthermore, in order to present its political strategies and to persuade the reader, the CAG uses a common means-end-argumentation: *this is necessary for that, to do this in order to get that*, etc. Consider the following examples:

–   making the national economy more competitive is key to spur sustainable growth and employment
–   to maintain and improve social cohesion increases adaptability and the willingness to change
–   to use structural reform to increase the margin for manoeuvre in macroeconomic policy
–   to promote social dialogue at all levels as the most important way to explain, consult as well as devise and implement the appropriate policies

This structure is again not surprising, because political strategies necessarily imply the presentation of means for reaching political goals. What is a little surprising is that the means are positioned as Theme, i.e. as a given, and the goals as Rheme, i.e. as the new information that is introduced. This gives the impression that the means are clear and unquestionably given, while the goals have to be introduced and explained. Usually, one would expect it the other way round: the goals as the given, and the strategies to achieve them as the important and relevant new information. Here, it is different, however, and even more surprising, since the general goals had already been introduced in the sections preceding the recommendation part. The fact that the strategies are construed as an unquestionably given, ideologizes the text even more insofar as the argument (certain strategies/means in order to achieve general goals) is put beyond any critical discussion. In other words, the policy paper is an argumentative text that does not allow any argumentation about the arguments presented. And indeed, as Wodak showed in Chapter 4, the fundamental argument of the whole paper — to increase competitiveness as the only way to increase employment in a global (market) world — is the given political position that must not be put into question. The *whisperer* is not willing to enter into a critical discussion; what s/he advises is based on his/her expert knowledge — and who would dare to question expert knowledge. Nevertheless, it is important for her/him not to appear as a politician on the stage but to remain the expert behind the scenes, because as a politician s/he would have to expose him/herself to the political debate; as an expert s/he does not have to. This is one of the reasons why the committee regime is so successful.

The analysis of the CAG policy-paper has demonstrated that the Commission's expert committees do not represent a politically neutral space. They rather take positions, develop strategies, build political programs; in other words, they make policies. Here, the expert is no neutral *Fachmensch im Dienst der Sache*, but a policy-entrepreneur. Interestingly enough, in interviews conducted with Commission officials, this was even explicitly stated. Consider the following sequence from such an interview. This excerpt was preceded by the interviewer asking his interlocutor, i.e. the Commission official, to compare his experience in the European Commission with having worked in other multinational organizations like the OECD:

(1)   [...] the European Union is by fa:r ah the most efficient
(2)   and ah closest to the governments
(3)   the closest to the member states.
(4)   cause here we don't make only analysis.
(5)   or we don't make only standards
(6)   we make policy here
(7)   and ah actually
(8)   the Union is is a or Commission is an exTENsion of the — national policy making.

Although the speaker starts with *European Union* as a whole, by using *we* in lines 4–6 he refers to what the Commission is doing. In line 8, this is even strengthened by the shift from *Union* to *Commission* which is described as an *extension of national policy making*. In contrast to the MEPs we interviewed and who identified themselves strongly with their respective political parties (see Straehle 1999), the Commission officials do not describe their policy-making in terms of political parties, interests or programs; from the point of view of the Commission's self-interpretation, there seem to be no party interests and ideological positions involved in the Commission's policy-making beside the one major goal of creating a common Europe — quasi as a *dispositif idéel* (M. Godelier). Commission officials give themselves the image of *idealistic* policy-makers — beyond the (party) struggles of everyday-politics, so to speak.

It is high time to correct the widely accepted image of the Commission as an institution serving no interests other than the purely European and, therefore, embodying the "European idea" *per se* (Cini 1996; Edwards and Spence 1997). This picture diminishes the reality. The committee regime is not only an administrative regime but also a regime that makes policy; and as such it is shaped by a variety of different interests, political positions and ideologies. It absorbs ever more political-strategic functions from the "true" decision-making bodies, i.e. the EP and the Council. The Commission's expertocracy produces, reproduces and transforms political and ideological positions of various kinds. This is not necessarily a bad thing, but one has to be aware of the consequences. The idealistic image of serving only European interests, for instance, becomes less idealistic and more ideological, when it comes to the point of what European interests actually are, what Europe means, what a common Europe should look like, and so on. The fact that these questions are increasingly answered by expert committees 'behind closed doors' changes not only the mechanisms of policy-making but the foundation of Western politics in general. At first sight, such a development definitely does not lead to more democratic participation of the citizens. It seems rather to question the relation between public space and democratic-republican politics as developed in Western nation states. To determine the new constellation we have to investigate the interdependency of politics, public space and democratic participation.

4.   Models of Public Space

S. Benhabib (1992) distinguishes three normative models of public space corresponding "three main currents of Western political thought" (Benhabib 1992: 89): the "agonistic" (H. Arendt, Aristotelian tradition), the "legalistic" (J. Rawls, liberal tradition) and the "discursive" model (J. Habermas, democratic-proceduralist tradition). The first model is rooted in the Athenian polis and Aristotle's idea of the *agora* as the place of common debate, shared reasoning and contestatory public speech of a democratic elite. It can also be called a *civitas* approach that presupposes a community of free, equal and self-governing citizens. In our century, this agonistic approach was significantly elaborated by H. Arendt, for whom political power — in a normative sense — could only result from the free communication of citizens:

> On this model, public space is the space 'where freedom can appear'. It is not a
> space in any topographical or institutional sense: a town hall or a city square
> where people do not 'act in concert' is not a public space in this Arendtian sense.
> But a private dining room in which people gather to hear a *Samizdat* or in which
> dissidents meet with foreigners become public spaces; just as a field or forest can
> also become public space if they are the object and the location of an 'action in
> concert', of a demonstration to stop the construction of a highway or a military
> base, for example. These diverse topographical locations become public spaces in
> that they become the 'sites' of power, of common action coordinated through
> speech and persuasion. (Benhabib 1992: 93)

Action in concert, in this sense, means the manifestation of differences and the argumentative competition (*agon*) between these differences. The "music" that comes out of such a concert is the manifestation of political power. For Arendt, political power, public space and free communication are intimately linked with each other. Accordingly, she sees a decline of public space when politics and the freedom of common action and debate are separate from each other; power is then replaced by violence, and self-determination by external determination (see also Vecchiarelli-Scott/Chelius-Stark 1996). Although Arendt was quite aware that her normative ideas are hardly to be found in historical reality, there are, however, certain limitations in applying them to modern and pluralistic societies (Benhabib 1992: 94f).

The liberal model, drawing mainly on Kant's practical philosophy, focuses on the neutrality of public dialogue, the idea of justice and the problem of the legitimacy of the political in general. Political liberalism is driven by the "search for a just, stable and tolerant political order" (Benhabib 1992: 100). In this search, the idea of neutrality of "free public reason" is essential insofar as it must guarantee the public coexistence of differing and competing conceptions of the good life. This "dialogic neutrality" allows disagreement between parties in discourse, it does not, however, allow disagreement about the fundamental principle of neutrality itself. In this sense, Rawls makes a strict separation between what is a legitimate issue of public and political discussion and what is not. The "private" sphere of the individual's assumptions concerning the good life must not be exposed to political debates, i.e. politicized. Consequently there are two forms of rights between which a political system must clearly distinguish: the rights of political participation and debate, and the rights of individual freedom and privacy. A political system, for Rawls, is just when the latter stands not only outside but also *above* the former. The political liberties, finally, play an "instrumental role" (Rawls) for the preservation and protection of the liberties of an individual's privacy (see also Habermas 1997: 91). Such a strict division between the good, the moral and the private on the one side, and the just, the legal and the public on the other, raises several problems, mainly because, as Benhabib points out, even in modern pluralistic societies "politics is about something other than 'neutrality'" (Benhabib 1992: 99) (also McElhinny 1997 on the blurred distinction between public and private):

> The liberal principle of dialogic neutrality, while it expresses one of the main principles of the modern legal system, is too restrictive and frozen in application to the dynamics of power struggles in actual political processes. A public life, conducted according to the principle of liberal dialogic neutrality, would not only lack the agonistic dimension of politics, in Arendtian terms, but perhaps more severely, it would restrict the scope of the public conversation in a way which would be inimical to the interests of oppressed groups. All struggles against oppression in the modern world begin by redefining what had previously been considered 'private', non-public and non-political issues as matters of public concern, as issues of justice, as sites of power which need discursive legitimation. In this respect, the women's movement, the peace movement, the ecology movements, and new ethnic identity movements follow a similar logic. There is little room in the liberal model of neutrality for thinking about the logic of such struggles and social movements. (Benhabib 1992: 100)

In spite of these limitations, however, there is one aspect crucial to modern political institutions which is strongly emphasized by Rawls' concept, namely that these institutions must not only be just but also be recognized as such. The public must recognize the justice of an institution, and it will do that only when the examination of the justice of this institution is seen as a public process — "open to all citizens to partake in" (Benhabib 1992: 101). For the legitimation of political power, this point is indeed of supreme importance.

J. Habermas' discursive model, based on a theory of communicative action (Habermas 1981), introduces a broader idea of public space. It extends public space from the political realm in a narrow sense — be it Arendt's *agora*, or just and neutral institutions in Rawls' sense — to practical discourses and their normative-rational conditions in general. In this way it also questions the strict division between political liberties on the one hand and private civil liberties on the other. Public space is then "viewed democratically as the creation of procedures whereby those affected by general social norms and by collective political decisions can have a say in their formulation, stipulation and adoption. [...] The public space comes into existence whenever and wherever all affected by general social and political norms of action engage in practical discourse, evaluating their validity." (Benhabib 1992: 105) Since citizens, today, engage in various kinds of practical discourses (e.g., in the frame of social movements), there are various kinds of public spaces, too. Modern societies are characterized by a plurality of public spaces. In any case, from a conceptual point of view, the procedures of communication, for Habermas, are its substance. What such a proceduralist approach focuses on, is, in his own words, "[...] die Kommunikationsvoraussetzungen und Verfahren einer diskursiven Meinungs- und Willensbildung, in der sich der *öffentliche Gebrauch der Vernunft* manifestiert" [..the communicative preconditions and procedures in the discursive formation of opinion and will in which the *public use of reason* is manifest] (Habermas 1997: 93). The *öffentliche Gebrauch der Vernunft*, indeed a crucial notion in Habermas' work, requires democratic procedures which guarantee and secure the political autonomy of citizens; and citizens are only politically autonomous when they can understand themselves as the authors of those laws they are subjected to. Without these democratic procedures a political and legal order would never gain the moral legitimacy it needs in modern and pluralistic societies (Habermas 1997: 92).

All three models described highlight different aspects of public space and have their respective plausibility. For Benhabib, it is clearly the discursive model that is more appropriate for understanding the situation of today than the others. She summarizes:

> Arendt's agonistic model is at odds with the sociological reality of modernity, as well as with modern political struggles for justice. The liberal model of public space transforms the political dialogue of empowerment far too quickly into a juridical discourse about basic rights and liberties. The discourse model is the

> only one which is compatible both with the general social trends of our societies
> and with the emancipatory aspirations of new social movements like the women's
> movement. The radical proceduralism of this model is a powerful criterion for
> demystifying discourses of power and their implicit agendas. (Benhabib
> 1992: 113)

5. Public space, democratic legitimacy and policy-making. The committee regime versus parlamentarian politics

Here, we cannot enter into the discussion of which model is best suited. Quite apart from the fact that such an evaluation is not, in any case, very helpful and mainly fulfils the demands of academic labeling, we want rather to take up those ideas and tools of the various models which can be applied to the specific problems analyzed in this book. At this point, we return to the committee regime of the EU described above and, once again, quote Benhabib:

> Undoubtedly, our societies are undergoing tremendous transformations at the
> present. In western democracies, under the impact of corporatization, the mass
> media and the growth of business-style political associations, like PAC's (Politi-
> cal Action Committees) and other lobbying groups, the public sphere of demo-
> cratic legitimacy has shrunk. (Benhabib 1992: 112)

What Benhabib here calls *business-style political associations* and *PAC's* is precisely what we described as the committee regime of policy-entrepreneurs. The decision-making of these committees behind closed doors has indeed affected the *public sphere of democratic legitimacy*. What does this mean, however, in the case of the EU? The organizational space that is generally associated with the public sphere of democratic legitimacy in EU politics is the EP. In Chapters 5 and 6, the procedures of EP decision-making were analyzed. It was shown how EP decisions are connected to decisions of other parts of the EU organizational system, what decision premises are construed, what competing political positions appear in the debate, how this competition is recontextualized in the movement from print to talk to print, etc. To illustrate the difference between the EP and the CAG in recommending to the European Council, consider the following extract from the EP resolution.

> The European Parliament
> [...]
> 22. Calls on the European Council meeting in Luxembourg to determine the
> procedures for co-ordinating economic policy, drawing up the employment
> guidelines, carrying out monitoring and drawing up annual reports, so that the
> Amsterdam conclusions in the field of employment can be put into practice
> immediately and so that lasting economic growth and ecology, sustainable em-
> ployment, and social security become the top priorities of the economic policy of
> the Union and the Member States; calls on the European Council to declare that

the Monti proposals on the internal market should be adopted as soon as possible given the very positive effect they are expected to have on employment.

This excerpt is taken from the last section of the resolution: *Co-ordination of economic policy*. Like the CAG, the EP assumes an advisory position in the communication to the European Council. The EP recommends just as the CAG does. There are, however, significant differences in how the recommendations are structured. As shown in Chapter 6, the resolution (as well as the preceding Van Velzen report) construes specific discourse identities by positioning the EP in an advisory or commanding role (participant) and some group, entity or institution in the role of the receiver of the advice (co-participant). The receivers alternate between the different points of recommendation: here it is the *European Council meeting in Luxembourg*, the adviser remains the same throughout the resolution, namely the EP. In the CAG paper, by way of contrast, we do not find these participant roles, i.e. discourse identities, in the recommendation section. Neither does the CAG appear as adviser, nor any specific group or body as the receiver of the recommendation. The CAG recommendations show only infinitival constructions without any participant roles (*to contribute to making..., to maintain and improve social cohesion..., to take advantage..., to review social protection systems...*, etc., see appendix). This omission of explicit adviser and receiver can be interpreted as a form of de-agentivization and de-institutionalization of the recommendations. In other words, the CAG, when advising, positions itself at a level that transcends political subjects and institutional contexts, as it were. The expert committee seems to give the following signal: we do not feel bound to political positions and institutional procedures but only to the *Dienst an der Sache*. We do not act as political subjects but as neutral experts — and as such our position is a truly objective one. It is the factuality and objectivity of the expertise that the CAG demonstrates. Consequently there are no personal pronouns to be found in the text either. Furthermore, in almost all clauses which have a subject in the grammatical sense, the object of the expertise takes on the role of the grammatical subject (e.g., *But **measures** [...] will hurt...,Only through collective effort will **structural reform** [...] be fruitful, ...the **balance** among the variety of taxes [...] is optimal with respect..., **Proper social protection** is even more necessary, The **reform** of social protection systems must consider..., **Pay-as-you go pension systems** are threatened by..., **Health insurance systems** also face the consequences, **Lifelong learning** has become...*, etc. see Appendix 3). The image of factuality and objectivity of what is stated in the recommendations is also emphasized by the many relational and existential processes dominating the text (relational: *Both **are** necessary, ... which **is** key to, It would **be** a dangerous error, It would **be** deplorable and dangerous if, proper social protection **is** even more necessary, Eliminating abuse and fraud **is** necessary but will not **be** enough, It **is** important that unemployed people, improving education and training **is** also* *indispensable,* etc.; existential: ***There is** a need to ensure,* ***There is*** *evidence,* ***There are*** *three priorities*; see Appendix 3). On the other hand, as was said above, relational processes, particularly those showing Value/Token structure, are linguistic tools to incorporate ideological values into the text (Halliday 1994: 126). They evaluate and ideologize messages but — and this is the decisive point — in the CAG paper they do so by *hiding* the evaluating subject behind it. The CAG does not appear as adviser, and it does not address any specific receiver of the advice. Here we find policy-making without political subjects. When political subjects are missing, however, then the responsibility for policy-making is not *suable* either. Political responsibility requires a political subject that can be held responsible.

The EP recommendations are different. They clearly show us who the adviser is, and who is the receiver of the advice. Here, political responsibility is not hidden, rather it is precisely the goal of the text to point to the specific political responsibilities of those groups, organs, institutions to which the recommendations are directed: *The EP calls on the Member States to improve..., The EP urges the Commission to exercise..., The EP calls on the Commission and the Council to assess..., The EP calls on Ecofin to devote..., The EP calls on the European Council to make..., The EP calls on the two sides of industry to...,* etc. It is visible who has to do what and who is responsible for what (even if the recommended action remains rather vague, Chapters 5 and 6). The text does not focus on what is good and what is bad (in the sense of ideology or *Weltanschauung*) but on what has to be done by whom. Accordingly, we find almost no relational processes in the whole resolution. This does not mean, of course, that the EP operates beyond ideologies. On the contrary, the EP, just like any parliament in the Western world, is naturally dominated by struggles between various political parties and ideologies. But these struggles take place in the committee sessions and the plenary debates preceding the final resolution (see Chapter 6). The final resolution itself does not so much present political arguments as the result of arguments and counter-arguments debated in various EP committees and the plenary session. And the result necessarily has to refer to institutional procedures, tasks and responsibilities. In contrast to the (hidden) ideological-argumentative character of the CAG text, we might call the EP resolution an institutional-procedural text. This does not mean, however, that political positions or ideological compromises are not manifest in the resolution. It means rather that the latter does not primarily develop a political program, a *Weltanschauung*, but a catalogue of organizational duties and responsibilities within the given institutional-procedural frame. This point becomes evident when we look at the prominence of institutional vocabulary occurring in the text (e.g., *European Council, Council, Commission, Ecofin, Employment Committee, Monti proposals, White paper, Community Charter,* etc.). Furthermore, as was shown in Chapter 5, the decisions taken by the EP continuously refer to previous EU decisions and canonical texts in the field of employment policies as *decision premises* of the actual decision. In other words, the EP resolution is deeply embedded in the organizational system of the EU and its history of decision-making on employment. The CAG paper, in contrast, does not show any of these premises. It seems to stand outside the EU organizational system and its institutional procedures; on the other hand, it certainly does represent this system, since the latter is more and more dominated by expert or advisory groups (Bach 1999).

Both the EP resolution and the CAG paper took an advising position vis-à-vis the European Council meeting in Luxembourg. Now one question is of course of immediate interest: Did the European Council follow this advice, did it take it into consideration at all? Although it is difficult to say with certainty what impact these two documents had concerning the Presidency Conclusions of the summit, a comparison of the EP resolution and the Presidency Conclusions shows that virtually nothing from the resolution was recontextualized into the European Council document (see Chapter 6). With regard to the CAG paper, it is even more difficult to say because -as already shown — this text develops a very general economic-political program without becoming too specific about particular measures, and about who has to do what. Certainly the overall dominance of globalization rhetoric and competitiveness as the *sine qua non* of employment policies that characterizes the CAG paper is not to be found in the Presidency Conclusions. For instance, the term *globalization* does not occur a single time in the Conclusions. Nevertheless, the idea that "strengthening the competitiveness of the European economy" (European Council Doc/97/23: 6) is the major tool for increasing employment is present throughout the Conclusions. In the section *Community policies in support of employment*, the heading of the first paragraph even says *Internal market competition and competitiveness* (European Council Doc/97/23: 5). However, the document that influenced the Presidency Conclusions most was the Commission's *Proposal for Guidelines for Member States Employment Policies 1998* (Chapter 6). The second part of the European Council document which introduces the actual employment guidelines — *Improving employability, Developing entrepreneurship, Encouraging adaptability in businesses and their employees, Strengthening the policies for equal opportunities*– and therefore presents what is really the crucial information of the whole document, is almost exclusively taken from the Commission's proposal.

6.   Ideological Experts and Powerless Politicians?

Let us now, on the basis of these results, return to the problem of public space. Does Benhabib's verdict that the *public sphere of democratic legitimacy has shrunk* apply to EU policy-making? Do our results confirm such a shrinking?

This question cannot be answered by a simple yes or no — at least not on the basis of the studies conducted in this book. The problem is too ambivalent and certainly would require further investigations of EU decision-making procedures and discourses. What does follow from our analyses, however, is that the tendencies of both *bureaucratization* of political decision-making processes and *politicization* of the administration (Bach 1999: 32) significantly shape the relation between organizational, political and public space. The main point here is the emergence of ever more organizational spaces (even in a topographical sense) that are at the same time political but not public spaces. The many so-called expert committees and groups — like the CAG — meeting 'behind closed doors' somewhere in the Commission buildings in Brussels do increasingly constitute political spaces that cannot be considered public spaces in a normative sense for several reasons: (1) these groups do not represent a democratic elite in the Arendtian/Aristotelian sense of the *polis* but a *functionary elite*; they are not based in a *demos* nor a *civitas* but in a transnational network of interest and lobbying groups;[2] it is not the power of arguments in Arendt's sense (rationality, objectivity and factuality) that decides the outcome of the communication but the power of ideologizing arguments efficiently, i.e. making a subjective position look objective and constructing factuality by leaving out the facts of (economic) reality. (2) The committee regime does not illustrate a just institution in Rawls' sense, for it operates largely in a legal vacuum. Furthermore, since committee policy-making is not "open to all citizens to partake in", it will not be recognized as just by the public either, and, therefore, not only lacks political legitimation but also undermines the legitimacy of EU policy-making as a whole. (3) The expert committees do not constitute practical discourses in Habermas's sense but rather the reverse, namely technocratic discourses. The increasing technocratization of political discourse goes hand in hand with a decrease in the political autonomy of citizens. Accordingly, from a proceduralist perspective which views public space "democratically as the creation of procedures whereby those affected by general social norms and by collective political decisions can have a say in their formulation, stipulation and adoption" (Benhabib 1992: 105), the EU committee regime not only affects but rather contradicts an emancipatory idea of public space. The use of technocratic rationality in the exclusive club of transnational functionaries certainly does not relate to Habermas's *öffentlicher Vernunftgebrauch*.

---

2. Although one could argue that, as in the case of the CAG, this network includes the social partners representing different interests of different parts of the European *demos*, it is clearly the case that certain parts of this *demos* (e.g., the industrial and financial sector) have a strong "voice" in the committee-*action in concert*, while others (e.g., the unemployed) have none at all (which is also evident from the CAG data).

7. Depoliticizing politics. The rhetoric of globalization and competitiveness

Although it is not easy to say to what extent the CAG policy paper actually influenced the decision-making of the European Council in Luxembourg, the mere existence of such an advisory group giving recommendations to the heads of state, and the very fact that it is difficult to say what influence it had, document very well the dominance of the committee regime in EU policy-making. We should not forget that the European Council does not decide about various everyday-political questions, but about the overall political-strategic guidelines of the Union. At such a level, the advice can *per se* not be technical but only strategic. Also, the CAG was asked for its contribution not by the European Council itself but by the President of the Commission — which is a further indicator for the Commission's dominating role even at the highest level of Union politics. On the other hand, the EP which, to a large extent, fulfils the criteria of all three models of public space, adopted an institutional-procedural catalogue of what has to be done by whom in order to increase employment. This catalogue, although formally serving as a decision premise of the decision to be taken by the European Council, apparently did not have much influence on the Presidency Conclusions. Altogether, it is the following picture of EU policy-making that emerges: an expert committee operating beyond a clear legal framework and democratic legitimacy supplies the heads of state with a *political program*, while the EP, as a truly political organ with democratic legitimacy, limits itself to a catalogue of procedural measures within a given institutional fame. In the first case, we have an organizational, non-public space that, under the cloak of an expertise, takes over political-strategic functions, while in the second case an organizational and at the same time public space sacrifices general political strategies in favor of practicable measures. This seems to be a perfect example of the technocratization of political discourse which — as we have shown — by no means represents a *Versachlichung* of political questions through neutral experts but a hidden ideologization through policy-entrepreneurs. On the other hand, when we go into the content of the CAG's political program we face a paradox: the goal of this 'political' program is precisely to deconstruct unemployment as a *political* problem. The overall dominating globalization rhetoric which positions the competitiveness of an economy in the argumentative center implies that unemployment is not so much a political problem as an economic one. It follows the well known neo-liberal argument that it is not the government that creates jobs but only the economy itself; it is not politicians who create jobs but entrepreneurs; all that politics can do is to let the economy work, so to speak. Accordingly, governments should not politically intervene in the market. On the contrary, the only thing they can do is to guarantee the liberty and flexibility that market forces require. This is the heart of the neo-liberal position which dominates the CAG paper and which very much limits the catalogue of political measures to create employment. For the EP resolution, as opposed to the CAG, unemployment is, however, clearly a political problem. Although, as shown in Chapter 5, the competitiveness and flexibility discourse is present in the document too, the EP asks for political measures and goals in order to improve the employment situation. In other words, we face the paradox that the *institutional-procedural* text of the EP is much more political in terms of actual employment *policies* than the *political* text of the CAG. The political program of the latter consists primarily of depoliticizing the problem, that is of transferring the problem from the *primacy of politics* to the *primacy of the market.* This is of course a delicate enterprise because what preceded the extraordinary European Council meeting in Luxembourg was precisely the claim to put un/employment on the Union's *political* agenda. The difficulty lies in putting something on the political agenda and at the same time depoliticizing it. How did the CAG manage to do this? The answer is: through globalization rhetoric and *the magic formula* of competitiveness. In Chapters 2 and 4 it was shown how globalization rhetoric functions and what central role it takes in neo-liberal economism in general and in the CAG paper in particular. Basically, globalization rhetoric constructs one global economic market where everybody has to compete with everybody. It is, however, not only individuals and enterprises that are constructed as worldwide competitors by this rhetoric but also states, national economies and supranational trade blocks such as the EU. The problem here is that the concept of competition and competitiveness is taken out of its original context, namely a market situation where economic actors compete with each other for profits, and put into a new context where fundamentally non-economic actors, like governments or states, are submitted to the principles of a universal economism. Political actors are then reduced to economic actors and states to big corporations. Politics becomes *ersatz* economics just as, from the contrary perspective, economics becomes *ersatz* politics. According to P. Krugman,

> "[...] the rhetoric of competitiveness — the view that, in the words of President Clinton, each nation is 'like a big corporation competing in the global marketplace' — has become pervasive among opinion leaders throughout the world. [...] A whole industry of councils on competitiveness, 'geo-economists' and managed trade theorists has sprung up in Washington." (Krugman 1998: 4)

Now we can add: this industry has sprung up in Brussels too. As described in various chapters throughout our book, the rhetoric of globalization and competitiveness has little to do with either economic or political reality. It neglects the real economic facts and political problems in many respects. The decisive shortcoming, however, is the construed analogy between political entities and economic entities. Let us summarize with Krugman:

> Most people who use the term 'competitiveness' do so without a second thought. It seems obvious to them that the analogy between a country and a corporation is reasonable and that to ask whether the United States is competitive in the world market is no different in principle from asking whether General Motors is competitive in the North American minivan market. In fact, however, trying to define the competitiveness of a nation is much more problematic than defining that of a corporation. The bottom line for a corporation is literally its bottom line: if a corporation cannot afford to pay its workers, suppliers, and bondholders, it will go out of business. So when we say that a corporation is uncompetitive, we mean that its market position is unsustainable — that unless it improves its performance, it will cease to exist. Countries, on the other hand, do not go out of business. They may be happy or unhappy with their economic performance, but they have no well-defined bottom line. As a result, the concept of national competitiveness is elusive. (Krugman 1998: 6)

Nevertheless, Krugman does not forget to mention that this rhetoric serves certain functions: "Finally, many of the world's leaders have found the competitive metaphor extremely useful as a political device. The rhetoric of competitiveness turns out to provide a good way either to justify hard choices or to avoid them." (1998: 16) This is indeed the crucial point when analyzing political discourse. The rhetoric of globalization and competitiveness has become an argumentative vehicle for disciplining the aims of social justice and welfare by economic arguments. As we have illustrated, the argumentation goes as follows: there are international/global constraints, and in the face of these constraints we cannot pay higher wages, we have to reduce jobs as well as social benefits; the welfare state has to reduce its duties in order to make itself more competitive. Those — like trade unions — who still promote the idea of social justice in the distribution of income have to learn that things have changed. Global competitiveness is the key; and, in order to become competitive states have to use all available means to keep their currency strong and be flexible — flexible in any respect. At the end of the twentieth century, we have to jump again into the "Darwinian Ocean" — as L. Thurow (1996: 166) puts it.

The process of disciplining works essentially on fear. In this, unemployment undoubtedly plays a major role. Here a certain degree of distinction must be made between the primary experience of unemployment (i.e. immediate experience affecting oneself, or a partner, or a family member), and secondary experience (i.e. indirect or acquired experience that there are more and more unemployed, that society is running out of work, and that it could affect me at any time.) This uncertainty and fear of losing one's job is spreading everywhere, it is undermining self-respect and disturbing social relationships even in the most private domains. To put it slightly more cynically: the fundamental problem that undermines a society is not an unemployment rate of 10% but the *fear of unemployment* in the other 90%. Instability and uncertainty are becoming a norm. Again, in the words of R. Sennett: "personal fears are intimately connected to new capitalism" (Sennett 1998: 128).

Let us summarize the two constitutive discourse figures marking the rhetoric of globalization and competitiveness: (1) the de-politicization of socio-economic fields of activity: here the role of the financial markets is important; (2) the passing of the nation state, which is also a passing of the welfare state ("impotence" of the nation state in the face of "new economic constraints"). What is happening in the first figure, in simple terms, is the following: a particular sector of the economy, the financial market, is being made into a universal horizon for the whole of the economy. Simultaneously it is being depoliticized, since it is explained as an inevitable destiny. It is no longer an area of control in the field of political activity, but rather the inalienable framework for this field of activity. Political action then no longer questions this framework but is content to fulfill it adequately; i.e. by guaranteeing competition and flexibility. The construction of economic constraints by the "global" financial markets leads directly to the second discourse figure, namely to the deconstruction of the nation state as an effective and above all responsible political entity. It thereby leads simultaneously to the invocation of new supra-national units of action. Confronted by these economic constraints, the nation state is said to be overburdened, or powerless, and supranational entities such as the EU must take its place. Now even if the nation state is by no means as powerless as it is said to be, this type of argument does have a degree of plausibility. The snag with this is that an effective and integrated supranational entity of this sort does not yet exist — particularly in the area of social policy and welfare. Precisely in this area the EU is still a "project in a state of uncertainty" (H.-P. Müller 1997: 817). This uncertainty between the end of the old model (nation state) and the development of a new model (supranational institutions) opens up a political vacuum that permits the financial players in particular to play their game without too much interference from political regulations. The rhetoric of competitiveness promotes an anti- or at least apolitical liberalism. This apolitical liberalism strengthens the position of economic experts and policy-entrepreneurs in political discourse. This leads us back to the committee regime and the CAG. In the CAG paper, the problem of unemployment is depoliticized through globalization and competitiveness rhetoric, and, at the same time, it is ideologized. Here we can very well apply the three functions of ideology proposed by Mumby (1988: 86) following Giddens (1979) (see Chapter 1): (1) *The representation of sectional interests as universal.* It is primarily one sector of the economy, namely the financial market, that is being made into a universal horizon of the whole of the economy, and, in a further step, also of politics. (2) *The denial or transmutations of contradictions.* As elaborated by Muntigl in Chapter 1, this point implies that opposing interests are reformulated as superficial or wrong. In the CAG paper, this was realized through the "Contrary to what many people believe"-constructions, i.e. by positioning opposing interests and concepts as the "belief of the people" — in contrast to the "knowing of the experts" — into the realm of irrationality; (3) *The naturalization of the present through reification*, meaning that "hegemonic relations, hierarchies, unequal participation [...] are socially constructed as natural, ahistorical, and devoid of time and space" (Chapter 1). In the CAG paper, this was realized by the two-step argumentative transformation, described in Chapters 2 and 4, of contingency into necessity, and necessity into virtue. In other words, an economic development — financial markets, competitiveness, flexibility — which, like any development across time and space, is contingent, is declared to be a necessity determined by destiny, and in a further step this necessity becomes a virtue.

The economic ideology underlying all of this is basically Neo-liberalism. Although many interviewees and also members of the CAG continuously stress the new European identity that should differ from the "Asian tigers" and the USA, the proposed ideologies and recommendations are very similar. Only further investigations of the new employment policies of the member states will allow insight into the implementation of the general recommendations and illustrate the impact of globalization and competitiveness rhetorics in the EU debates.

Since the Maastricht Treaty the EU considers itself to be a *political* union. And as a political union it must be able to solve political problems. If mass unemployment is the major political problem in Europe — which it apparently is from the perspective of the "bulk of the population" — , then the legitimacy of the EU as a political union will crucially depend on how this problem is dealt with: whether it is dealt with by a transnational elite of policy-entrepreneurs or on the basis of a *public sphere of democratic legitimacy* (Benhabib). Admittedly such a union is still a project in the making. So far, however, it is the committee regime with its non- or pseudo-institutional frame which seems to be characteristic of the emerging EU policy complex. The formation of the political union is also impeded because the EU still lacks a common constitution (Henningsen 1998). And a political entity lacking a political constitution is a rather questionable entity. On the other hand, if the EU manages to give itself a constitutional frame built on the European model of democracy, public space, welfare state, social justice and individual freedom, then Europe will be able to maintain or regain the primacy of politics — even in the face of highly dynamic financial markets. A European Union without an institutionalized "social appeal" (Henningsen), however, is only an illusion — a dangerous illusion that might sooner or later explode in one direction or another.

Appendix

Appendix 1. Competitiveness Advisory Group (CAG): long sequence from meeting 19 September 1997, Jean-Claude Paye: pp. 2–3

Paye:
I don't know what- ……..
…peut être réunion en cadre plus restreint qu'il n'était, qu'il n'était prévu, puisque nous avons reçu eh y compris à la dernière minute eh des regrets de quelques membres qu'ils n'ont pas pu venir, certains d'entre eux ont envoyés des papiers, eh, Mr.Monks a envoyé un papier, Mr.Tronchetti Provera a envoyé un papier, qui s'ajoute à ceux que nous avons reçu notamment du Premier Ministre Eyskens et de Mr.Vallance, et de Mr.Fanjul que nous avions déjà. J'ai pour ma part comme je vous l'avais promis eh, essayé de eh, regrouper dans un document qui vous a été diffusé je pense au début de la semaine quelques idées sur… pour orienter la discussion aujourd'hui, vous vous rappellerez en tout cas ce que était la à notre précédente réunion que eh, premièrement nous avons décidés de faire un document pour la session spéciale du Conseil Européen sur l'emploi, qui va se tenir, la date est maintenant certaine, le 21 novembre, nous avons décidés que étant donné la brièveté des délais nous ferions eh, nous-même ce document c'est à dire sans faire appel à des, à des experts extérieurs et que nous essayerions de faire un document qui soit eh, aussi bref, aussi punchy, aussi pédagogique eh, et aussi concret que possible. Car ça fait évidemment beaucoup de eh, d'objectifs eh, qui ne sont pas aisé a rendre conciliable mais je vois qu'il faut s'y efforcer.

Le document que je vous ai envoyé eh, dans la lettre qu'il accompagnait j'ai expliqué aussi clairement que je pouvais mais aussi brièvement possible que je ne le considérais pas comme eh, le projet du document à envoyer au eh, Chefs d'État et de gouvernements. Je le considérais comme eh, une espèce de, de check-list en quelque sorte eh, pour nous aider aujourd'hui a vérifier eh, deux, deux choses, la première c'est que nous restons d'accord sur eh, la ligne que nous avions eh, définie eh, à notre précédente réunion, c'est à dire eh, et que je viens de rappeler, c'est à dire de faire eh, un rapport eh, court, pédagogique, punchy et concret, et deuxièmement et surtout eh, passer en revu les différentes lignes d'action possibles de telle sorte que eh, nous voyons entre nous, premièrement que nous n'oublions pas de secteurs ou il y aurait des recommandations ins-importantes a faire et deuxièmement que nous essayons dans chaque secteur d'identifier, et ce n'est pas fait dans le papier, d'identifier quelques ehz, actions eh, concrètes sur lesquelles nous voudrions mettre eh,l'accent. Je, je suis parti eh, en faisant ce papier des convictions qui sont, qui sont les miennes et que je vous avais exposés, eh, c'est à dire que eh, la situation européenne en terme de compétitivité n'est pas aussi bonne qu'elle pourrai l'être et par conséquent eh, il faut à la fois être eh, alarmiste et optimiste parce que eh, la réalité fondamentale fait que nous avons en Europe eh, des atouts eh, importants, et qu'il faut savoir exploiter au plus vite. La deuxième conviction ou constatation que, que je fais c'est que eh, nous avons les uns et les autres eh, des convictions, des origines, des expériences qui sont différentes. Et que il nous faut essayer de tirer profit de cette diversité mais arriver à quelque chose qui si possible soit eh, la vue commune que eh, nous avons. Donc ce document je le répète est simplement eh, un, un canvas eh, et eh, si vous en êtes d'accord je voudrais suggérer que nous le passions en revue rapidement et que vous me disiez très, très directement, très franchement eh, si eh, cela vous parait eh, utilisable eh, comme, eh, base en suite pour le document final, mais le document final devrait être à mon avis très différent dans sa présentation, c'est à dire qu'il devra être plus eh, politique si je puis dire et plus concret à la fois c'est à dire qu'il faut qu'on sélectionne-sélectionnions un petit nombre, un petit nombre eh, de de thèmes et d'action eh, proposés, un petit nombre de recommandations. La une des difficultés que nous avons, que nous aurons à l'évidence en, en sélectionnant des actions, c'est que eh, y, il faut nous tenir à mi-chemin entre eh, deux dangers eh, opposées. Et un premier danger qui est eh, vous n'êtes pas assez concrets, vous restez trop générales, trop dogmatiques en quelque sorte et vous affirmez sans démontrer. Ca c'est un premier danger et si eh, nous ne remédions pas à ça, si nous n'évitons pas ce danger, le, le papier n'aura pas d'impacte. Et à l'autre extrême, eh, le danger quand on propose des actions concrètes c'est que eh, en certain nombre de pays auxquels nous nous adressons eh, disent: "Ah oui, mais ça a marché au Pays-Bas, ça a marché en Nouvelle-Zélande, ça marche aux États-Unis mais, ça ne peut pas marcher chez nous, parce que la situation est différente, parce que les traditions sont différentes etcetera etcetera."

Donc il faut, il faut faire attention à mon avis eh, à à ne pas eh, sortir une liste d'action qui soit simplement une espèce de de d'inventaire et surtout d'inventaire trop long dans lequel finalement personne ne retiendrai les choses parce que certaines actions, les pays diraient, certains pays diraient: "Mais nous les avons déjà faites" et d'autres actions les pays diraient „Elles ne sont pas réalisables chez nous." Donc c'est la je crois le, le, la difficulté eh, de de notre tâche, c'est à dire eh, trouver le, le juste, le juste milieu entre ce qui apparaîtra comme de l'affirmation dogmatique ou de l'acte de foie et ce qui à l'opposé apparaîtrai comme des recommandations pratiques mais eh, non-généralisables parce que trop liées à eh, au, aux spécificités de tel ou tel pays. Une fois que nous aurons eh, discuté un petit peu cela je voudrais si vous en êtes d'accord que eh, nous commencions à réfléchir eh, entre nous eh, à, à la suite des opérations après le 21 novembre, c'est à dire que eh, j'aimerai que nous commencions et on peut le faire notamment au cours du déjeuner que nous allons passer ensemble que nous essayons de, de voir quelles sont les, les thèmes que nous voudrions eh, retenir et, et approfondir eh, lors des prochains rapports que nous devrons faire, là à priori je pense que i, i, il faudra que nous nous inspirions un peu de la, la pratique de nos prédécesseurs eh, c'est à dire eh, avoir quelques, quelques eh, eh, thèmes sur lesquelles on concentre le, le rapport et eh, avoir eh, une, une bonne base eh, de scientifique si je peux dire eh, afin, apporter une démonstration et en même temps en tirer eh, des recommandations qui soient, qui soient concrètes. Mais il y a une eh, grande variété de, de sujets sur lesquels je crois que notre groupe pourrait se, se pencher et, et j'aimerais bien que nous en, en parlions à déjeuner si vous le voudriez. Je ne sais pas si Mr. Jacquemin à ce stade quelque chose a, a ajouter, peut-être un mot sur votre papier si vous l'avez diffusé, Mr. Jacquemin.

Appendix 2: CAG policy paper *Employment for Europe*, final version: pp.4–13

Competitiveness Advisory Group, Competitiveness for Employment, Report to the President of the Commission and the Heads of State and Government for the European Jobs Summit (*November 1997*)

COMPETITIVENESS FOR EMPLOYMENT

The CAG considers that the highest priority for EU countries is the creation of jobs and the reduction of unemployment. It is the conviction of the Group that the only way to reach this goal fully and sustainably is through competitiveness. Europe's ambition must be to return to the top rank of the world economy. That is what will win the fight for employment.

The challenge is formidable. The world economy has embarked on an ever-faster process of trade expansion and technological progress, and now has moved to ever-fiercer competition. The consumer benefits and every country in the world has the opportunity to become part of the broad stream of collective development. Globalisation is therefore an irreversible process.

But it is also a demanding process, and often a painful one. Economic progress has always been accompanied by destruction of obsolete activities and creation of new ones. The pace has become swifter and the game has taken on planetary dimensions. It imposes deep and rapid adjustments on all countries — including European countries, where industrial civilisation was born. Social cohesion is threatened by a widespread sense of unease, inequality and polarisation. There is a risk of a disjunct between the hopes and aspirations of people and the demands of a global economy. And yet social cohesion is not only a worthwhile political and social goal; it is also a source of efficiency and adaptability in a knowledge-based economy that increasingly depends on human quality and the ability to work as a team.

It is more than ever the duty of governments, trade-unions and employers to work together
- to describe the stakes and refute a number of mistakes;
- to stress that our countries should have high ambitions and they can be realised; and
to implement the necessary reforms consistently and without delay.

Failure to move quickly and decisively will result in loss of resources, both human and capital, which will leave for more promising parts of the world if Europe provides less attractive opportunities.

I. Explaining the stakes and refuting the mistakes

Contrary to the belief of many people, unemployment is not the unavoidable consequence of a globalised economy. All countries are exposed to globalisation and yet the unemployment rate is lower in the USA or Japan than in Europe. And within the European Union, the situation differs vastly from one country to another and among regions within countries.

Contrary to the belief of many people, competition from developing countries characterised by low wages and weak social and environmental standards is not the main cause for unemployment in European countries. Again, the example of other major industrialised countries proves that. Furthermore, most EU countries run a positive trade balance with developing countries.

Contrary to the belief of many people, employment has not fallen in Europe. But it is true that employment creation has been unable to match the growth in labour force due to demography and the increasing number of women in the labour market.

Contrary to the belief of many people, even though there is a long-term trend towards less working time because of productivity gains, work sharing, to the extent that it rests on the static assumption that there is a given amount of work to share, is not the best way to create sustainable employment. Economic activity is a collective creation: work creates employment.

Contrary to the belief of many people, house keeping in accordance with the Maastricht criteria does not cause unemployment. It is a prescription for health and ensures credibility with markets which, in today's economy, is critical for growth and employment. Those countries, inside and outside Europe, that meet these criteria of good management, are often the countries with falling unemployment.

Contrary to the belief of many people, laws to protect existing jobs do not enhance job creation. They serve worthwhile purposes of human dignity and increase the motivation for investing in human capital. But they often deter entrepreneurs from hiring, out of fear of not being allowed to reduce their staff if necessary. This is particularly true of smaller enterprises, even though they are the main potential source for job creation. When laws hamper firms' capacity to innovate and adapt, they eventually trap the workers they intend to protect in doomed companies.*

Contrary to the belief of many people, the growing gap between the direct wages for non-skilled and skilled workers — which is evident in the USA — does not mean necessarily that the actual disposable income of the poorer is declining. There are means to move from the direct wage inequality — which the market economy uses to reflect differences in skills — to the level of collective fairness that European countries deem appropriate.

II. Strong points of Europe

In facing worldwide competition, Europe has a number of strong points that justify the ambition it should have for strong competitiveness, growth and employment.

The economy is now more than ever based on knowledge and the ability to exploit it. The education level, research capacity and cultural diversity which characterise Europe are decisive factors contributing to creativeness, and therefore innovation and progress.

European countries have long practised the rule of law, through solid institutions and rules which provide security, justice, accountability and predictability. Such values are indispensable for strong economic development.

European countries have a commitment to social cohesion, which promotes the full realisation and optimal use of each individual's potential. The less the fear of the future and the sense of unfairness in the society, the more people will be willing to change and will increase European competitiveness.

European countries are irreversibly engaged in building a union which, by virtue of its size and approach, with enable each country to take full advantage of its wealth of human resources.

But these qualities can be exploited only if crucial reforms are quickly and resolutely undertaken across the range of policy areas. The Group offers some recommendations that are not intended to be detailed or exhaustive, but that are, in its views, absolute priorities.

III. Recommendations

To subject any government policy to two criteria. Both are necessary, but the first ranks first:
– to contribute to making the national economy more competitive, which is key to spur sustainable growth and employment;
– to maintain and improve social cohesion, which increases adaptability and the willingness to change. But measures designed to enhance social cohesion will hurt, over time, the very people they intend to help if they actually impair competitiveness.

To take advantage of the current economic recovery and the renewed optimism which that instills to accelerate the process of structural reform. It would be a dangerous error to allow economic improvement to detract from necessary reforms.

To use structural reform to increase the margin for manoeuvre in macroeconomic policy. The higher the rate of non-inflationary growth, the more sustainably and the faster the rate of unemployment will fall.

To promote social dialogue at all levels as the most important way to explain, consult as well as devise and implement the appropriate policies. Only through collective effort will structural reform, macro-economic policy and the quest for corporate efficiency be fruitful. It would be deplorable and dangerous if that collective spirit failed to meet the challenges of

---

* The three trade union leaders in the CAG are not **convinced** of the evidence of this assertion on the effects of labour laws. Future work of CAG could assess these effects.

modernising social protection systems, adapting working time and maintaining appropriate wage moderation. But it is also a shared responsibility to ensure that social dialogue effectively contributes to action.

To review all public sector activities that bear on the economy. Governments create wealth by providing services, especially in the fields of security, justice and social cohesion. But the public sector in European countries has become much heavier than in our main competitors, particularly the USA and Japan. Even accounting for tradition and cultural differences, governments must ensure that taxpayer's money is effectively used to enhance competitiveness.

To give priority to assessing how best the reform of tax systems can contribute to sustainable job creation and increased competitiveness. There is a need to ensure that the overall tax burden is matched by adequate level and quality of public sector activities, the balance among the variety of taxes — including taxes on labour — is optimal with respect to employment, and no harmful tax competition takes place among Member States.

To review the legal and administrative environment for doing business, in order to make it less complex and unwieldy. Despite the good intentions of lawmakers and regulators, this red tape is increasingly resented as a straight jacket which deters initiatives, slows down innovation and prevents job creation.

To review social protection systems. Proper social protection is even more necessary when people feel threatened by economic development. But it must foster individual responsibility, mobility and adaptation, and offer the freedom to choose the quantity of work one wants to deliver.

The reform of social protection systems must consider the overall incentive structure to identify where labour policy and social policy, taken together, skew in favour of not working, rather than working. Often unemployment and related welfare benefits, once due account is taken of the interactions with the tax system, combine to provide an income that discourages working for some of the unemployed (the unemployment trap) or prevent them from working harder when they get a part-time or low-paid job (the poverty trap).

Elements to be reviewed include:

Pay-as-you-go pension systems are threatened by demographic pressures. The risk is aggravated in a number of countries by a tendency to delay entry into professional life, to promote earlier retirement and to discourage retirees from any paid activity. It is indispensable in most European countries that reforms be implemented to ensure the sustainability of pension schemes.

Health insurance regimes also face the consequences of demographic change. They are also badly affected by the steadily rising cost of medicine. Eliminating abuse and fraud is necessary but will not be enough to prevent the risk of a costly drift, which would hit European competitiveness and thus employment. Health insurance must be reviewed to determine how best to reconcile greater individual responsibility with social solidarity.

Unemployment insurance systems were generally designed to provide a replacement income for workers who were likely to soon find a job that was more or less identical to the one just lost. These systems must adapt to take into account today's realities and be clearly designed as insurances for adaptation to new demands on the labour market. They should in no way deter the unemployed from seeking a job because of a combination of taxes and a loss of a range of benefits that would make taking work unattractive. It is important that unemployed people be back onto the ladder of gainful employment, even at a lower rung than they might eventually reach. In that case, in-work benefits could be used to help compensate for too low an income. The experience of countries where such benefits exist (including the earned income tax credit) should be assessed carefully.

To enhance worker's employability. Reforming social protection systems will make an important contribution, but improving education and training is also indispensable. Lifelong learning has become a well-recognized requirement, but it is far from being implemented completely. It is hard to define what needs to be learned in order to ensure genuine employability in a rapidly changing economy. Close cooperation among employers, workers, and public and private educational institutions is of the essence.

To encourage innovation in all fields. There is evidence that the state can guide and stimulate scientific research, particularly in funding major projects — including defence — where the return on investment is difficult to predict. The state can also be a force in helping businesses to implement scientific breakthroughs in order to launch new products and services. Yet the state's most important contribution for innovators — often smaller firms or even individuals — is assistance with entrepreneurial risk taking, particularly by reducing red tape, fostering the creation of supportive infrastructures and promoting more efficient forms of financing innovation. In this respect, establishing a system of insurance-credit for innovative projects at the European level, could prompt European financial and banking systems to catch-up rapidly with the United States in the area of venture capital.

To take advantage of the European dimension:

The single market is far from complete. Yet its completion would constitute a powerful engine for growth and employment by speeding up structural adaptation and giving the public the confidence and ambition that is now lacking. In addition to further progress in opening national economies to competition, there are three priorities:

- agreement on the European company statute;
- harmonised evolution of tax systems towards levels and contents that meet the two criteria of competitiveness and social cohesion;
- development of trans-European networks for transport and telecommunications.

Moving towards Economic and Monetary Union has already yielded a remarkable convergence in economic results among Member States. Shifting to the Euro will give European countries increased margin for manoeuvre and a solid common base for economic efficiency. Provided, of course, that the macro-economic and structural policies on which the success of the Euro depends are implemented consistently.

Conclusion

Only by rapidly improving competitiveness can the employment problem be solved sustainably. This requires deep change in many areas. It would be disingenuous to conceal this. But experience shows that, in European and non-European countries alike, such changes are feasible and do pay off.

Countries will achieve greater and faster results if they prove willing to undertake reforms and create a context for modernisation and cause for ambition.

They must learn from the experiences of those around them, inside and outside Europe, and use systematic benchmarking of policies.

They must also ensure that all parts of society feel that the pain and the gain are shared equitably.

All parts of society must feel that they have obligations as well as rights and that they have the chance to prove their merits and ability. They must believe that their taxes are put to the best use in order to achieve the twin — and complementary — goals of economic efficiency and social cohesion. Otherwise social cohesion is threatened.

Anxiety amongst the people of developed countries as well as the recent turbulence in financial markets in the emerging economics of Asia show that globalisation is neither an easy nor a linear process. History will not be kind to political, business and labour leaders who would fail to understand, explain and act in order to rise to the challenge.

Appendix 3. Report on the Proposal of the European Parliament to the Extraordinary European Council Summit on Employment (20–21 November 1997)–(C4–0389/97)

Committee on Employment and Social Affairs
Rapporteur: *Mr Wim J. van Velzen*

Contents
1. A. MOTION FOR A RESOLUTION
2. B. EXPLANATORY STATEMENT
3. Opinion of the Committee on Economic and Monetary Affairs and Industrial Policy
4. Opinion of the Committee on Research, Technological Development and Energy
5. Opinion of the Committee on the Environment, Public Health and Consumer Protection
6. Opinion of the Committee on Women's Rights
7. Opinion of the Committee on Culture, Youth, Education and the Media
8. Opinion of the Committee on Regional Policy
9. Opinion of the Committee on External Economic Relations

By letter of 17 July 1997 to Mr Gil-Robles Gil-Delgado, President of the European Parliament, Mr Juncker, acting President of the European Council, asked for the European Parliament's contribution to the Extraordinary Summit.

At the sitting of 18 July 1997 the President of Parliament announced that he had referred this request to the Committee on Employment and Social Affairs as the committee responsible, and to the committees concerned for their opinions.

At its meeting of 2 July 1997, the Committee on Employment and Social Affairs appointed Mr W.G. van Velzen rapporteur.

The Committee on Employment and Social Affairs considered the draft report at its meetings of 3 September, 24 September, 6 October and 7 October 1997.

At the last meeting it adopted the motion for a resolution by 23 votes to 3, with 2 abstentions.

The following took part in the vote: Hughes, chairman; Menrad and Ojala, vice-chairmen; van Velzen, rapporteur; Andersson, Boogerd-Quaak, Cabezon Alonso, Chanterie, Ettl, Fayot (for Blak), Hernandez Mollar, Jöns, Lulling (for Mann pursuant to Rule 138(2)), Malangré (for Castagnetti), McMahon, Megahy (for Carniti), Oddy (for Correia), Peter, Pirker (for Donnelly), Pronk, Reding (for Glase), Schiedermeier, Schmidbauer (for Malone), Skinner, Titley (for Morris), Van Lancker, Weiler and Wolf.

The opinions of the Committee on Economic and Monetary Affairs and Industrial Policy, the Committee on Research, Technological Development and Energy; the Committee on the Environment, Public Health and Consumer Protection; the Committee on Women's Rights, the Committee on Culture, Youth, Education and the Media; the Committee on Regional Policy and the Committee on External Economic Relations are attached to this report.

The report was tabled on 9 October 1997.

The deadline for tabling amendments will be indicated in the draft agenda for the part-session at which the report is to be considered.

A. MOTION FOR A RESOLUTION

Resolution on the Proposal of the European Parliament to the Extraordinary European Council Summit on Employment (20–21 November 1997)–(C4–0389/97)
The European Parliament,
– having regard to the decision of the Amsterdam European Council of 16–17 June 1997 to call

for an extraordinary meeting of the European Council under the Luxembourg Presidency to review progress in the creation of employment opportunities (SN 150/97),

– having regard to the letter of Mr Juncker, acting President of the European Council, to Mr Gil-Robles Gil-Delgado, President of the European Parliament, asking for Parliament's contribution to the extraordinary summit (C4–0389/97),

– having regard to the report by the Committee on Employment and Social Affairs and the opinions by the Committees on Economic and Monetary Affairs and Industrial Policy; on Research, Technological Development and Energy; on the Environment, Public Health and Consumer Protection; on Women's Rights; on Culture, Youth, Education and the Media; on Regional Policy; and on External Economic Relations (A4–0307/97),

1. Considers that, in the light of decisions taken by the Amsterdam European Council on employment, definite agreements should be reached at the Luxembourg Employment Summit concerning the creation of employment in the form of verifiable convergence criteria with quantitative objectives based on bench-marking and best practices. The combined effort of the Member states and the EU must aim to increase the current employment rate of 60,4% to 65% within 5 years and a reduction of the unemployment rate to 7%; youth unemployment should be reduced to 50% of its current level within three years;

2. Favours the adoption of a norm for the inactive/active ratio, which reflects the ratio between the active and the portion of the population aged between 15 and 65 in the three best performing Member states and asks the Employment and Labour Market Committee to further elaborate the indicators in the various fields and ensure that Member states apply them; this norm should include criteria for underrepresented groups and be linked to social criteria such as the provisions of the European Social Charter, the Community Charter of the Fundamental Social Rights of Workers;

a. Training
3. Calls upon all parties, in future, to link the training of unemployed young people and the longterm unemployed to a guarantee that the retrained unemployed will be given paid employment for at least a year. Special attention should be devoted to groups particularly badly affected by unemployment;

4. Calls on the Member States to align their efforts to promote training by gearing their national budgets to the mean of the three best-performing Member States and undertaking to increase average spending on the education, professional training of adults and RTD by 0.5% of GDP. As a result, the Member States will progressively transfer resources destined to alleviate the consequences of unemployment (passive measures) into active employment measures, in order to raise employment without putting public funding or social protection systems at risk;

5. Calls on the Member States, in conjunction with the two sides of industry, instructors and training institutes to develop a system of training, employment and work experience such that no person aged under 25 need draw unemployment benefit and that after the age of 25 everyone should have the right to receive two years' paid training over the whole of their lifetime as part of the 'lifelong learning' process; looks to occupational training schemes to become more flexibly aligned with the needs of the market;

6. Calls on the two sides of industry to conclude agreements on creating jobs which can be assigned to the young and the long-term unemployed after completion of training and to agree on the creation of (temporary) jobs by means of combinations of job rotation, parental leave and lifelong learning; urges the Member States particularly to assist SMEs in complying with this obligation, and calls on employers to make training of staff (and future staff) part of their strategic and investment planning;

b. Organization of working time
7. Calls on the Member States and the two sides of industry to remunerate overtime in the form

of time off or of vouchers (for services or courses) or longer career breaks or sabbaticals, and to conclude agreements for flexible working time on the basis of the Commission study and to support proposals involving the collective shortening of working hours by lowering social security contributions, thus enabling (partial) compensation for workers' loss of income to be guaranteed; such proposals should principally be a matter for collective agreement between the social partners, and stresses that fundamental working time standards should be governed by national and European legislation;

8. Calls on the Commission and the two sides of industry to make proposals concerning 'atypical' employment to ensure that the irregular work which is prevalent in it is accompanied by adequate social security and employees' rights equivalent to those for full working-time;

c. Financial measures

9. Calls for a social or lowest VAT rate to be introduced for labour-intensive services, particularly in the case of work experience and training places and the *'Third System'* ; the Summit should immediately permit trials of reduced VAT rates;

10. Urges that decisions be taken without delay to reduce taxation of labour by means of European agreements on transferring taxation to the environment, natural resources, energy and capitalintensive production, as proposed in the White Paper on Growth, Competitiveness and Employment;

11. Calls on the Member States to transfer 30% of the budgetary resources devoted to passive employment measures to education and training for reintegration into the labour market; these resources could also be used to help finance paid jobs in the *Third System* and to combat the informal economy;

12. Calls for the elimination of bureaucratic obstacles to investment, for the review and simplification of the administrative burdens on SME's and for coercive measures to dismantle legal and financial obstacles to the founding of businesses;

13. Calls on the Commission and Council in future to assess all relevant policy measures in the light of their impact on employment; demands also the Commission to undertake a review of the employment impact of all sections of the EU budget and in the same framework to gear more significantly the Structural Funds towards the prevention of long-term unemployment, the promotion of higher skills, entrepreneurship and adaptability; urges also Member states to devote at least 50% of their structural fund allocations towards the development of human resources;

14. Calls on ECOFIN to devote its next meeting primarily to support for and elaboration of the measures decided at the employment summit;

15. Calls on the Heads of Government to make it possible for under-utilized European budget headings to be used for action to enhance employment, notably in connection with local employment initiatives and territorial pacts for the 'Third System', and especially to create a guarantee fund for loans from the European Investment Bank to Small and Medium-sized Enterprises;

16. Calls on the European Council to take the initiative of bringing forward the use of the remaining appropriations entered in the ECSC budget starting in 1998 to fund operating budgets beyond 2002 for job-creation measures and that to this end special funds be allocated to the EIB;

d. Coordination of economic policy

17. Calls on the European Council, at the Luxembourg Summit, to determine the procedures for coordinating economic policy, drawing up the employment guidelines, carrying out monitoring and drawing up annual reports, so that the Amsterdam conclusions in the field of employment can be put into practice immediately and that economic sustainable growth and ecology, sustainable employment, and social security become the top priorities of the economic policy of

the Union and the Member States.

18. Asks the Luxembourg Extraordinary Summit for Employment to conclude a binding "European Pact for Employment, Sustainability and Solidarity" as a complement to the Stability Pact concluded in Amsterdam;

19. Instructs its President to forward this resolution to the extraordinary European Council on Employment, to the Council, the Commission, the European social partners and the governments and parliaments of the Member States.

B. EXPLANATORY STATEMENT
Introduction

At the Amsterdam European Council, important instruments were adopted for the coordination of European employment policy. At the Essen European Council in December 1994, the foundations had already been laid for a European employment strategy by establishing common priorities. The European Councils in June 1995 in Cannes, December 1995 in Madrid and June 1996 in Florence lent further support to the multiannual programme adopted in Essen. However, apart from the agreement of declarations, not all that much has yet been achieved, partly because of a lack of specific, quantifiable objectives and penalties for Member States which fail to comply.

At the summit on employment in Luxembourg in November 1997, European heads of state and of government are to adopt practical measures based on the new Treaty provisions. This report aims to review the new possibilities created by those provisions and to derive from them a limited number of practical policy proposals for submission to the Luxembourg summit.

The report is based on the following premises:

a. At this stage, there is no point in working out new ideas. Previous Council, Commission and European Parliament reports already contain enough ideas which have yet to be elaborated in detail.

b. The main task is to find a strategy geared to a few practical objectives and instruments; a strategy whose implementation, both at European and at national level, can begin without delay and whose deployment and results can be monitored.

c. Maximum use will be made of proposals which have previously found support within the Council but have not resulted in Community action.

d. Apart from EMU, the Member States and the Union must now concentrate on a coordinated, active labour market strategy which will provide training and employment for the more than 18 million unemployed people in the Union. The prime target groups should be the young and the long-term unemployed.

1. *The new chapter on employment in the EC Treaty*

Three documents adopted at the Amsterdam summit are vital to the further development of a European employment strategy: the new chapter on employment to be inserted in the Treaty, the resolution on growth and employment and the conclusions of the Presidency on employment, competitiveness and growth.

In the new chapter on employment, four points are of particular importance. Firstly, the statement that the Member States regard promoting employment as 'a matter of *common* concern' and that they must therefore *coordinate* their measures in this field within the Council (Article 2). Article 3 is more specific about this:

'The Community shall contribute to a *high level of employment* by encouraging cooperation between Member States and by supporting and, if necessary, complementing their action. In doing so, the competences of the Member States shall be respected.'

In addition to this requirement of coordination, it is also important to note that ' *the objective of a high level of employment* shall be taken into consideration in the formulation and implementation of Community policies and activities' (Article 3).

A third important point is that the Council, acting by a qualified majority, may each year draw up employment guidelines in the light of which the employment policies of the Member States may be judged and recommendations made to individual Member States. These guidelines must be consistent with the broad economic guidelines (Article 4).

A further important innovation is that the Council may adopt *incentive measures* 'designed to encourage cooperation between Member States and to support their action in the field of employment through initiatives aimed at developing exchanges of information and best practices, providing comparative analysis and advice as well as promoting innovative approaches and evaluating experiences, in particular by recourse to *pilot projects* .' (Article 5)

2. European Council resolution on growth and employment

By means of its resolution on growth and employment, the European Council announced its intention of *linking* the monetary discipline of the Stability Pact to job creation. The resolution begins by noting that it is imperative to give a new impulse for keeping employment firmly at the top of the political agenda of the Union. A stronger link therefore needs to be established between a successful and sustainable EMU, an effective internal market and employment. Priority objectives are education, training, flexibility of the work-force and ensuring that labour markets respond well. Modernization of social security systems is intended to contribute to social integration and economic effectiveness.

It is intended that (as from 1998) employment should become an *integral element in the broad guidelines* for economic policy. Tax and social security systems must become more conducive to employment. The European Investment Fund and the European Investment Bank are assigned an important role in creating jobs, especially in small and medium-sized enterprises, in the fields of education, health, the urban environment and environmental protection and large infrastructure networks. After 2002, outstanding ECSC reserves are to be used for a research fund for sectors related to the coal and steel industry. Lastly, the two sides of industry are called upon to shoulder their responsibilities in full. All in all, the resolution is a welcome supplement to the new chapter in the Treaty, which it also serves to flesh out.

3. Conclusions of the Presidency on employment, competitiveness and growth

Here too, the European Council stresses that it is of the utmost importance to create the right conditions in the Member States to promote training and flexibility on the part of workers and to ensure that labour markets respond readily to economic changes. To this end, the Member States must intervene actively in labour markets to enable people to develop their potential to the full.

The Council repeats that it is desirable to reduce taxation, particularly of labour, and calls for a restrictive reallocation of public expenditure to encourage investment in human potential, research and development, innovation and the infrastructure vital to competitiveness.

In addition, the relevance to the labour market of training and permanent education must be increased, tax and social security benefits systems must be further reviewed in order to increase employment, and more active labour market measures must be adopted. Efficiency and equity must be improved by making more active use of social transfers and by turning benefit systems into proactive systems which improve the opportunities available to workers on the labour market.

At various points, the Amsterdam European Council displayed an awareness that immediate action was called for. In the conclusions, it urged the Council to strengthen the employment focus of the broad guidelines and to implement this approach *as soon as possible* . This request is repeated in the Resolution on Growth and Employment. The recognition that swift action is needed is encouraging, but it also of course creates obligations.

4. *Notes on the Resolution on the Employment Summit*

At the Luxembourg summit, heads of government will have the opportunity to show the public that they are just as serious about combatting unemployment as they are about EMU. This cannot be achieved by means of yet another ministerial declaration but only by concluding specific, verifiable and enforceable agreements which enter into force *immediately* . These should primarily relate to improving the position on the labour market of groups particularly hard hit by unemployment: unskilled young people and the long-term unemployed.

Some of the proposals in the resolution have been on the Council's agenda before. What is now needed is specific objectives, which must be pursued with the same determination as the EMU criteria. Further recommendations which entail no commitments will do nothing to assist the more than 18 million unemployed people in the Union. As it is principally the Member States or local authorities and the two sides of industry who are in the best position to judge which *instruments* are most appropriate to them, the Luxembourg Summit should primarily concern itself with the *common objectives* and a *common timetable* .

The Luxembourgish President of the European Council, Jean-Claude Juncker, has already proposed that the employment/unemployment ratio of the current three best-performing EU Member States be taken as a norm for the fifteen Member States. In principle, your rapporteur favours the adoption of a norm based on the 'i/a ratio' (the ratio of inactive to active persons on the labour market), but he considers that it should include criteria for groups under-represented on the labour market. An 'i/a ratio' must also be linked to social provisions, namely the European Social Charter, the Community Charter of the Fundamental Social Rights of Work-ers, and agreements on a statutory minimum income, a statutory minimum wage, and protection against dismissal. Without such a common foundation of social rights, an 'i/a norm' could lead to negative competition in social protection policy.

a. Training
Special attention should be devoted to the long-term unemployed: 50% of the 18 million unemployed people in the EU have been without work for more than a year, and 30% for two years or longer. Without retraining and a guarantee of a job to give them work experience (whether or not for the first time), it is very unlikely that members of this section of the population can be integrated into the labour market again. The second priority group consists of the young, 20% of whom are unemployed and 14 million of whom have no qualifications other than compulsory schooling. 5 of these 14 million have not even completed their compulsory schooling. A training and guaranteed jobs ('work experience jobs') plan is also very important. The disabled, between 50% and 70% of whom are unemployed, also require special attention. The necessary training measures will, at the minimum, necessitate an increase in the appropriate national budgets.

According to calculations by the Commission, 80% of the technology currently in use will be out of date within ten years, so that, unless they receive in-service training, 80% of employees will possess outdated knowledge and skills. Even now, it is often difficult to find suitable applicants for job vacancies. SMEs in particular complain that they often cannot find workers with the appropriate skills. In 1995, an average of 0.5% of national budgets was being spent on adult education and training. In 1985 the corresponding figure had been 0.25%. It seems essential to further increase the budget to a minimum of 1%.

It is wrong to hold government solely responsible for training and further training of workers. The two sides of industry should also take responsibility for ensuring that workers receive training or retraining in good time. Government and the two sides of industry can conclude agreements about training and job guarantees which include provision for national government and the EU to assist SMEs. Businesses should include training in their strategic and investment plans. Government and the two sides of industry must cooperate to ensure that unemployed young people who have undergone training find jobs as quickly as possible.

Together, they should offer 'contracts' to unemployed young people under which a job is guaranteed for at least a year after training has been completed.

b. Organization of working time

At present, a full-time job in Europe involves working 41.1 hours per week. Nearly 9 million workers work an average of more than 48 hours per week. In addition, a huge amount of *overtime* is worked in Europe. Where this overtime is of a structural character, enterprises and the two sides of industry should reduce it by creating more jobs. Where overtime is unavoidable, consideration should be given to paying for it in the form of free time or vouchers which can be used to pay for services and/or courses. Redistributing work by reducing working hours and overtime, job rotation, parental leave and 'lifelong learning' could create many new permanent and/or temporary jobs. In some Member States, this has already been tried out to good effect. The report by Michel Rocard contains suggestions for cutting working hours which ought to be implemented. Increasing productivity, inter alia thanks to the use of modern information and communication technologies, is liable to generate an ever larger group of 'outsiders' unless a more creative and fairer approach to time is adopted.

Many of the jobs which have been created in the 1990s are part-time. The days when full-time contracts were the only 'normal' ones are past. This state of affairs calls for new rules on the social and statutory rights of 'atypical workers'. The proposals for European Directives on 'atypical work' have been on ice for years, and now urgently need to be updated and adopted.

c. Financial measures

In Europe, unskilled work in particular is too costly. Reducing *labour costs* (without cutting net disposable income) could both preserve and create jobs. A start must be made as soon as possible on shifting *taxation* from employment to the environment and capital-intensive production. The analysis and recommendations contained in the Delors White Paper are still relevant. SMEs, especially in the services sector, have a key role to play in the job creation strategy, but this is being underexploited because labour-intensive services are relatively expensive. This results in much work being carried out in the black or grey economy. Reducing the disparity between gross and net wages is the appropriate way of reducing pressure on labour. This can primarily be done at national level. In addition, however, there is an instrument which could be adopted *immediately* at Union level: *reducing VAT on labour-intensive services to the lowest rate* . Following the decisions taken in Amsterdam, the European Council ought at the very least to allow Member States to carry out trials in certain designated sectors. These should also extend to the *'third system'*.

The budget line for the *Third System* proposed by the European Parliament affords a good opportunity to fund or part-fund pilot projects for this new employment. In addition, Member States should seek ways of using benefits actively for employment in this sector and supporting the establishment of voucher systems. An obvious course here is to assign a prominent role to local and regional organizations.

The decision of the Amsterdam European Council not to make any new funding available for employment policy was very disappointing. The assumption that a more active labour market policy will be budgetarily neutral is implausible. Moreover, countries which have both high unemployment and large budget deficits are confronted with conflicting objectives on the road to EMU.

The European Council could resolve this conflict by providing more generous subsidies for pilot projects to pursue active labour market strategies geared to the young and the long-term unemployed. In addition, the European Council could consider excluding investment in education and training from calculations of national deficits.

The Council could also make it possible for under-utilized budget headings to be used to create employment, particularly for local employment initiatives and territorial pacts for the 'Third System'. The ECU 170 billion not utilized by the Structural Funds could be used for these purposes. Greater financial leeway has also been created by the application of the deflator. In order to encourage SMEs to make more use of the funds of the European Investment Bank, it is desirable that the EIB should provide subsidies and/or guarantees to guarantee national bank loans. This would enable SMEs to secure loans at lower interest rates. The necessary funds could be obtained from various sources. Besides those already mentioned, the reserves of the EIB and the reserve of the ECSC should be considered.

The European Parliament should undertake a critical review of the budget of the European Union to ascertain where it is possible and desirable to transfer funds to employment objectives. However, the Council may also be expected to review past decisions in order to make more money available for a more active labour market policy.

d. Coordination of European economic policy
At Amsterdam, the European Council laid the foundations for coordination of economic policy at European level, which is intended to strike a balance between monetary stability and economic growth and employment.

An important instrument for this is the guidelines which are to be drawn up (see Article 4(2) of the chapter on employment) and which must be respected by the Member States in their employment policy. The procedures for this remain to be determined, but it would be logical for them to be similar to those for the broad economic guidelines. As the economic guidelines and the employment guidelines will need to be consistent with each other, a procedure must be found which will entrust the Ecofin Council and the Social Affairs Council with shared responsibility for the annual drawing-up of the two sets of guidelines on the basis of annual reports from the Member States. This procedure should ensure that economic growth and employment are the top priorities of the economic policies of the Union and the Member States.

Progress towards the creation of employment should be monitored with the help of verifiable convergence criteria based on quantitative objectives. Nonetheless, it must be acknowledged that the comparison of results (benchmarking) is a technique which needs to be developed and applied with prudence, since it is based on the comparison of practices, scenarios and results between economic agents of a similar nature; for that reason the results of such a comparison cannot be used immediately in the design of concrete measures without taking into account the real socio-economic situation prevailing in each Member State.

Appendix 4. Minutes of 21/10/1997–Provisional Edition
European Council on employment
A4–0307/97
Resolution embodying Parliament's proposal to the extraordinary European Council meeting on Employment (20–21 November 1997) (C4–0389/97)

The European Parliament,
– having regard to the decision of the Amsterdam European Council of 16–17 June 1997 to call for an extraordinary meeting of the European Council under the Luxembourg Presidency to review progress in the creation of employment opportunities (SN 150/97),
– having regard to the letter of Mr Juncker, President-in-Office of the European Council, to Mr Gil-Robles Gil-Delgado, President of the European Parliament, asking for Parliament's contribution to the extraordinary summit (C4–0389/97),
– having regard to the report by the Committee on Employment and Social Affairs and the opinions of the Committee on Economic and Monetary Affairs and Industrial Policy, the Committee on Research, Technological Development and Energy, the Committee on the

Environment, Public Health and Consumer Protection, the Committee on Women's Rights, the Committee on Culture, Youth, Education and the Media, the Committee on Regional Policy and the Committee on External Economic Relations (A4–0307/97),

A. whereas the portents of economic recovery in Europe, though faint, are undeniable and forecasts of growth have been revised upwards everywhere; whereas GDP will rise by an average of 2% in 1997, and growth will be between 2.5 and 3% in 1998; whereas in view of the structural improvement in the relationship between GDP growth and job creation, the return to normal growth will be reflected in the creation of more employment than at the time of previous economic recoveries, but whereas it will not be enough to reduce unemployment to a tolerable level,

1. Considers that, in the light of decisions taken by the Amsterdam European Council on employment, definite agreements should be reached at the Luxembourg employment summit concerning the creation of employment in the form of verifiable convergence criteria with quantitative objectives based on benchmarking and best practices; also believes that the combined efforts of the Member States and the EU must aim to increase the current employment rate of 60.4% to 65% within five years and to cut the unemployment rate to 7%; youth unemployment should be reduced to 50% of its current level;

2. Stresses the fact that despite the progress made with the free movement of goods and services, which has created new jobs and business opportunities, there is still much to be done to transform the fifteen national markets into a single large and homogenous market; too much national legislation is still adopted in a piecemeal manner, which increases distortions of competition in the fiscal, social, environmental, consumer protection and other spheres; too many directives are poorly transposed into national law; all these make the case for supporting the Monti proposals regarding the internal market;

3. Favours the adoption of a norm for the inactive/active ratio which reflects the ratio between the active population and the total population aged between 15 and 65 in the three best performing Member States, and asks the Employment Committee to develop further the indicators in the various fields and ensure that Member States apply them; considers that this norm should include criteria for under-represented groups and be linked to social criteria such as the provisions of the European Social Charter and the Community Charter of the Fundamental Social Rights of Workers;

4. Emphasizes the need for European economic, financial, income and monetary policies to be coordinated in order to achieve an appropriate policy mix in the EU that is capable of contributing to growth, investment and employment; emphasizes the need for this coordination to be consolidated by means of an economic, investment and tax pact;

Training

5. Calls upon all parties, in future, to link programmes of training and high- quality education aimed at developing market-relevant skills of the unemployed to a guarantee that the retrained unemployed will be given paid employment for at least a year; special attention should be devoted to groups which are particularly badly affected by unemployment;

6. Calls on the Member States to align their efforts to promote training by gearing their national budgets to the average of the three best-performing Member States and undertaking to increase average spending on the education, professional training of adults and RTD; as a result, the Member States should progressively use resources intended to alleviate the consequences of unemployment (passive measures) to finance active employment measures, in order to raise employment without putting public funding or social protection systems at risk;

7. Calls on the two sides of industry to develop a system of continuing training such that everyone should have a right to continuing training over the whole of their working life as part

of the 'lifelong learning' process;

8. Calls on the two sides of industry to conclude agreements on creating jobs which can be assigned to the young and the long-term unemployed after completion of training and to agree on the creation of (temporary) jobs by means of combinations of job rotation, parental leave and lifelong learning; urges the Member States particularly to assist SMEs in complying with this obligation, and calls on employers to make training of staff (and future staff) part of their strategic and investment planning;

Organization of working time

9. Believes that Member States need to address the issue of promoting flexibility in the labour market with regard to working hours, working time and working patterns (such as career breaks, sabbaticals, etc.) through a non-legislative, non-compulsory process based on social dialogue at the level of the individual enterprise, in particular having regard to the vital role of SMEs in job creation; notes the importance of enhancing labour market mobility through improved mutual recognition of diplomas, and through the portability of pensions, insurance and social insurance;

10. Calls on the Commission and the two sides of industry to make proposals concerning 'atypical' employment to ensure that the irregular work which is prevalent in it is accompanied by adequate social security and employees' rights which are equivalent to those for full working-time;

Financial measures

11. Calls for a social or minimum VAT rate to be introduced for labour- intensive services, particularly in the case of work experience and training places and the 'Third System'; the European Council should immediately permit trials of reduced VAT rates;

12. Urges that decisions be taken without delay to reduce taxation of labour by means of European agreements on transferring taxation to the environment, natural resources, energy and capital-intensive production, as proposed in the White Paper on Growth, Competitiveness and Employment;

13. Urges a shift towards reducing the overall tax burden for individuals and companies;

14. Calls on the Member States to improve the interaction between taxation and welfare systems in order to minimize the disincentives to accepting low- paid job opportunities, by further exploring innovations in the field of social policy such as basic income and negative income tax;

15. Calls on the Member States to secure a switch from passive to active employment measures and to take action to combat the informal economy;

16. Urges the Commission and the Member States to exercise increased vigilance when granting aid to undertakings by monitoring the use made of it so as to ensure that it contributes genuinely to creating stable jobs rather than facilitating business restructurings and relocations that can entail redundancies even when accompanied by 'social plans';

17. Calls for the stimulation and promotion of R&D by means of appropriate tax concessions, easy access to and availability of venture capital and close cross-border cooperation between undertakings, schools and research institutes, the elimination of bureaucratic obstacles to investment, a review and simplification of the administrative burdens on SME's and for coercive measures to dismantle legal and financial obstacles to the establishment of businesses;

18. Calls on the Commission and Council in future to assess all relevant policy measures in the light of their impact on employment; also calls on the Commission to undertake a review of the employment impact of all sections of the EU budget and in the same framework to gear more significantly the Structural Funds towards the prevention of long-term unemployment, the

promotion of higher skills, entrepreneurship and adaptability; urges also Member States to increase the efficiency of Structural Fund programmes with greater emphasis on employment;

19. Calls on ECOFIN to devote its next meeting primarily to support for and elaboration of the measures decided at the employment European Council;

20. Calls on the European Council to make it possible for under-utilized EU budget headings to be used for action to enhance employment, notably in connection with local employment initiatives and territorial pacts for the *'Third System'*, and especially to create a guarantee fund for loans from the European Investment Bank to SMEs,

21. Calls on the European Council to take the initiative of bringing forward the remaining appropriations entered in the ECSC budget to fund operating budgets after 2002 and, starting in 1998, use them for job-creation measures and calls for special funds to be allocated to the EIB for this purpose;

Coordination of economic policy

22. Calls on the European Council meeting in Luxembourg to determine the procedures for coordinating economic policy, drawing up the employment guidelines, carrying out monitoring and drawing up annual reports, so that the Amsterdam conclusions in the field of employment can be put into practice immediately and so that lasting economic growth and ecology, sustainable employment, and social security become the top priorities of the economic policy of the Union and the Member States; calls on the European Council to declare that the Monti proposals on the internal market should be adopted as soon as possible given the very positive effect they are expected to have on employment;

23. Calls on the European Council to take greater account of the economic interdependence of the Member States that has emerged with the transformation of fifteen national markets into a single large and homogenous market and increasingly limits the effectiveness of purely national economic policies; considers it absolutely essential, therefore, that further progress be made towards greater complementarity of the Member States' economic policies so that synergies may be achieved in the stimulation and promotion of innovation, research and technological development by means of appropriate tax concessions for SME's, the facilitation of access to and availability of venture capital for SME's operating in R&D sectors, the promotion of efficient research infrastructure and close cross-border cooperation between undertakings, universities and research institutions;

24. Asks the Luxembourg extraordinary European Council to conclude a binding "European Pact for Employment, Sustainability and Solidarity" as a complement to the Stability Pact concluded in Amsterdam;

25. Sees the development of European infrastructure , i.e. the trans-European networks proposed in the Delors White Paper, as a stimulus to employment that will have its impact within the EU because it also has a growth- promoting function and will encourage investment;

26. Calls on the Member States to continue their efforts to use, as a matter of priority, the room for manoeuvre released by the reform of public finances to reduce labour costs and shift the tax burden from labour to mobile factors; calls therefore for a European tax pact that puts an end to the ruinous tax race in the EU, eases the burden of taxation and other non-wage labour costs and brings about an ecological tax reform;

* * *

27. Instructs its President to forward this resolution to the extraordinary European Council on employment, the Council, the Commission, the European social partners and the governments and parliaments of the Member States.

References

Abélès, Marc (1994). A la recherche d'un espace public communautaire. *Pouvoirs, 69*, 117–128. Abélès, Marc (1996). La Communauté européenne: une perspective anthroplogique. *Social Anthropology, 4(1),* 33–45.

Abélès, Marc, Irene Bellier, & Mary McDonald (1993). *Approche Anthropologique de la Commission Europeenne: Executive Summary.* Unpublished manuscript. CNRS, Paris.

Abélès, Marc & Irene. Bellier (1996). La Commission Européenne du compromis culturel à la culture politique du compromis. *Revue française de science politique, 46(3),* 431–457.

Addison, John T. & W. Stanley Siebert (1997). *Labour Markets in Europe. Issues of harmonization and regulation.* London: Dryder.

Albrow, Martin (1998). *Abschied vom Nationalstaat. Staat und Gesellschaft im Globalen Zeitalter.* Frankfurt: Suhrkamp.

Antaki, Charles (1994). *Explaining and arguing.* London: Sage.

Archer, J. & V. Rhodes (1987). Bereavement and reactions to job loss: A comparative review. *British Journal of Social Psychology, 26(3),* 211–224.

Bach, Maurizio (1999). *Die Bürokratisierung Europas. Verwaltungseliten, Experten und politische Legitimation in Europa.* Frankfurt & New York: Campus.

Baecker, Dirk (1999). *Organisation als System.* Frankfurt: Suhrkamp.

Bahktin, Mikhail (1981). *The dialogic imagination.* Austin: University of Texas Press.

Bainbridge, Timothy & Anthony Teasdale (1996). *The penguin companion to the European Union.* London: Penguin.

Balla, Bàlint (1989). Konflikttheorie. In G. Endruwiet & G. Trommsdorff (Eds.), *Wörterbuch der Soziologie* (349–355). Stuttgart: Ferdinand Enke Verlag.

Barber, Benjamin R. (1995). *Jihad versus McWorld: How globalism and tribalism are reshaping the world.* New York: Ballantine.

Baumann, Zygmunt (1995). *Life in fragments: Essays in postmodern morality.* Cambridge: Blackwell.

Beaugrande, Robert A. de & Wolfgang U. Dressler (1981). *Einführung in die Textlinguistik.* Tübingen: Niemeyer.

Beck, Ulrich (Ed.) (1998). *Politik der Globalisierung.* Frankfurt: Suhrkamp.

Beck, Ulrich (1998). Wie wird Demokratie im Zeitalter der Globalisierung möglich? In U. Beck (Ed.), *Politik der Globalisierung* (7–66). Frankfurt: Suhrkamp.

BEIGEWUM (1997). *Was hat der Euro mit den Arbeitslosen zu tun?* Vienna: Wirtschaftsuniversität.

BEIGEWUM (1998). *Der NAP ist da! Wo bleiben die Jobs? Leitlinien einer emanzipatorischen Beschäftigungspolitik.* Vienna: Wirtschaftsuniversität.

Benhabib, Seyla (1992). *Situating the self: Gender, community and Postmodernism in contemporary ethics.* New York: Routledge.

Bernstein, Basil (forthcoming). Vertical and horizontal discourse: An essay. *Journal of Education.*

Billig, Michael, Susan Condor, Derek Edwards, Mike Gane, David Middleton, & Alan Radley (1988). *Ideological dilemmas.* London: Sage.

Billig, Michael (1991). *Ideology and opinions.* London: Sage.

Boden, Deirdre (1994). *The business of talk.* Cambridge, UK: Polity.

Boden, Deirdre (1995). Agendas and arrangements: Everyday negotiations in meetings. In A. Firth (Ed.), *The discourse of negotiation: Studies of language in the workplace* (83–99). London: Pergamon.

Born, Joachim (1999). Multilingualism and power: Vagueness as a strategic, text-constituting principle in supranational organizations. In R. Wodak, & C. Ludwig (Eds), *Challenges in a Changing World* (193–209). Vienna: Passagenverlag.

Born, Joachim & Wilfried Schütte (1995). *Eurotexte. Textarbeit in einer Institution der EG.* Tübingen: Gunter Narr Verlag.

Bostyn, A. & D. Wright (1987). Inside a community: Values associated with money and time. In S. Fineman (Ed.), *Unemployment: Personal and social consequences.* London: Tavistock.

Bourdieu, Pierre (1997). *Der Tote packt den Lebenden. Schriften zu Politik & Kultur 2.* Hamburg: VSA.

Bourdieu, Pierre (1998). *Gegenfeuer. Wortmeldungen im Dienste des Widerstands gegen die neoliberale Invasion.* Konstanz: Universitätsverlag.

Breuer, Stefan (1991). *Max Webers Herrschaftssoziologie.* Frankfurt & New York: Campus.

Burke, Kenneth (1966). *Language as symbolic action: Essays on life, literature, and method.* Berkeley and Los Angeles: University of California Press.

Burke, Kenneth (1969[1945]). *A Grammar of motives.* Berkeley and Los Angeles: University of California Press.

Burt, Ronald (1995). *Structural holes.* Harvard: Harvard University Press.

Callon, Michel & Bruno Latour (1981). Unscrewing the big Leviathan: how actors macrostructure reality and how sociologists help them to do so. In K. Knorr-Cetina & A. V. Cicourel (Eds.), *Advances in social theory and methodology: Toward an integration of micro- and macro-sociologies* (277–303). London: Routledge.

Christie, Frances & J. R. Martin (1997). *Genre and institutions: Social processes in the workplace and school.* London: Cassell.

Cicourel, Aaron (1964). *Method and measurement in sociology.* New York: The Free Press.

Cicourel, Aron (1992): The interpenetration of communicative contexts: Examples from medical encounters. In A. Duranti & C. Goodwin (Eds.), *Rethinking context. Language as an interactive phenomenon* (291–310). Cambridge: Cambridge University Press.

Cicourel, Aron (1994). Theoretical and methodological suggestions for using discourse to recreate aspects of social structure. In A. Grimshaw, P. Burke, & (Eds.) *What's Going on Here? Complementary studies of professional talk* (Vol. 2. 61–94). Norwood: Ablex.

Cilia, Rudolf de, Martin Reisigl, & Ruth Wodak (1999). The discursive construction of national identities. *Discourse & Society, 10(2),* 149–174.

Cini, Michelle (1996). *The European Commission. Leadership, organisation and culture in the EU administration.* Manchester & New York: Manchester University Press.

Clark, D. Y. (1987). Families facing redundancy. In S. Finman (Ed.), *Unemployment: Personal and social consequences.* London: Tavistock.

Clark, Ian (1997). *Globalization and fragmentarization. International relations in the twentieth century.* New York: Oxford University Press.

Collier, Jane (1994). Regional disparities, the single market and European monetary union. In J. Michie & J. G. Smith (Eds.), *Unemployment in Europe* (145–159). London: Academic Press.

Corbett, Richard, Francis Jacobs & Michael Shackleton (1995). *The European Parliament* (3rd ed.). London: Cartermill.

Dahrendorf, Ralf (1994). *Der moderne soziale Konflikt.* Munich: Deutsher Taschenbuch Verlag.

Dittgen, Herbert (1997). Welt ohne Grenzen? Überlegungen zur Zukunft des Nationalstaats. *Merkur. Deutsche Zeitschrift für europäisches Denken, 9/10(51),* 941–949.

Drew, Paul & John Heritage (1992). *Talk at work: Interaction in institutional settings.* Cambridge: Cambridge University Press.

Drew, Paul & Marja-Leena Sorjonen (1997). Institutional dialogue. In T. A. van Dijk (Ed.), *Discourse and social interaction: Discourse studies, Vol. 2–A multidisciplinary introduction* (92–118). Newbury Park, CA: Sage.

Edelman, Murray (1977). *Political language.* New York: Academic Books.

Edwards, Derek & Jonathan Potter (1992). *Discursive psychology.* London: Sage.

Edwards, Geoffrey & David Spence (1997). *The European Commission* (2nd ed.). London: Cartermill.

Ehlich, Konrad & Jochen Rehbein (1994). Institutionsanalyse. Prolegomena zur Untersuchung von Kommunikation in Institutionen. In G. Brünner & G. Grafen (Eds.), *Texte und Diskurse: Methoden und Forschungsergebnisse der Funktionalen Pragmatik* (287–327). Opladen: Westdeutcher Verlag.

European Commission (1994). *White Paper on growth, competitiveness and employment.* Brussels.

European Commission (1997). *Jobs Summit: Three documents adopted by the European Commission on 1st October 1997.* Brussels.

European Commission (1997). *Employment in Europe 1997.* Luxembourg: Office for Official Publications of the European Communities.

European Commission (1998). *Employment policy guidelines.* Brussels.

Fairclough, Norman (1999). Democracy and the public sphere in critical research on discourse. In R. Wodak & C. Ludwig (Eds.) *Challenges in a changing world* (63–86). Vienna: Passagenverlag.

Fetterman, David M. (1989). *Ethnography step by step.* Newbury Park: Sage.

Field, John (1995). *Employment policy. European Union policy briefings.* London: Cartermill.

Firth, Alan (1995a). *The discourse of negotiation: Studies of language in the workplace.* London: Pergamon.

Firth, Alan (1995b). Introduction and overview. In A. Firth (Ed.), *The discourse of negotiation: Studies of language in the workplace* (3–39). London: Pergamon.

Fries, Peter (1998). *Theme and new in written advertising.* Paper presented at the Systemic Functional Linguistics Workshop, Cardiff, UK.

Garkinkel, Harold (1984). *Studies in ethnomethodology.* Cambridge, UK: Polity.

George, Stephen (1996). *Politics and policy in the European Union.* Oxford: Oxford University Press.

Giddens, Anthony (1979). *Central problems in social theory: Action, structure, and contradictions in social analysis.* London: Hutchison.

Giddens, Anthony (1984). *The constitution of society.* Cambridge, UK: Polity.

Giddens, Anthony (1989). *Sociology.* Cambridge: Polity Press.

Giddens, Anthony (1991). *Modernity and self-identity: Self and society in the late modern age.* Stanford: Stanford University Press.

Goffman, Erving (1979). Footing. *Semiotica, 25,* 1–29.

Goodman, S. F. (1996). *The European Union* (3rd ed.). London: MacMillan.

Goodwin, Charles (1994). Professional vision. *American Anthropologist, 96(3),* 606–633.

Goodwin, Marjorie Harness (1990). *He-said-she-said: Talk as social organization among black children.* Bloomington and Indianapolis: Indiana University Press.

Greenwood, Justin (1997). *Representing Interests in the European Union.* London: MacMillan.

Gregory, Michael (1996). Clause and sentence as district units in the morphosyntactic analysis of English and their relation to semiological propositions and predications.

Grint, Keith (1991). *The sociology of work: An introduction.* Cambridge, UK: Polity Press.

Gruber, Helmut (1996). *Streitgespraeche.* Stuttgart: Westdeutscher Verlag.

Gunnarsson, Britt-Louise, Per Linell, & Bengt Nordberg (1997). *The construction of professional discourse*. London: Longman.

Habermas, Jürgen & Niklas Luhmann (1971). *Theorie der Gesellschaft oder Sozialtechnologie — Was leistet die Systemforschung?* Frankfurt: Suhrkamp.

Habermas, Jürgen (1981). *Theorie des kommunikativen Handelns*. 2 Volumes. Frankfurt: Suhrkamp.

Habermas, Jürgen (1997). *Die Einbeziehung des Anderen. Studien zur politischen Theorie*. Frankfurt: Suhrkamp.

Habermas, Jürgen (1998a). Jenseits des Nationalstaats? Bemerkungen zu Folgeproblemen der wirtschaftlichen Globalisiserung. In U. Beck (Ed.), *Politik der Globalisierung* (67–84). Frankfurt: Suhrkamp.

Habermas, Jürgen (1998b). *Die postnationale Konstellation. Politische Essays*. Frankfurt: Suhrkamp.

Halliday, M. A. K. (1994). *An introduction to functional grammar* (2nd ed.). London: Edward Arnold.

Hodge, Robert & Gunther Kress (1993). Language as ideology (2nd ed.). London & New York: Routledge.

Hammersly, M. & P. Atkinson. (1983). *Ethnography*. London: Tavistock.

Hayes-Renshaw, Fiona & Helen Wallace (1997). *The Council of Ministers*. London: MacMillan.

Henningsen, Manfred (1998). Die politische Verfassung Europas. *Merkur. Deutsche Zeitschrift für europäisches Denken*, (5, 52), 454–461.

Hirst, Paul & Grahame Thompson (1996). *Globalization in question: The international economy and the possibilities of governance*. Cambridge: Polity Press.

Höffe, Otfried (1999). *Demokratie im Zeitalter der Globalisierung*. Munich: C. H. Beck.

Huffschmid, Jörg (1997). Globalisierung — das Ende von Wirtschaftspolitik. In BEIGEWUM (Ed.), *Wege zu einem anderen Europa* (230–254). Köln: Papyrossa.

Iedema, Rick (1995). *The language of administration: Write it right literacy in industry research project* (Stage III). Erskinville, NSW: Disadvanted School Program.

Iedema, Roderick (1997). The language of administration: Organizing human activity in formal institutions. In. E. Christie and J. R. Martin (Eds), *Genres and institutions: Social processes in the workplace and school* (73–100). London: Pinter.

Iedema, Roderick (1999). Formalising organizational meaning. *Special Issue, Discourse & Society,10(1)*, 49–65

Iedema, Rick & Ruth Wodak (1999). Introduction: organizational discourses and practices. *Discourse & Society, 10(1)*, 5–19.

Jahoda, Marie, Paul Lazarsfeld & Hans Zeisel (1975). *Die Arbeitslosen vom Marienthal. Ein soziographischer Versuch*. Frankfurt: Suhrkamp.

Klein, Josef (1988). *Politische Semantik. Bedeutungsanalytische und sprachkritische Beiträge zur politischen Sprachverwendung*. Opladen: Westdeutscher Verlag.

Koch, Claus (1997). Im Diesseits des Kapitalismus. *Merkur. Deutsche Zeitschrift für europäisches Denken*, 9/10(51), 763–777.

Kress, Gunther & Theo van Leeuwen (1996). *Reading images: the grammar of visual design*. London & New York: Routledge.

Krugman, Paul (1994). *Peddling Prosperity. Economic sense and nonsense in the age of diminished expectations*. New York: Norton.

Krugman, Paul (1998). *Pop internationalism*. Cambridge (Massachusetts): MIT Press.

Latour, Bruno (1987). *Science in action*. Milton Keyes: Open University Press.

Latour, Bruno & Steve Woolgar (1986). *Laboratory life: The construction of scientific facts*. Princeton, NJ: Princeton University Press.

Lebaron, Curtis & Jürgen Streeck (1997). Built space and the interactional framing of experience during a murder interrogation. *Human Studies, 20*, 1–25.

Lemke, Jay L. (1995). *Textual politics*. London: Taylor and Francis.

Lepsius, M. Rainer (1995) Institutionenanalyse und Institutionenpolitik. In B. Nedelmann (Ed.), *Politische Institutionen im Wandel. Kölner Zeitschrift für Soziologie und Sozialpsychologie*, Sonderheft 35 (392–403). Opladen: Westdeutscher Verlag.

Linell, Per (1998). Discourse across boundaries: On recontextualizations and the blending of voices in professional discourse. *Text, 18(2),* 143–157.

Linell, Per & Srikant Sarangi (Eds.) (1998). Discourse across the professions — Special issue on professional discourse studies, *Text 18(2)*.

Lipset, Seymour (1959). *Consensus and conflict*. New Brunswick: Transaction Books

Luhmann, Niklas (1984). Soziale System. Grundriß einer allgemeinen Theorie. Frankfurt: Suhrkamp.

Luhmann, Niklas (1996). *Organisation und Entscheidung*. Bielefeld: Unpublished Manuscript.

Luhmann, Niklas (1997). *Die Gesellschaft der Gesellschaft*. 2 Volumes. Frankfurt: Suhrkamp.

Martin, Hans-Peter & Harald Schumann (1996). *Die Globalisierungsfalle. Der Angriff auf Demokratie und Wohlstand*. Reinbeck: Rowohlt.

Martin, J. R. (1991). Nominalization in science and humanities: Distilling knowledge and scaffolding text. In E. Ventola (Ed.), *Function and systemic linguistics: Approaches and uses* (307–337). Berlin and New York: Mouton de Gruyter

Martin, J. R. (1993b). Technology, bureaucracy and schooling. *Cultural Dynamics, 6(1),* 84–130.

Martin, J. R., Christian Matthiessen, & Clare Painter (1997). *Working with functional grammar*. London: Edward Arnold.

Maynard, Douglas (1984). *Inside plea bargaining: the language of negotiation*. New York: Plenum.

McElhinny, Bonny (1997). Ideologies of public and private language in sociolinguistics. In R. Wodak (Ed.), *Gender and discourse* (106–139). London: Sage.

Michie, Jonathan & Frank Wilkinson (1994). The growth of unemployment in the 1980s. In J. Michie & J. G. Smith (Eds.), *Unemployment in Europe* (11–31). London: Academic Press.

Mouzelis, Nicos (1995). *Sociological theory: What went wrong? Diagnosis and remedies*. London: Routledge.

Müller, Hans-Peter (1997). Spiel ohne Grenzen? *Merkur. Deutsche Zeitschrift für europäisches Denken, 9/10(51)*, 805–820.

Mumby, Dennis K. (1988). *Communication and power in organizations: Discourse, ideology and domination*. Norwood: Ablex.

Mumby, Dennis & Robin P. Clair (1997). Organizational discourse. In T. A. van Dijk (Ed.), *Discourse as social interaction* (181–205). London: Sage.

Muntigl, Peter (1999). Creating and effacing differences in speeches on unemployment. *Text, 19(1)*, 111–141.

Muntigl, Peter (forthcoming). Reading speeches politically. In P. Chilton & C. Schäffner (Eds.), *Politics as text and talk: Analytic approaches to political discourse*. Amsterdam & Philadelphia: John Benjamins.

Nugent, Neill (1994). *The government and politics of the European Union*. London: MacMillan.

O'Neill, Michael (1996). *The politics of European integration: A reader*. London: Routledge.

Pedler, Robin H. & Guenther F. Schaefer (1996). Preface. In R. H. Pedler & G. F. Schaefer (Eds.), *Shaping European law and policy. The role of committees and comitology in the political process* (ix-xi). Maastricht: European Institute of Public Administration.

Perraton, Jonathan, David Goldblatt, David Held & Anthony McGrew (1998). Die Globalisierung der Wirtschaft. In U. Beck (Ed.), *Politik der Globalisierung* (134–168). Frankfurt: Suhrkamp.

Potter, Jonathan (1996). *Representing reality*. London: Sage.

Richardson, Jeremy (1996). Policy-making in the EU: Interests, ideas and garbage cans of primeval soup. In J. Richardson (Ed.), *European Union: power and policy-making* (3–23). London: Routledge.

Sacks, Harvey (1992). *Lectures on conversation* (Ed. G. Jefferson, 2 vols). Oxford and Cambridge, MA: Blackwell.

Sarangi, Srikant (1998). Rethinking recontextualization in professional discourse studies: An epilogue. *Text, 18(2),* 301–318.

Schaefer, Guenther F. (1996). Committees in the EC policy process: A first step towards developing a conceptual framework. In R. H. Pedler & G. F. Schaefer (Eds.), *Shaping European law and policy. The role of committees and comitology in the political process* (3–24). Maastricht: European Institute of Public Administration.

Schegloff, Emanuel (1992). On talk and its institutional occasions. In P. Drew & J. Heritage (Eds.), *Talk at work: Interaction in institutional settings* (101–34). Cambridge: Cambridge University Press.

Schegloff, Emanuel (1997). Whose text? Whose context? *Discourse & Society, 8(2),* 165–187.

Schubert, Alexander (1998). *Der Euro. Die Krise einer Chance.* Frankfurt: Suhrkamp.

Sedlak, Maria (1997). *'The European Council requests...': The question of agency in the European Council's Presidency Conclusions.* Working Paper. Vienna: Research Center Discourse, Politics, Identity.

Sennett, Richard (1998). *Der flexible Mensch. Die Kultur des neuen Kapitalismus.* Berlin: Berlin Verlag.

Stillar, Glenn (1998). *Analyzing everyday texts: Discourse, rhetoric, and social perspectives.* Thousand Oaks, Calif.: Sage

Straehle, Carolyn (1999). *'We are not Americans, we are Europeans'. Looking inside the European Union.* Unpublished manuscript. Research Center Discourse, Politics, Identity; Vienna, Austria.

Straehle, Carolyn, Gilbert Weiss, Ruth Wodak, Peter Muntigl & Maria Sedlak (1999). Struggle as metaphor in European Union discourses on unemployment. *Discourse & Society,* 10/1, 67–100.

Streeck, Jürgen (1996). How to do things with things. *Human Studies, 19,* 365:384.

Suchman, Lucy & Randall Trigg (1993). Artificial intelligence as craftwork. In S. Chaiklin & J. Lave (Eds.), *Understanding practice: Perspectives on activity and context* (144–178). Cambridge: Cambridge University Press.

Tannen, Deborah (1998). *The argument culture.* New York: Random House.

Taulègne, Béatrice (1993). *Le Conseil européen.* Paris: Presses Universitaires des France.

Thompson, Geoff (1996). *Introducing functional grammar.* London: Edward Arnold.

Thurow, Lester (1996). *The future of capitalism. How today's economic forces shape tomorrow's world.* New York: Penguin.

Titscher, Stefan, Ruth Wodak, Michael Meyer, Eva Vetter (Eds.). (1998). *Methoden der Textanalyse.* Opladen: Westdeutscher Verlag.

Todd, Emmanuel (1999). *Die Neoliberale Illusion. Über die Stagnation der entwickelten Gesellschaften.* Zürich: Rotpunktverlag.

Tomaney, John (1994). Regional and industrial aspects of unemployment in Europe. In J. Michie & J. G. Smith (Eds.), *Unemployment in Europe* (160–176). London: Academic Press.

Townsend, Alan R. (1997). *Making a living in Europe. Human geographies of economic change.* London: Routledge.

Van Dijk, Teun A. (1993). *Elite discourse and racism.* Newbury Park, Calif.: Sage.

Van Leeuwen, Theo (1995). Representing social action. *Discourse & Society, 6(1),* 81–106.

Van Leeuwen, Theo & Ruth Wodak (1999). Legitimizing immigration control. A discourse-historical analysis. *Discourse Studies Vol 1* (1), 83–118.

Van Schendelen, M.P.C.M. (1996). EC committees: Influence counts more than legal powers.

In R. H. Pedler & G. F. Schaefer (Eds.), *Shaping European law and policy. The role of committees and comitology in the political process* (25–38). Maastricht: European Institute of Public Administration.

Vecchiarelli-Scott, Joanna & Judith Chelius-Stark (1996). Rediscovering Hannah Arendt. In *H. Arendt, Love and Saint Augustine* (115–211). Chicago: University of Chicago Press.

Waters, Malcolm (1995). *Globalization*. London: Routledge.

Warr, P. (1983). Work and unemployment. In P. Drenth, H. Thierry, D. J. Willems & C. J. de Wolff (Eds.), *Handbook of work and organizational psychology*. London: John Wiley.

Weber, Max (1976). *Wirtschaft und Gesellschaft. Grundriss der verstehenden Soziologie*. Tübingen: J.C.B. Mohr.

Weiss, Gilbert (1999). Some remarks on decision-making in committees of the European Union. In R. Wodak & C. Ludwig (Eds.), *Challenges in a changing world. Issues in critical discourse analysis* (157–192). Vienna: Passagenverlag.

Weiss, Gilbert & Ruth Wodak (1998). *Organization and communication. On the relevance of Niklas Luhmann's systems theory for a discourse-hermeneutic approach to organizations.* Paper presented in Kopenhagen, Denmark.

Weiss, Gilbert & Ruth Wodak (forthcoming). European Union discourses on employment: strategies of depoliticizing unemployment and ideologizing employment policies. *Concepts and Transformations*.

Wodak, Ruth (1986). *Language behavior in therapy groups*. Los Angeles: UCP.

Wodak, Ruth (1987). Kommunikation in Institutionen. In U. Ammon, N. Dittmar, & K. Mattheier (Eds.), *Handbuch der Soziolinguistik* (799–821). Berlin: de Gruyter.

Wodak, Ruth (1996). *Disorders in discourse*. London: Longman.

Wodak, Ruth (1999a). *Theories in applied linguistics*. In C. Schaner-Wolles & J. Rennison (Eds.), Festschrift for Wolfgang Dressler.

Wodak, Ruth (1999b). *Rekontextualisierung und Bedeutungswandel. Diskursive Entscheidungsprozesse in der EU*. In R. Sverje-Rindler (Ed.), Diskurse in Europa.

Wodak, Ruth, Rudolf de Cillia, Martin Reisigl, Karin Liebhart, Klaus Hofstätter & Maria Kargl (1998). *Zur diskursiven Konstruktion nationaler Identität*. Frankfurt: Suhrkamp.

Wodak, Ruth, Florian Menz, Richard Mitten, & Frank Stern (1994). *Die Sprachen der Vergangenheiten*. Frankfurt: Suhrkamp.

Wodak, Ruth, Peter Nowak, Johanna Pelikan, Helmut Gruber, Rudolf de Cillia, & Richard Mitten (1990). *Wir sind all unschuldige Täter: Diskurshistorische Studien zum Nachkriegsantisemitismus*. Frankfurt: Suhrkamp.

Wodak, Ruth & Martin Reisigl (2000). *Discourse and discrimination*. London: Routledge.

Wodak, Ruth & Maria Sedlak (1999). *"We demand that foreigners adapt to our life-style ..." Political discourse on immigration laws in Austria and the United Kingdom.* Unpublished manuscript. Research Center Discourse, Politics, Identity; Vienna, Austria.

Wodak, Ruth, Stephan Titscher, Michael Meyer, & Eva Vetter (1997). *Sprache und Diplomatie. Ein Forschungsbericht*. Unpublished manuscript. University of Vienna.

Wodak, Ruth & Eva Vetter (1999). Competing professions in times of change. The discursive construction of professional identities in TV talk shows. In R. Wodak & C. Ludwig (Eds.), *Challenges in a changing world. Issues in critical discourse analysis* (209–238). Vienna: Passagenverlag.

Wodak, Ruth & Gilbert Weiss (2000). *"We are different than the Americans and the Japanese!" — A critical discourse analysis of decision making in EU-meetings about employment policies.* Unpublished manuscript. University of Vienna.

Yin, Robert K. (1989). *Case study research: Design and methods*. Newbury Park, CA: Sage.

Index

In the series DIALOGUES ON WORK AND INNOVATION the following titles have been published thus far or are scheduled for publication:

1. NASCHOLD, Frieder and Casten VON OTTER: *Public Sector Transformation: Rethinking Markets and Hierarchies in Government.* 1996.
2. TOULMIN, Stephen and Björn GUSTAVSEN (eds): *Beyond Theory. Changing organizations through participation.* 1996.
3. GUSTAVSEN, Björn, Bernd HOFMAIER, Marianne EKMAN PHILIPS and Anders WIKMAN: *Concept-Driven Development and the Organization of the Process of Change. An evaluation of the Swedish Working Life Fund.* 1996.
4. MERRELYN, Emery: *Searching. The theory and practice of making cultural change.* 1999.
5. PÅLSHAUGEN, Øyvind, Björn GUSTAVSEN, Dag ØSTERBERG and John SHOTTER: *The End of Organization Theory? Language as a tool in action research and organizational development.* 1998.
6. GUSTAVSEN, Björn, Tom COLBJØRNSEN and Øyvind PÅLSHAUGEN (eds): *Development Coalitions in Working Life. The 'Enterprise Development 2000' Program in Norway.* 1998.
7. ENNALS, Richard and Björn GUSTAVSEN: *Work Organization and Europe as a Development Coalition.* 1999.
8. GREENWOOD, Davydd J. (ed.): *Action Research. From practice to writing in an international action research development program.* 1999.
9. VAN BEINUM, Hans (ed.): *Ideas and Practices in Action Research. An institutional journey.* n.y.p.
10. KALLIOLA, Satu and Risto NAKARI (eds): *Resources for Renewal. A participatory approach to the modernization of municipal organizations in Finland.* 1999.
11. LJUNGBERG VAN BEINUM, Ingrid: *Using the Lamp instead of Looking into the Mirror. Women and men in discussion about the relationship between men and women in the work place.* 2000.
12. MUNTIGL, Peter, Gilbert WEISS and Ruth WODAK: *European Union Discourses and Unemployement. An interdisciplinary approach to employment policymaking and organizational change.* n.y.p.